THE CONVICT SETTLERS OF AUSTRALIA

THE CONVICT SETTLERS
OF AUSTRALIA

*An Enquiry into the Origin and Character
of the Convicts transported to New South
Wales and Van Diemen's Land 1787-1852*

L. L. ROBSON

*Lecturer in History
University of Melbourne*

MELBOURNE UNIVERSITY PRESS

First published 1965
Reprinted 1970, 1973

Printed in Hong Kong by
Dai Nippon Printing Co. (H.K.) Ltd for
Melbourne University Press, Carlton, Victoria 3053

U.S.A. and Canada: ISBS Inc., Portland, Oregon 97208

ISBN 0 522 83994 0
Dewey Decimal Classification Number 365

Preface

This book seeks to answer two questions—what sort of people were the convicts transported to New South Wales and Van Diemen's Land, and what sort of lives did they lead in Australia? I have tried to consider these questions because prisoners made up most of the population of Australia for many years, and because the origin of the founding felons has never been systematically investigated. This enquiry is grounded on a careful sample of prisoners transported, and I urge the reader who is interested in my statistical methods to scrutinize Appendices 1 and 4 before he reads the text. This will help explain the basis of a book which attempts to marry statistical analysis with more conventional ways of writing history.

L.L.R.

Acknowledgments

It is pleasant to thank people, but it would be more of a pleasure if one could mention everybody who helped in the production of this book. It is based on a Ph.D. thesis written in the Department of Demography, Institute of Advanced Studies, at the Australian National University, Canberra, and I thank Professor W. D. Borrie of that Department and Professor C. M. H. Clark, Department of History, School of General Studies, the Australian National University, for their assistance, tolerance and guidance. Thanks are due to Mrs B. R. Penny and Mr L. F. Fitzhardinge of the Australian National University for helpful suggestions and observations. Dr Norma McArthur of the Department of Demography helped me with the design of punched cards used for recording the data concerning the convicts, and Dr John Cobley of Sydney placed at my disposal his great knowledge of the prisoners transported to early New South Wales. Grateful acknowledgment must be made to the Department of History of the University of Melbourne for financial assistance in preparing the MS. for publication, and to Mr Geoffrey Blainey of the Department of Economic History who read through the final draft and made useful comments.

A large debt is owed to Mr Peter Eldershaw, State Archives Officer, Hobart, who fostered my interest in the technique of sampling and who guided me through the material in the Tasmanian State Archives. I must also record my grateful thanks to the Tasmanian State Library Board for permission to examine and use their records. The Archives Authority of New South Wales granted me permission to examine their holdings and cite them, and I thank Mr R. F. Doust and his staff, together with the staff of the Mitchell Library, Sydney, for their assistance. Material on microfilm was examined in the National Library of Australia, Canberra, and I thank Mrs P. Fanning and the staff at the Parkes Annexe for their willing assistance. I also wish to thank the officers of the British Museum Newspaper Library and the officers of the Public Record Office, London, together with Miss M. E. Bryant, who undertook vital work for me in

England. The substance of chapter 4 was published in *Historical Studies, Australia and New Zealand,* vol. 11, no. 41 (1963); I am indebted to the editors for permission to reproduce it.

Unpublished Crown-copyright material in the Public Record Office has been reproduced by permission of the Controller of H.M. Stationery Office.

Contents

CONVICTS IN AUSTRALIA

CONVICTS IN BRITAIN

1

Introduction

The village Hampdens of that generation sleep by the shores of Botany Bay.[1]

Idiots, madmen and cripples, with boys, ignorant clerks and weakly idle pickpockets, constitute a considerable proportion of every importation of convicts.[2]

Transported convicts made up most of the population of Australia in its early years. As late as 1841, approximately one-fifth of the population of New South Wales was described as 'bond', and twenty years previously the proportion of transported convicts had been only slightly less than that described as 'free'. Van Diemen's Land was even more saturated with prisoners.[3]

The importance of the convicts to Australia's development cannot, therefore, be discounted: they and their children numerically dominated the country from the first settlement in 1788 to the 1820s, and they formed the great labour force which laid the foundations of Australia prior to the gold rushes of the 1850s. It is fitting that their origin, character and fate in Australia be examined.

Observations on the origin of the convicts transported to Australia vary greatly, principally because observers have looked at the unusual offences. Some have held that the founding felons were village Hampdens, torn from their native heath by harsh landed-class legislation for trivial offences committed from economic necessity, flung across the world, and now sleeping by the shores of Botany Bay. Others have gone to the other extreme, and maintained that the convicts were persistent criminals from the city slums, and that 'political' offenders were less than half of one per cent of all prisoners sent to the penal colonies.[4]

It is clear that the truth of the origin of the convicts could be established by listing all the prisoners ever placed on ships bound for Australia, and then counting them. Assuming that the particulars are recorded, we could then state that a certain proportion were old men, a certain number poachers, and so on. But because more than 150,000 individuals were transported, this task would present great practical difficulties, and be extremely tedious

3

and laborious. However, there is a short cut available, and this is the application of a sampling technique, which is described fully in Appendix 1.

By use of this sampling method, the general picture of the origin of the convicts can be sketched once the total number transported has been calculated. There are a number of official returns of convicts sent to the two colonies, but it is clear that these calculations were often inaccurate (see Appendix 2 for a comparison of the various sets of figures). It is therefore worth establishing for a start that the total number of convicts sent to New South Wales and Van Diemen's Land was 122,620 males and 24,960 females. To this total should be added some other prisoners if it is wished to calculate the grand total of felons sent to all the colonies of Australia at all times. Thus, with the addition of 9,688 men sent to Western Australia between 1850 and 1868, 1,173 sent to New South Wales as experimental shipments of 'exiles' in 1849, and approximately 4,580 sent directly to Norfolk Island, Port Phillip and Moreton Bay, the final total of convicts is 163,021, of whom 24,960 were women. Nineteenth-century writers give various grand totals, some wildly inaccurate, or calculate totals per year, but no evidence has been found that a careful official calculation was made of all convicts ever sent to Australia.

If these numbers are broken down, it is possible to compare the two main penal colonies: to New South Wales between 1787 and 1840 went 67,980 men and 12,460 women, a total of 80,440 persons, and to Van Diemen's Land between 1803 and 1852 were directed 54,640 men and 12,500 women, a total of 67,140 prisoners.

These were the numbers sent, and the numbers which arrived were very similar because deaths caused by disease, over-crowding, and wilful neglect by ships' masters, were very heavy in only isolated cases. For example, the Second Fleet set out in 1790 with 1,017 convicts, of whom no less than 267 died on their way to Sydney. There was also heavy mortality because of typhoid on board the *Hillsborough* in 1798, which lost 95 out of 300 men, and on the *Royal Admiral (II)** in 1800, 43 men out of 300; the *Atlas (I)* in 1801, lost 65 out of 179 men because of overcrowding.

* Voyages made by ships of the same name were numbered to distinguish them.

Over all, in the period between 1787 and 1852, only 1·8 per cent of the men and women transported to New South Wales and Van Diemen's Land were lost. This amounts to 2,834 persons (of whom 577 were women), and, of these, 283 drowned in the shipwreck of the *George III* off Van Diemen's Land in 1834, and in the wreck of the *Waterloo* at the Cape of Good Hope in 1842.[5]

It is therefore true to say that, despite popular belief about the conditions on convict ships, mortality was extremely low indeed; there is no foundation for a general charge of inhumanity resulting in death on the convict ships. No doubt some prisoners were brought to a premature end by the conditions under which they travelled to the colonies, but the notorious Second Fleet was not typical. Because of the low death rates during the whole transportation period, the number of convicts who left Britain for Australia is virtually the same number who disembarked at Sydney or Hobart Town, except in isolated cases.

The punishment of transportation was not new when the first ships of convicts bound for Australia left England in 1787. People had been banished from England from early times, and transportation of a sort was sanctioned by Act of Parliament in the reign of Elizabeth I, and formed part of the basis of the Poor Law. In the early seventeenth century undesirables were sent to the galleys: John Knox, for example, served at the oars for a time, and so did St Vincent de Paul; but with the coming of galleons and ships which could do without oarsmen, transportation of this sort ceased, though the twin objects of punishment and service to the injured state were accomplished during and after the American War of Independence by housing criminals on old ships, known as hulks, anchored in ports of the kingdom.

Transportation proper was established by an Act of Parliament in 1717 (4 George I, c. 2), which noted the great want of servants in America, and provided for the transportation there of persons convicted of certain felonies. Thus was a new legal punishment created, for, prior to this legislation, convict transportation had been tied closely to the granting of pardons by royal prerogative.

In the course of the eighteenth century, a number of Acts made transportation to America common under the provision of the corner-stone legislation of 1717. Calculations have been made concerning the total number of persons transported, and it appears that certainly 30,000 prisoners were conveyed from Britain during the eighteenth century.[6] Transportation ceased when the

American war started, and though the home government endeavoured to resume transportation after the hostilities, no more than one shipload of prisoners was landed in the United States. An Act of 1776 (16 George III, c. 43) had provided that men sentenced to transportation should be kept on hulks in the Thames, pending despatch to America.

The second important Act of Parliament concerning transportation was that of 1779 (19 George III, c. 74), by which the courts were enabled to order transportation to any place beyond the seas. Five years later it was enacted (24 George III, c. 56) that the Crown could appoint places to which felons might be sent, and it was under the provisions of these Acts that convicts were first transported to Australia.

Not a punishment by summary magisterial jurisdiction, transportation was awarded by courts of Quarter Sessions and Assizes as a rule, though a handful of men was transported by courts-martial, and a few by special commission, such as that established after the 1830 agrarian outrages in southern England. To qualify for transportation, a man or woman must have been convicted by due process of law, though a few men claimed in New South Wales that they had been transported from Ireland at the turn of the century without a trial. Because of the troubled state of the country at that time, this need not be doubted, but should be regarded as a very unusual and belated form of banishment. By and large, only the Assizes and Quarter Sessions transported convicts to Australia, and, although the law and its administration changed, and varied in England, Ireland and Scotland, most convicts sent out to New South Wales and Van Diemen's Land were convicted under procedures which did not differ very much from those of today.

If some allowance is made for changes in the law, and efficiency of the police, a prospective Australian settler might appear in the following circumstances. A man going from his business in London along the Strand towards home pauses to look into a shop. A moment or two later, he misses his watch, looks around, and pursues a youth whom he thinks has purloined it, at the same time drawing the attention of a constable or passers-by to him by crying out 'Stop thief!'. Upon being caught, the youth is taken before a magistrate and formally charged at the wish of the injured party. If the magistrate considers there is enough evidence, the prisoner would be detained for trial at the Old Bailey. Otherwise he might be convicted summarily, by the Justice sitting alone, to a period in the House of Correction. If the prisoner is to be tried at the Old Bailey, he would be cast into gaol to await trial.

Whether he appeared before the superior court depended on the circumstances of the theft, whether the magistrate or police recognized the offender as one who had been before them previously, and, fundamentally, on the willingness of the prosecutor to carry the case forward. When tried, and if found guilty, the pickpocket might be awarded a prison sentence, or might be sentenced to transportation, or death, which was subsequently and usually commuted to transportation. The prisoner would then be taken to a hulk at Sheerness, from where he might or might not be sent out to Australia. What evidence there is suggests that former offences and character played a large part in the decision to transport him to a penal colony. If it were decided to transport this convict, he would be placed on board a vessel for Australia along with approximately two hundred other men. Men and women were transported on the same ships for the last time in 1815, and the practice became increasingly rare after 1805.

The law was reformed during the transportation period, and therefore the course of that reform must be examined, especially as it affected larceny, which was by far the most common offence for which men and women were transported.

Statute laws concerning larceny passed in the eighteenth and early nineteenth centuries were guided by little principle. What there was turned on the common interest of members of parliament who introduced severe laws because they had suffered at the hands of criminal depredators, and therefore wished to deter and punish by awarding a heavy penalty for a repetition of the offence. There were hundreds of crimes for which a man might be sentenced to death, and perhaps have that punishment commuted to transportation, and the letter of the law was extremely severe. However, no one expected it to be applied to the letter, and some of the offences for which a man could be sentenced to death were so unusual that a mere listing of them is quite misleading as a criterion of transportation. Such offences as 'breaking down the head of a fish-pond, whereby fish may be lost', and 'cutting hop-binds', caused the transportation of a negligible number of persons to Australia.

Reformers of the law had little notice taken of them till well into the nineteenth century, and certainly not till the end of the struggle with France, when in 1818 a parliamentary committee of enquiry recommended three steps: the repeal of obsolete statutes, reduction of punishment for certain types of larceny from death to transportation or imprisonment, and punishment by transportation for forgery, also a capital offence. Such was the opposition in Parliament that very little reform was accomplished, and the Peel reforms of the 1820s were principally a consolidation of the laws scattered in such extraordinary carelessness across the statute book. Nevertheless, they did include alleviation of punishment for certain felonies from death to seven years' transportation or a prison sentence, as well as abolition of the distinction between grand and petty larceny, and abolition of capital punishment for certain forms of larceny.[7]

After Peel's time, his Acts were progressively revised. Lord Auckland succeeded in abolishing the death penalty for coinage offences in 1832, and William Ewart repealed capital punishment for animal stealing, and for stealing in a dwelling-house to the value of £5, in the same year. In 1833 changes were made in punishments for housebreaking and housebreaking with larceny, and capital punishment was replaced by transportation. In short, the letter of the law came closer to the manner and spirit of its administration.[8]

The effect of these and subsequent changes in the law on transportation was slight. All they meant was that men who previously ran the risk of being hanged were now certainly transported (they usually were anyway), and that men who were formerly likely to be transported, might escape with a gaol sentence. The important point to stress is that the types of offences for which men were transported to Australia altered scarcely at all. This could be summed up by saying that a man found guilty of stealing money in, say, 1790 might be hanged, though he would probably be transported for life, whereas the same offence in, say, 1840 would be punished by seven years' transportation, or perhaps a period in prison.

The origins of the convicts can be stated briefly in the form of tables concerning the countries of trial, offences for which transported, and so on, but to avoid subjecting the reader to such an intensive barrage, the tables concerning these points have been placed in Appendix 4. Particulars of female convicts are in chapter 3 and the appendices. These tables lead to the following conclusions about the convicts:

Approximately 123,000 men and 25,000 women were transported to New South Wales and Van Diemen's Land, and 1·8 per cent died on the voyage out.

Most of them (130,000) came after 1815, half were sent out for seven years, and a quarter for life.

Two convicts out of every three were tried in England, about one in three in Ireland, and a few in Scotland and abroad.

The average age was twenty-six years, approximately 75 per cent of the prisoners were single, and nearly all were from the labouring classes.

Certainly one-half, and probably two-thirds, had formerly been punished, usually for forms of theft.

Eight out of every ten were transported for larceny of various kinds.

Two-thirds were Protestants, and one-third Roman Catholic.

These are the very general findings, but it is to particular places of trial, and particular offences and circumstances, that attention is drawn in the following chapters.

2

The Places of Trial

A number of slang phrases current in St Giles's *Greek* bid fair
to become legitimized in the dictionary of this colony . . .
The London mode of *pronunciation* has been duly ingrafted
on the colloquial dialect of our Currency youths . . . this is
accounted for by the number of individuals from London and
its vicinity, who speak in this manner.[1]

The overall characteristics of the prisoners, numerically dominated by English, have been recorded in the preceding chapter,
but the English and Irish backgrounds were very different indeed
during the transportation era: Ireland was economically and poli-
tically subject to England; one country became industrialized, the
other did not. Is there, then, a difference between the English
and Irish prisoners transported to Australia?

One observer certainly fancied he noticed a difference between
the national groups; Scottish convicts were considered the worst
and Irish the best in Van Diemen's Land and New South Wales
because, in his view, the English law was more severe for minor
crimes: 'A man is banished from Scotland for a great crime, from
England for a small one, and from Ireland, morally speaking,
for no crime at all'.[2] Whether this is true or not can only be
determined by examination of many case histories, but a comparison of the English and the Irish does highlight some differences, and modify the general picture sketched earlier.

Briefly, the Irish were older than the English by about two
years on the average, included more married men among their
number than did the English, had been less in trouble with the
police prior to transportation,[3] were sent to Australia for shorter
periods than the men tried in England, included a relatively high
proportion of unskilled workers, and had not moved from their
counties of birth as often as the English.*

The Irish convicts, therefore, do not conform to the general
pattern, and the reasons for this will become apparent when
individual counties and offences are examined. But it is absurd

* For differences between offences committed by Irish and English convicts, see the chapter on individual offences.

to analyse each and every county of Britain for variations from
the 'typical' convict; the table of counties of trial (see Appendix
4) indicates that only a few are worth individual attention.
London must be the main one.

Convicts sentenced to transportation and subsequently sent to
Australia from London formed 17 per cent of the total number
of men forwarded to New South Wales and Van Diemen's Land
between 1787 and 1852. In the early years, moreover, the Londoner was even more often to be found in the ranks of Australia's
unwilling settlers; at 1809 the men tried in the metropolis numbered no less than 27 per cent of the total convicts transported
to Australia. Thus the early governors were accustomed to receive London men, incapable of honest labour unless they were
driven to it,[4] and hard to control because of their depraved morals.[5]

Details of trials, and particulars on the convict indents, show
that Londoners were drawn heavily from the Stepney and Poplar
districts, the areas north of the City around Clerkenwell, and the
locality of St Giles's, north of the Strand and centred upon
Seven Dials, Soho. On the south bank, a lesser number of Australian convicts had lived in Bermondsey, and in the north again,
another smaller group in the vicinity of Marylebone.

Here were the poorest parts of London both in the eighteenth
and nineteenth century,[6] and here lived the *classe dangereuse*
from whose ranks Australian convicts were drawn. The 'Rookery
of St. Giles's', home of thieves, prostitutes and 'cadgers'* at the
height of the transportation era, was an endless and teeming
intricacy of squalid courts and yards, and was matched in notori-
ety by another prominent landmark, the large and dirty building
called 'Rats' Castle', which also housed thieves, prostitutes and
boys who lived by plunder.† Cheap lodging-houses and thieves'
kitchens abounded, and even after the Rookery was broken up
to make way for New Oxford Street, twelve to thirty people lived

---

* Beggars. For slang and cant expressions, see Partridge, *Dictionary of
Slang*. St Giles is the patron saint of beggars.

† When it was removed in 1845, there was found the foundation of a
hospital built in the twelfth century. It was here that criminals were tradi-
tionally permitted a bowl of ale on their last journey up to Tyburn. Note
Swift's verses on *Clever Tom Clinch, Going to be Hanged*:

> As Clever Tom Clinch, while the rabble was bawling,
> Rode stately through Holborn to die in his calling,
> He stopt at the George for a bottle of sack,
> And promised to pay for it when he came back.

in one room. Thirty-eight men, women and children were found lying on the floor of one apartment in 1851.[7]

Another part of London which was the haunt of potential un-solicited Australian settlers was the district now designated E.1, where, in Spitalfields, very dangerous thieves' dens also existed. Burglars, pickpockets and thieves' associates congregated there, and helped pass away the time by amusedly watching their numer-ous dogs kill rats in a wooden enclosure. One rookery in this area contained about eight hundred thieves, vagabonds, beggars and prostitutes in the 1830s and 1840s.[8]

Such parts of London were positively dangerous for respect-able inhabitants during the transportation era. The 'Thatched House' in Field Lane, notorious for its receivers of stolen property, was a centre of vice in 1817. The beadle of St Andrew's reported that when he followed a person there to arrest him, he stirred up a hornet's nest at the 'Thatched House', for twenty or thirty men tried to rescue the man he had taken prisoner; the beadle was compelled to get more assistance. On Sunday mornings at Saffron Hill there were to be found on the streets three hundred to five hundred people, most of them drunk. The Irish were especially prone to intoxication. On one occasion three subscriptions were taken up for the wake of an unfortunate girl who had perished in the work-house, but all three were spent on drink, until at last the parish had to bury the corpse, by which time six other inmates had succumbed.

Receiving houses, or 'Hell Houses', were numerous around the City. One had a half-door opening inwards, through which thieves running to escape arrest tossed their booty. A charge laid had resulted in the woman proprietor and her maid being transported.[9] And so powerless were the authorities in the unsavoury parish of St Giles's that, in 1817, when on one occasion a malefactor was chased there, the pursuers were obliged to go away and leave the thief because his companions appeared, and 'they set us at defiance'.[10] St Luke's was little better: on Sundays, persons passing down the street before eleven o'clock on their way to Divine Service had to walk in the middle of the thoroughfare, and were liable to insult. Irish inhabitants of this district were to be found drunk as early as five o'clock on a Sunday morning.[11]

It was not to be wondered at that people led brutish and criminal lives in such areas, though there existed respectable dwellings side by side with the most unsavoury. Criminal activity was, for some, a way of life and the principal source of income. For instance, one couple who were both thieves had six children who all started off in life by being sent out to steal. The eldest one married a girl whose father was transported. They both made their living by theft, and were often in prison, until at last the man was taken up and sentenced to penal servitude, leaving his wife with three young children. She was frequently in custody after that for robbing drunken men, and had an illegitimate child. Her eldest daughter was taken to the Refuge Aid Society, and the second son was repeatedly in gaol for uttering base coin, until he, too, was finally transported. Another daughter married a man who was transported at last, and she was then imprisoned, and delivered of twins while in Newgate. Upon being reprieved, she was apprehended shop-lifting, and returned to gaol.[12]

Not all London thieves, however, operated on a family basis, for gangs existed in plenty at Paddington, Covent Garden, Gray's Inn Lane, and in Spitalfields, where there were several bands devoted to the commission of crime.[13] They trained pick-pockets and defrayed the expenses of defending any of their number brought up to trial. Members were distinguished by marks,[14] and organized into gangs under a 'captain'.[15] One such group met regularly at the 'Virginia Planter' inn at Spitalfields,[16] which was a 'flash' house, or a house that harboured criminals, of the sort at Snow Hill described in *Oliver Twist*.[17]

There were many of these in the metropolis, and the 'Brown Bear' was directly across the street from Bow Street police office. Another, the 'Red Lion', was near the Fleet Ditch. Sometimes known as Jonathan Wild's house, it was there a sailor was robbed and flung naked into the Fleet, for which offence two men were transported. Human bones were found in the cellar, and there was a secret door leading to the neighbouring house. All 'flash' houses had some exit from the back for pursued customers.[18]

James Hardy Vaux, who was three times transported to New South Wales, found the attraction of the 'Butcher's Arms' 'flash' house in Clare Market so strong that he could not resist going there for the evening when he knew full well that his description was known, and the police out after him. He was arrested on the premises.[19]

There is little doubt that numbers of London offenders lived around the City because of the attraction of 'flash' houses in Smithfield, Whitechapel and Shoreditch,[20] and there was general agreement on this point by those people who took the trouble to investigate the nature and incidence of crime in the metropolis.[21] Typical addresses of London convicts were significant: 34 Chapel Street; St Georges-in-the-East; Whitecross Street near the City Road; 28 Longfield, Poplar, near the 'Three Tuns' public house; Tottenham Court Road; 20 Caroline Place; Marlborough Road, Chelsea; Bethnal Green; Westminster; Brookes' Market; Holborn; Whitechapel; Gray's Inn Lane.

At least 4 per cent of the men tried in London were of Irish birth, and it is reasonable to suppose that more Irish were among those who had no information in their records concerning native place. Most of the London Irish also lived in the poorest and most crowded parts of the capital, particularly near Brook Street, Ratcliffe Cross (near the London docks), down both sides of the Commercial Road, and in Rosemary Lane.* Here could be observed the shawl-clad women with luxuriant hair, who smoked clay pipes so short in some cases that the owner's nose reached over the bowl. But the houses were unexpectedly neat for such an area, and the men, though apparently lazy and idling about, could perform great feats of exertion for which the English were almost unfitted.[22]

The convicts who came from such areas to Australia were aged 23·9 years on the average. The mean age for all male convicts was 25·9 years, so at first sight the age of the Londoners does not vary much from the norm. One noteworthy difference is, however, masked by the average. This is the proportion of prisoners aged nineteen years or under, because the numbers make up between 27 and 30 per cent of the London-tried men, whereas the figure for all the prisoners transported lies between only 20 and 22 per cent. Because so many of the convicts tried in the capital were relatively young, it will be necessary to dwell further on these lads.

There is an extraordinary record of a meeting of young thieves, who included a 'cadger' six years of age and several of ten. It was possible to tell how long each boy had been out of gaol by noting the length of his hair and the style of his hair-cut. The meeting

---

* Properly Royal Mint Street. Rosemary Lane was as unsuitable a popular name as Petticoat Lane for Middlesex Street was appropriate.

was like feeding-time at a menagerie: 'At one moment a lad would imitate the bray of a jack-ass, and immediately the whole hundred and fifty would fall to braying. Then some ragged urchin would crow like a cock, whereupon the place would echo again with a hundred and fifty cock-crows.'

Eighty-six of the boys at this curious meeting admitted that they had been in prison on many occasions, and when one lad said he had been gaoled twenty-nine times, the whole body of the meeting rose to look at him in awe, some chalking on their hats the number of times they had been in gaol. The adventures of Jack Sheppard and Dick Turpin, together with the *Newgate Calendar* and *Lives of the Robbers and Pirates,* formed their chief reading, and after a policeman present was asked by the chairman to leave, they applauded heartily, hissed, groaned and cried 'throw him over!'[23]

Active detestation of the police by the costermongers in particular was noticeable in London, and fighting considered to be a vital part of a lad's education, he who had the largest muscles being an object of envy and admiration. To serve out a policeman was regarded as the bravest of admirable acts, and one youth followed an officer for six months in order to get revenge. Finally, he saw the policeman in a brawling crowd outside a public house, whereupon he ran in and kicked him savagely, crying, 'Now you b——, I've got you at last'. He was given twelve months' imprisonment, though his victim was injured for life, and the lad was warmly applauded by the court where he lived.[24]

Many of the thieves at the mass meeting were induced to speak of their lives, and most of them had seen executions but thought nothing of their deterrent effect, and picked pockets under the very gallows. Some had been flogged in prison, but the general feeling was that it hardened them.

It was calculated that there were at least 6,000 boys of this sort practising crime in 1819 in London,[25] and that there were approximately 8,000 criminals under seventeen years of age in the capital.[26] They lived in the areas from which Australian convicts came: St Giles's, Seven Dials, Drury Lane, Marylebone, Clerkenwell, Saffron Hill, Chick Lane, Shoreditch, Spitalfields, Bethnal Green, Whitechapel, Ratcliffe Highway, Kent Street, and at the back of the mint in the Borough.[27]

Gambling in the streets by boys was also general in these districts of London, and one boy sentenced to transportation to

Botany Bay* had bet in units as high as £1. Youths assembled at 'flash' houses, divided into gangs, and selected their captain for the current criminal enterprise. One party split up £400 in plunder on one night.[28]

No one observed with satisfaction the appalling plight of children in London where, in the 1840s, thousands between the ages of eight and fourteen rose every morning with no idea of how they were to get food for the day ahead, or where they were to lay their heads at night.[29] Such was the London background of some convicts observed by the infamous George Barrington, pickpocket *extraordinaire*, who was transported to Australia and affected to be painfully shocked by the behaviour of his fellows on their way from prison to the transport: 'Many were scarce a degree above brute creation, intoxicated with liquor, and shocking the ears of those they passed with blasphemy, oaths and songs, the most offensive to modesty.'[30]

Descriptive evidence of the character of London convicts is confirmed by consideration of former offences, for the number of prisoners previously taken into custody by the police was relatively high. Earlier punishments of Londoners, said to be indisputably the worst of the convicts sent out to Australia,[31] were mainly for forms of larceny, but the most telling fact was the periods spent in gaols, which in some cases did not classify their inmates, so that the innocent and the guilty, those convicted and those waiting to be tried, the insane and the depraved, were thrown willy-nilly in together. An earlier estimate of the effect of imprisonment was still relevant: prisons enclosed wretches for the commission of one crime and returned them, if alive, fitted for the perpetration of thousands.[32] Youths while in gaol were instructed how to commit crimes more cleverly,[33] and one lad was taken up three times between the ages of nine and twelve. He was a member of a gang which became decimated when its members were transported.[34]

Prisons had vicious effects, then, especially on those who had never been gaoled previously. Boys in one exercise yard formed a circle with one of their number going around to pick the pockets of the rest to see who was most dexterous[35]. A London apprentice boy who had been gaoled stated that prison was no use to him

* Botany Bay was a general, popular term for the Australian penal settlements. It may have been kept in currency by ballads, because it was a much more useful rhyme than 'New South Wales' or 'Sydney Cove', and, of course, had the advantage of alliteration. 'Van Diemen's shore' was sometimes used in a similar way.

or any one else as a reformatory—he had committed an offence on the very day he was released.[36] But in the conditions of the time, there was little else he could do: persons imprisoned could only return to their former dissolute lives.[37] It was scarcely possible more effectively to vitiate and corrupt than to confine youths in London gaols.[38]

Some previous offences illustrate the forms of theft for which youths were being cast into gaol and then transported to New South Wales and Van Diemen's Land on subsequent charges: Joseph Johnson, for instance, had received fourteen days 'for a till', one month for picking pockets and three months 'for a till' again; George Roffey, transported in 1838, had been imprisoned seven times for theft; and George Thomas, transported the same year, had been in gaol for two months on suspicion of stealing a sovereign; George Phillips, transported in 1837, had been in prison for one month on a charge of theft, and for six weeks for garden robbery; and Frederick Strike in 1834 was sent to Van Diemen's Land after having been in gaol twice on suspicion of picking pockets.*

Occupations of the London-tried men throw further light on their origin, because although the number of labourers did not vary much from the overall proportion for all convicts, there was a relatively large number of transport workers, personal servants, and such persons as boot-makers and building workers, but relatively few metal and textile workers. Agricultural workers appeared scarcely at all among the London men.

Little but commonplace can be added in explanation of the great numbers of labourers, but the number of workers in transport and communications demands some comment. Most usual occupations under this head were those of errand boys and stable hands, with a few carters and sailors. Men engaged in personal service were mainly servants, though there were some chimney sweeps and barbers, as well as those offering 'errand boy' as their calling. On this point, a prisoner who gave evidence to a parliamentary enquiry at the end of the transportation era reflected that most young thieves in the metropolis were, he considered, errand boys, not led into a life of crime by poverty, but more by mischief and parental carelessness.[39] One such lad was errand boy to a common-councilman of London, and he waited at a neighbouring

* For the sources of information concerning convicts mentioned by name in the text, see Appendix 11.

public-house. This inn was a resort of thieves and loose women with whom he became acquainted, the upshot being that he robbed his master's premises, and was transported for seven years,[40] a period for which a relatively large number of Londoners were sent to Australia.

The youthfulness of the prisoners tried in the metropolis[41] suggests that they included a large number of single men, and certainly the number of married men and widowers was relatively few. However, the lack of data on this point hampers a firm conclusion.

The offences for which these men were sent to Australia will be examined at a later point, but descriptive and quantitative evidence scrutinized suggests most strongly that the areas around the City of London such as St Giles's and Spitalfields were the places where lived the *classe dangereuse,* and where Hogarth's 'Gin Lane' appears a true picture of the background of a sizeable number of Australia's early settlers. There is, furthermore, reason to believe from the evidence of those competent to judge that the youthful convicts were persistent criminals, if not habitual ones, and that they lived a hand-to-mouth street-Arab existence. Convicts from London seemed to have been inured to crime by their environment, the doubtful efficiency of the police, and the general atmosphere of brutality in which the labouring classes lived, an atmosphere unknown to the middle and upper classes of the late eighteenth and early nineteenth centuries:

> In St. James's they keep up their spirits with wine,
> In St. Giles's they're drunk on 'blue ruin' by nine.
>
> . . .
>
> In St. James's fraternity goeth ahead,
> In St. Giles's they fraternize ten in a bed.
>
> . . .
>
> In St. James's they sleep on down pillow and snore,
> In St. Giles's the same, but it's down on the floor.[42]

The counties which transported most male convicts to New South Wales and Van Diemen's Land were London, Lancashire, Dublin, Yorkshire, Warwickshire and Surrey. These six counties alone accounted for the trial of 39 per cent of the prisoners, and it will now be considered whether the convicts from these counties, other than London, conform to the general pattern, or vary from it in the same way as the capital.

The age of their convicts confirms that most of them resembled London, because Lancashire, Dublin and Warwickshire all sent out to Australia relatively large numbers of prisoners aged nineteen years or under, though in the cases of Yorkshire and Surrey the difference from the average was not very great. Relatively large numbers of single men also came from these five counties, and a similar trend to youthfulness among the prisoners was also evident in other industrialized counties such as Staffordshire and Lanarkshire. Gloucestershire and Cork also transported young men, from the City of Cork and from Bristol.

Because the Irish prisoners were generally older than the English, those tried in counties other than Dublin and Cork must have been considerably older than the average. Every way the analysis of age and county of trial is regarded, evidence appears of the prevalence of juvenile criminals in towns. For instance, the inspector of the Irish prisons remarked that 'many' boys aged between thirteen and sixteen were transported from Dublin and Cork,[43] and an official of Worcester Gaol commented on the incorrigible nature of some Birmingham boys; indeed, he held that this was the case with the Birmingham people in general. They were ill-behaved, and those re-committed came from Dudley, Stourbridge and Birmingham.[44]

The character of the people who appeared before him was also remarked upon by the chairman of the Warwickshire Quarter Sessions in 1828. Imprisonment had a most unfortunate effect on boys, he considered, and he had known them committed again on the very day he had discharged them, whereupon they became impertinent, thanked him if he transported them, and sometimes used improper language to the Bench.[45] Crime in Warwickshire meant crime in Birmingham, he pronounced: 90 per cent of the prisoners were from that city, and more than half were boys. Only 5 per cent stole because of distress, the rest pilfered 'in a trumpery way'.[46]

The extent of such pilfering prior to transportation was relatively high in Lancashire, Yorkshire and Warwickshire, though Dublin and Surrey did not differ from the overall figure. It is significant, however, that among other counties which sent relatively large numbers* of previous offenders out to Australia were again Staffordshire and other industrial counties.

Did the main counties conform to the general picture that approximately a third of the convicts were born outside their counties of trial? A relatively large number of men were born outside the counties of Yorkshire, Surrey and Warwickshire, and it is noteworthy that a very large number indeed were born outside the county of Lancashire. More than 10 per cent were Irish-born, and this is not surprising, because in the mid-1830s the city of Manchester was believed to be one-fifth Irish, and the 1841 census listed the number of Irish in the county as 106,000, of whom approximately 34,000 were in Manchester and 50,000 in Liverpool.[47]

The Irish capital itself was the only one of the five counties here examined to show any significant variation from the point of view of period of transportation, the county of Dublin transporting a relatively large number of men for the minimum seven-year period. However, the maximum sentence of transportation for life was awarded relatively few times in Lancashire and Surrey, as well as Dublin.

The five counties also tended to follow the London model in respect of occupation of prisoners transported to Australia; in both Lancashire and Dublin there were few farm workers among the convicts, though there was a relatively large number of textile workers in the case of the former county, and a similar abundance of transport workers and personal servants in Dublin. Among Yorkshire and Warwickshire transportees appeared many textile and metal workers but, again, few farm labourers. Surrey produced a relatively large number of carpenters for Australia, but it should be stressed that, in absolute numbers, labourers predominated in all these counties except Warwickshire, which had metal workers as the largest single group.

To sum up, this concentration of facts shows that the general findings apply fairly well to the five big counties of Lancashire, Dublin, Yorkshire, Warwickshire and Surrey, and that their convicts had similar characteristics to the London ones. It is noteworthy that age and former offences were the only variables to differ much from the general findings for all Britain. That is to say, these urban prisoners tended to be young, and to have been

* For the use of the word 'relatively', see Appendix 1.

punished relatively often. Their urban background goes a long way to explain this.

There is a famous description of the living conditions of the poor in Manchester in 1844,[48] and although there is not enough information to say so with certainty, who will doubt that the convicts sent to the penal colonies of Australia included in their ranks many men from the factory towns so dramatically described by Engels? Among the features of life in 'little Ireland' in Manchester was the practice of drinking illicitly-distilled whisky in houses crammed with Irish on Saturday nights. Such was the quality of this brew that bands of men spilled mad drunk from these dens, armed with weapons such as pokers, and roamed the streets looking for others to assault, especially Irish from other than their own provinces.[49] Brawls and sprees were repeated throughout the factory towns, and although it is impossible to say whether the men from Lancashire were of the lowest class inhabiting the cellars of that city (there were reckoned to be 20,000 such wretched cellar dwellings in 1832),[50] numbers of previous convictions and types of offences committed, together with data on occupation and age, suggest strongly that the convicts were, as in London, recruited heavily from the poorest areas. It must not be considered that all English, or all the convicts, were typified by factory workers in the large towns, but there need be little doubt that descriptions of working-class areas are most relevant to discussion of the background of many involuntary Australian settlers.

There is also reason to believe that most of the men transported from Dublin were living in the working-class areas of that city, the poorest districts of which were among the worst in the world.[51] At the time of the Union, Dublin had a larger population than any of the cities of England with the exception of London,[52] so the large number of convicts from the city is not surprising; Dublin appeared no exception to the general picture of overcrowded, insanitary and rapidly-growing towns. Even an admirer of the eighteenth century cannot make a picture of the life of the poor in Dublin very attractive, for lack of government action to alleviate acute distress was characteristic of the period.[53] Voluntary associations there were in plenty, but the social history of Dublin in the years up to the Great Famine is a similar one to that of London or Manchester, Birmingham or Bristol where, in the last case, a typical occurrence was the withdrawal of respectable inhabitants from certain parishes such as St James's, which was left to fester with the poorest and lowest people.[54]

The growth of slums harbouring a *classe dangereuse* was typical of the cities of this period. It was also the case in Scotland. Although few records give the particular part of Glasgow and Edinburgh in which the convicts lived, the few that do note that prisoners inhabited the poorest quarters. Both cities contained areas that were medieval in character, and the Irish, together with the Highlanders driven from the north, existed in wynds and closes of Glasgow considered to house the very lowest of unskilled labourers and criminals.[55] In these sordid and squalid surroundings were people for whom theft and prostitution were not only the principal sources of income, but a settled way of life.[56]

Though a substantial number of Australia's convicts were transported from the cities of Britain, the English and Irish countryside also supplied the penal colonies with a labour force. Data do not permit the clear establishment of origin of enough convicts for the investigator to say for certain that such and such a man was country born and bred. All that can be done is to examine a few counties which were of rural character throughout the transportation period. Thus Dorset, Wiltshire, Bedfordshire and Cambridgeshire will be treated as one, though other counties could just as well be selected.[57]

Briefly, this test of the overall picture showed divergences which ran counter to those of the urban areas. The men from these non-industrialized counties included relatively few under twenty years of age, and a relatively large number of married convicts. Extent of former offences, however, was as expected, i.e. approximately one-third had certainly been in trouble previously, and probably more. Relatively few received a seven-year sentence, and a relatively large number was transported for life. There were very many farm labourers, and one-third of the prisoners were born outside the county of trial.

Whether this one-third was part of a shiftless class cannot be determined without looking intently at what details there are of trials of these men, together with any statements made by them, and it is seldom that enough data are available. Nevertheless, there is some secondary evidence concerning the rural offender, and although it has been shown that emphasis laid on poaching as an immediate cause of transportation has been misplaced, there is no doubt that rural crime was exercising the minds of witnesses before committees of enquiry. The few rural prisoners transported do not permit or justify an enquiry into the laws of settlement, the effect of Speenhamland methods of relief, and the state of the agricultural labourer in general. However, some impression of the life of the farm-worker would not be out of place.

That the conditions of life of the rural worker deteriorated in the years after 1815 appears certain. Not all parishes were filled with poverty-stricken labourers dying of starvation and demoralized to an extreme point, but there were some where only the devil took the hindmost. Before 1830, in some districts with what observers chose to call a 'surplus' population, wages or relief were sufficient only to sustain life. And if unemployment existed, there followed law-breaking by men who idled away the day and made the roads dangerous at night.[58]

Causes of offences for which men were transported can only be understood in relation to specific crimes, but there is not a little evidence that the condition of some rural workers during the period was grave. Crime was caused by the low rate of wages and want of employment, it was said, together with the vicious system of supporting numbers of young men from the poor rate, and the population was tragically increased by early marriages to avoid the charge of bastardy, or to receive a better allowance from the parish.[59]

Such degradation was not typical of all counties, however. In Cumberland, for instance, no wages were paid out of the poor rates in 1826, and the level of earnings was higher there than in almost any other county. There had been no increase of crime among the agricultural labourers in 1827, one inhabitant of the county congratulated himself, though some persons, he admitted, indulged themselves with poaching because they loved sport.[60]

Rather was it in the southern counties that the rural workers' plight grew so desperate in the 1830s that machines were broken and arson committed. In Bedfordshire degradation of the labourer reached a point where, prior to 1824, all the unemployed were lined up on Monday mornings for the farmers to bid for their services.[61] Such was one result of paying wages out of the poor-rate.

Though crime could not be simply explained by methods of poor relief, many criminal acts did arise from the fact that no matter how hard they worked, men could not maintain their families without relief from the parish. The worker then sank to poaching, and was gaoled because he was unable to pay the fine, whereupon he grew bolder and stole poultry, becoming a confirmed criminal and depredator in the course of time. Counties suffering most were Suffolk, Sussex, Bedfordshire, Dorset and Wiltshire, where the paying of wages out of the poor-rate had gone the furthest. Norfolk, Huntingdonshire and Devonshire were also affected.[62]

It was nevertheless not clear to everyone that men were being driven to crime by economic necessity. In Essex, it was held, the idle and dissolute were the ones who lived by theft, but stern police action had resulted in their going back to honest work.[63] And the Constabulary Force Commissioners, after listening to a great deal of evidence on the subject of rural crime in 1839, concluded that in scarcely any cases was crime caused by want or destitution. 'The notion that any considerable proportion of the crimes against property are caused by blameless poverty or destitution we find disproved at every step.'[64]

Even in the rural counties approximately one-third of the convicts had been born outside the county of trial, and there is evidence to suggest that some of these men were not law-abiding and that they made a profession of preying on the countryside, for a large proportion of rural and provincial crime was committed by migrant depredators, or by men only loosely connected with the particular neighbourhood.[65] In Herefordshire, the countryside was infested with vagrants,[66] and it was considered in 1839 that the main body of delinquents in the rural districts were of that group. This body fell into two classes. One was composed of the habitual criminals, such as horse-stealers and housebreakers, and the second of mendicants. Both these groups travelled the country from town to town and from fair to fair in search of dishonest gain. As well, there were other individuals who made incursions from the provincial towns upon the surrounding countryside, returning to their headquarters with booty.[67] There is some confirmation of this finding in a return from Knutsford (Cheshire) House of Correction in 1837, for of ninety-four convicted persons lodged there in custody, twenty were from Lancashire, four from Staffordshire, four from Yorkshire, seven from other English counties, and nine from Ireland.[68]

The commissioners whose report reveals such a wealth of evidence from those in a position to know the truth about the nature and extent of crime in the country, could find no proof that any but very occasional offences were committed because of want,[69] and the existence of a substantial number of men, possibly professional marauders, away from their counties of birth has been shown. Although the immediate cause of an offence may not have been want, degradation of the rural workers in some areas could do little but create a climate which encouraged criminal activity, whatever the cause. An atmosphere of lawlessness (in the southern English counties in particular) was created, at least partly, by the demoralization springing from under-employment and the handing out of relief. In addition to this, the system of police changed only slowly and well behind necessity, with the result that the creation of a competent force in one county drove the shiftless into another, the habits of vagrancy receiving considerable impulse from the operation in provincial towns of new police methods based on the metropolitan organization established by Peel in 1829.[70]

There appeared to be less vagrancy in Ireland, and it now remains to examine some Irish non-industrialized counties. Five selected at random were Tyrone, Meath, Galway, Kerry and Kilkenny. The number of men convicted and transported from these counties was small, however—only 3 per cent of the total number of men transported, and 13 per cent of those tried in Ireland. The principal difficulty in analysis is the same as that for English 'rural' counties—it is difficult to know whether the convicts were town or village dwellers, or whether they lived in isolated places deep in the country. And although these Irish counties were not industrialized, it is not true to maintain that they were non-urban up to the famine of 1845. Nevertheless, the exercise should give an indication of the characteristics of Irish convicts not tried in the two principal counties of Dublin and Cork.

It is at once apparent that relatively few men were under twenty years, and that the number of married men was relatively high. In number of former offences, too, the Irish here isolated differed from the average figure for all convicts, for the number of men without earlier convictions was very high, as was the number sentenced to the minimum period of transportation. In addition, examination of their records showed that few had moved from their counties of birth and that, again, relatively large numbers were farm labourers and ploughmen and such-like. In short, the

characteristics of these Irish from non-industrialized counties probably differed more sharply from the 'typical' convict than any
other group so far examined. The reasons for this are connected
with the system of land occupation in Ireland.

The sorry story of Ireland during the period, as well as before
and after, can only be touched on, because the offences for which
the Irish came to Australia will afford a better and more fruitful
opportunity of filling in the background. This is not to say that
the Irish convicts from outside Dublin and Cork were all innocent
victims of Ireland's perennial troubles, but if the two principal
cities are set aside then the Irish may have more claim than most
prisoners to the title of 'village Hampdens'.

The regard in which English town criminals were held by witnesses who should have known what they were talking about has
been noticed, and on all sides there is evidence of the quite dissimilar character of the Irish. One observer thought transported
Irish considered themselves well-off, and that they were more to
be pitied than blamed, being mere peasants transported on very
minor charges. He also recorded a difference between the English
and Irish on the transports: the Irish were always anxious to
oblige and were civil, whereas the English had none of these
characteristics. They had to be driven to everything and considered work as degrading, whereas the Irish appeared determined
to work hard, and make the best of their new lives.[71]

No one who has read the report of the Devon Commission,
undertaken just prior to the Irish famine of the mid-forties, could
fail to agree with the grave judgment that it was impossible to
describe adequately the wretched state of the Irish peasantry.
The report noted that: 'In many districts their only food is the
potato, their only beverage water, that their cabins are seldom a
protection against the weather, that a bed or a blanket is a rare
luxury, and nearly in all, their pig and manure heap constitute
their only property.'[72]

From such a background came some Australian convicts considered to be not nearly so inured to crime as the English and
Scottish. Bigge thought that they arrived in a very healthy state,
and his report leaves a strong impression of bewilderment among
the Irish which ill fits confirmed criminals—they were obedient
en route, the commissioner noted, and the separation from their
native country made a deep impression upon their minds.[73]

Whether Ireland was over-populated or not before the famine

is a question which cannot be simply answered, but marriage was at an early age and families large. 'Vive la pomme de terre!' wrote one traveller, and Disraeli calculated that on arable land the population density was greater than that of China[74] for, in 1841, there were over eight million inhabitants in Ireland, many of the densely-populated western counties being the least productive. Undoubtedly there were areas of the country where the birth-rate and the system of 'farming', if it can be so dignified with the name, combined with history to make the life of the peasantry one of misery. Though the Devon Commission's conclusions were not utterly pessimistic, the general picture is of a potentially rich farming country being wasted by the crazy sub-letting and con-acre* systems. The result was at the same time tragic and comic. For instance, such was the paucity of farm buildings that farmers were driven to thatch their cattle with straw to protect them from the weather.[75]

It is easy to blame the absentee landlords for Ireland's plight, and ignore those whose actions were improving their holdings and the lot of their tenants. But they sinned, rather by omission than commission, and must take a large part of the blame for agrarian crime and the horrors of famine caused by failure of the potato. Two factors dominated the life of the rural Irish, and led at least in part to circumstances precipitating transportable offences.

The first was an increase of over 100 per cent in the population from 1770 to 1841, without industrialization, and the second was the obsession of the Irish peasant for securing and hanging on to a piece of land, even if it were only as big as a postage stamp. The landlords and larger farmers were at fault in that they permitted subletting on the scale they did; one estate consisted of 10,996 acres and 'supported' 10,129 persons.[76] This sort of economy was so delicately balanced that any shortage of food was bound to create even more misery than that already experienced by families living from hand to mouth in single-room cabins in a country where, in a normal year, over one million people were in a state of beggary. Conditions were worse than anywhere else in Europe,[77] and Gladstone was unhappily correct when he spoke of 'Ireland, Ireland that cloud in the West, that coming storm'.[78]

When people lived literally on water and potatoes, and were

* Con-acre was the letting by a tenant of a small portion of land prepared for crop.

uneducated, it needed little to blow an always-smouldering fire
into flames of violence. The smell of peat and gunsmoke hung
over a country in which incipient warfare existed between Irish
and English, Roman Catholic and Protestant, landlord and tenant,
tenant and sub-tenant, and sub-tenant and sub-sub-tenant, not
to mention feuds between families that had been going on for so
long that no one remembered why they had started. There was a
nightmare violence in Ireland that was no dream, and to which
the population had become accustomed. The condition of the
peasantry, then, was miserable in the extreme. 'The people had
an alarmed and unsettled aspect and . . . seemed to labour under
some strong and insatiable want that rendered them almost
reckless.'[79] The offences of the Irish convicts reflect the state of
the society from which they sprang.

3

The Offences

'How will he stand in the Newgate Calendar? P'raps not be
there at all. Oh, my eye, my eye, wot a blow it is!' 'Ha! Ha!'
cried Fagin, '. . . see what a pride they take in their profession,
my dear. Ain't it beautiful?'[1]

The offence of *other larcenies* caused the transportation of every
third convict sent to Australia. Over 80 per cent of the group
were tried in England, and about one-third of all male convicts
were thieves convicted in England and sent to Australia for
'other larcenies'. London transported more of them than any other
single county, though courts in Surrey and Lancashire also convicted relatively large numbers of thieves, and there is a clear
association between urban areas, youthfulness of criminals, and
former offences.

London men, who stole objects left where thieving hands could
remove them, illustrate the type of 'other larcenies' leading to
transportation. Joseph Wright, for instance, was in 1787 sent out
of the country for seven years on a charge of stealing lead, and
Jacob Bellett, also on the First Fleet, left his country for his
country's good for the theft of manufactured lining. Other typical
offences included those of James Cartland, transported in 1791
for purloining two and a half bushels of coals from a barge at
Puddle Dock, and John Tucker, who came out in 1790 for the
theft of some lining and wearing apparel taken while the prisoner
was living with a linen draper. And Thomas Robson was transported at the age of thirty-two for seven years for stealing papers
at the Navy Office. He was a clerk, and left for Australia in 1806.

In the *Old Bailey Sessions Papers*[2] there is often available a
verbatim account of proceedings in London trials, and that of
Charles Peeler, charged with theft of some muslin, was reported
in considerable detail. It transpired that the prisoner's wife was
also involved, or so it was suspected, but a charge against her in
the previous sessions had not been successful, and now her husband was indicted. The prisoner at the bar was a weaver and
evidently feeling bitter towards the officers who had lodged him
in custody for he threw himself about violently and stated during

his trial 'that if it was not for the bloody Nosers* we should not get half the Swags we did', and further observed to a witness, 'you are a bloody villain, for the sake of a pound or two, these fellows would swear any man's life away'. He was transported for seven years and behaved in a most insolent manner when being removed from the court.

Levy Lyon was transported in 1809 for stealing over the value of forty shillings. His trade was buying and selling old clothes, and the sentence of execution was commuted. The dangerous character of some parts of the metropolis in Georgian times was graphically illustrated here, for during the trial it was stated that the prisoner had resisted arrest at George Street, an area in which the apprehender found himself surrounded by 'a parcel of girls', one of whom was flourishing a knife. They failed to rescue the struggling prisoner.

Other articles stolen included two blankets, a watch, money, fifty pounds of sugar from a cart in Friday Street, and money from a till. James Cameron was transported in 1802 for rifling the till, and the case is of some interest because it was one of those rare occasions when a prisoner pleaded a reason for his offence, claiming in this case that he stole 'through distress' and that 'it was made up among them [the police officers]'. His appeal for mercy was no use, and he received sentence of transportation for seven years.

Another London convict was John Webb, who was tried and found guilty in 1795 of stealing four gallons of rum valued at £3; and Joseph Willoughby, transported in 1801, apparently took advantage of his position in the City, for he stated that he was 'inn-porter' to the Lord Mayor of London at the Mansion House. He was sent to New South Wales for stealing one hundred and fifty pounds of iron from the roof of those premises. James Bowing in 1818 stole a tub with one hundred oysters in it. He was another individual who nearly escaped arrest through the intervention of a gang of girls, this time in Bailey's Court near Cable Street (running east from Royal Mint Street), and William Pearce was transported to Van Diemen's Land for actually stealing from the mint, he related. Upon arrival at the Derwent he disclosed that he had been employed at the mint with his father cleaning sovereigns. He stole, according to him, forty-seven of the objects of his work.

* A 'noser' was a police informer or paid spy.

There is little evidence from the trial reports, and from an assessment of the objects stolen, that contradicts previous observations on the character of the London thief. Admittedly not all the trials have been followed up, and though an observer's comment that most convicts were useless in Australia, especially the London pickpocket who was a worthless, good-for-nothing blackguard,[3] may not be completely true, extenuating circumstances were few and far between.

Stealing from the person was also a very common form of larceny among the London men transported. One was noted as 'most daring', but John Andrew, sent to Van Diemen's Land in 1825, claimed that this report on his conduct was understandable but wrongly-based, because he was repeatedly punished on the hulk and behaved badly in order to get away. Such an admission was most unusual, although it was reported on and off during the years of transportation that convicts tried to get sent to Australia. Life transportation was awarded in 1818 to another man, John Harris (2),* for stealing a watch from the person at Purim Fair in Duke's Place. Thieves congregating at fairs to ply their trade were for long a source of public annoyance.[4]

Another case of picking pockets was that of Albert James Avery, who was tried in 1818. This convict was a boot-closer aged eighteen, and his case was a curious one in that prisoner, and a twenty-one-year-old confederate charged with stealing a handkerchief from a gentleman, told the court that 'the officer said he would get us transported right or wrong'. The details are interesting because they are almost identical with those which caused the transportation of the notorious James Hardy Vaux.[5] Vaux's account of his apprehension is full of unrighteous indignation, but, considered in conjunction with Avery's case, it has the ring of authenticity: the thieves' London is readily recognizable. Another handkerchief thief was Benjamin Edmondson, who was transported for the abstraction of a silk handkerchief valued at 2s. 6d., the prosecutor stating that the offence occurred on Fish Street Hill, and was 'dexterously done'.

Thieves did not steal handkerchiefs in order to wipe their noses, and though some were worn as neckerchiefs, the one piece of working-class finery, the articles were sold as a rule to 'fences', i.e. receivers of stolen property. These receivers operated all over London, but especially near the City, and Dickens was des-

* Persons of the same name were numbered to distinguish them.

cribing a true scene (Field Lane?) in *Oliver Twist* when he
spoke of a thoroughfare leading to Saffron Hill. In its shops were
great bundles of second-hand handkerchiefs for sale; the street
was 'the emporium of petty larceny'.[6]

Convicts transported did not, as a rule, assess the value of the
handkerchiefs they stole, but one of the criminal classes, interviewed in mid-nineteenth century, talked about his career and
noted that 'the best handkerchiefs then brought 4s. in Field-lane',[7]
and another said that when he came first to London, he had no
'fence' or 'pals' for a time, and sold the handkerchiefs he stole to
Jews in the streets, mainly in Field Lane, for 1s. 6d. Sometimes
he received 3s. 6d. for the best handkerchiefs, 'those that have
the pretty-looking flowers on them'.[8]

Thirdly, articles were stolen, and then pawned. John Mason,
for instance, who was transported in 1818, was a lodger who
later sent his victim a letter with the pawn duplicates enclosed,
and promised to pay for the stolen articles. Notwithstanding, he
was cast for death, but subsequently had his sentence commuted.
Another convict also stole from his lodgings. This was John Hindle
alias Thorpe, who was sent out to Van Diemen's Land in 1844.
His wife was also transported because she had engaged in the
same enterprise.

Yet division of 'other larcenies' into groups is unrealistic, because it is not always clear why the theft was committed. Sometimes, however, there are pieces of information which suggest
the character of the person. For instance, a bed was stolen by
William Guion in 1827, and he felt obliged to tell the police in
Hobart Town that his wife and child were with his father, a retired
coach-master, at Prospect Place, New Kent Road, and that he
had a cabriolet of his own which stood in ranks. And James
Dennis, transported for stealing a ring in 1838, intimated upon
arrival at the Derwent that he had misbehaved on the passage
out: 'I am one of those who wanted to rise and stab the officers
of the ship; Webb was the one who proposed.'

Offences, then, were many and various. A random list includes,
for example, stealing a parcel out of a cart, a cheese, a gold
watch, two nets, and eighteen pennies from a cap. William Player
stated in 1824 that he stole blankets from an undertaker in Shoreditch: 'I got seven years for a watch before and spent six at
Sheerness. I was out twelve months and now am again transported.' Whether this was said in a spirit of cheerful irresponsibility

or gloom it is impossible to say. Other things stolen were calico, a cotton bed valence during a fire, three beds and carpets, shoe-buckles, pewter dishes from Dicey Quay, ten quartern loaves of bread, a cask and two gallons of peppermint from a cart in Fen-church Street, a looking-glass, sugar tongs, a Cheshire cheese, candlesticks, and three half-guineas and thirty-nine half crowns valued at 39s.

This last case was an instance of stolen articles deliberately undervalued to enable the prisoner to escape the sentence of death. Prosecutors for the offence of stealing in a dwelling-house to the amount of upwards of 40s., and privately stealing in shops goods over 5s. in value, generally undervalued the property lest the prisoner be capitally convicted. The juries of London, mainly tradespeople and shopkeepers, sought every opportunity to reduce the value of articles stolen in a dwelling-house to below 40s.,[9] and this practice had occurred as early as the end of the seventeenth century. Such action by juries meant that many capital statutes virtually ceased to exist, though they were, in all their savagery, on the statute book.[10]

A few more instances of offences must suffice. In 1791 Joseph Audery was sent to New South Wales for stealing eleven silk handkerchiefs from a shop, and detected by the sharp-eyed officer of a patrol who saw him wearing one, untrimmed, around his neck, Richard Richardson, a boy known as 'One-Ey'd Gunner', stole three beds and carpets, and Thomas Winstan was one of the many Londoners who took money that was not his. According to the account of his trial, this he did by asking a little girl in the street for change of half a guinea, and, when she gave him the money, running away without giving up his coin (if he had one).

Although we must wonder what to think of Thomas Rogers, a boy transported on the Second Fleet for seven years because he stole twenty-eight yards of woollen stuff, and who told the court that his father had been scalded to death and that his mother was in the work-house, the reader of London trials is driven to the conclusion that there was nothing particularly noble about the convicts sent out to Australia from the capital. Very few and far between were any suggestions of victimization. Examination of many records, particularly the admissions made in Van Die-men's Land, leaves the reader with a very strong impression of nimble minds and impertinence. Noting that juvenile thieves took fruit from nursery gardens in London as if they had a right to it, a police magistrate correctly remarked that the boys in the town were 'much sharper and readier'.[11]

It has been observed that London and Lancashire were alike in some respects, both from the point of view of urbanization and the characteristics of the convicts who were tried and transported. 'Other larceny' cases leading to the prisoner setting out for Australia were also similar in the two areas. Typical of objects stolen in Lancashire were one hundred yards of stuff valued at £5, a spying glass, a pencil case and 5s. 1d., ten pounds of sugar, wet linen from a field, sixteen pounds of lead fixed to a roof, and watches. The list could be extended for pages, and cases cited similar to those described in connection with London.

As in Lancashire and the metropolis, so in Dublin. Here there was the same variety of objects purloined: brass cocks, sacks, money, lead, a trunk, hay, potatoes, leather, bacon, furniture, a watch, lead piping, candlesticks, and spectacles. The Dublin men sent out did not in general enlarge upon the circumstances of their offences, though a few from outside the capital did so: Thomas Armstrong of Co. Mayo, who was transported for taking £10 that did not belong to him, explained that 'I was prosecuted by Edward O'Neill, my cousin; I took it from his house at night; he was a hatter and I his apprentice, and after having left him I stole it from the till.' William Johnston of Antrim was another of the few to add remarks to the statement of offence ('I have lived twelve months by stealing'), but there is no evidence to suggest that the character of the offences in Dublin was not similar to those perpetrated in other urban areas of Britain.

'Other larcenies' were not only committed in the urban and industrialized areas of Britain, though most of them were. An unusual provincial case, in that it was later incorporated into a book, was that of Samuel Clare from Northamptonshire, who was transported in 1838 for stealing thirty-five sovereigns from a stable, and the account of his apprehension by an officer of the famous Bow Street police affords a rare chance to get the view of an officer of the law. Goddard, the officer in question, had been called in to investigate a robbery, and, as he could obtain no clue, went to Weedon fair, where he heard that potential culprits such as poachers, idlers, thimble-riggers and horse-stealers would be present. At the fair, a friend of Goddard's saw two brothers challenging anyone to toss for a sovereign, and his suspicions were aroused, for he knew that these two had until that day been poverty-stricken. Goddard followed up the brothers, and arrested one of them when he found a jemmy and ten sovereigns in his possession. They were subsequently found guilty of stealing, and transported.[12] Both were sent to Van Diemen's Land, and one of the brothers admitted when he reached Hobart Town that the robbery had indeed been committed by them. He was Samuel Clare, aged twenty-three, single, and a 'rough carpenter' by trade. His record stated he had been previously gaoled, and he confirmed that he had served three months for poaching.

Other provincial cases make it clear that, with the exception of theft from the person—typically an urban offence needing a crowd of people for successful execution—men were transported for taking much the same type of objects as previously mentioned, though there was a greater proportion of 'country' objects stolen, e.g. a bullock-hide, meat, beef, a quart pot, mutton, a plough, sacks, wool, butter, wheat, herrings, a plough share, whips, harness and two trusses of grain.

Robert Bence, however, was transported in 1790 for stealing clothes from a house, and had been 'seduced by the instigation of the Devil'. On the other hand, John Avery, aged sixty-four, was tried at Kent Quarter Sessions in 1832 for stealing three sheepskins, and had no such excuse recorded. He had been twice imprisoned before, said his gaol report, and for some years had lived chiefly by pilfering. The prisoner protested that this was not so: 'I have lived by buying rabbit skins, travelling about Kent; I have followed that trade for the last twenty years; before that I was at sea.' A newspaper report of his trial stated that he was convicted for stealing the sheepskins, the property of Robert Lake, at Thanington, and 'having been twice before convicted of felony, the prisoner was sentenced to seven years' transportation.' When he arrived in Van Diemen's Land, Avery stated that he had received stolen sheepskins, and had been in prison for three months on one occasion and for twenty-one days on two other occasions.

A few observations on the character and disposition of the prisoners are available, but in general they say little. However, the character of a man transported for stealing cloth was thought to deserve comment: Charles Redman, tried by Gloucester Assizes in 1827 and sent to New South Wales, was 'a very bad character; belonged to a gang of cloth stealers. His brother seven years last Assizes.' Another man, William Bray from Herefordshire, was transported for the theft of hay, and considered 'idle and disorderly'; and the case of George Whitehead from Derby, transported to New South Wales for stealing copper money, was written up in some detail:

'Whitehead's real name it is believed is George Almond, he answers to the description of a person of that name and the following account of him has been furnished by Mr. Wild, a constable at Sheffield—"He is a very bad character; in 1817 he was tried at Rotherham for uttering base coin; he was tried and convicted once after that and imprisoned again. Tried in October 1820 and transported for seven years and returned back to Sheffield. We have missed him about three weeks." Stedman of *Leviathan* hulk believes him to be Almond who had been on board that vessel. His conduct during his imprisonment has been very bad, so much so that it was found necessary to place him in irons to prevent a violent attempt to escape. Since his conviction he has declared his intention to escape within six months after he is delivered on board the hulk.'

Now these sort of remarks cannot be held to be typical, yet Cunningham, an experienced surgeon-superintendent on convict vessels, confirmed in the 1820s that 'I soon discovered, before the end of the voyage, that no juries had ever made fewer mistakes!'[13]

This leads to consideration of earlier offences, and the number of times the men sent out to Australia for 'other larcenies' had been previously lodged in gaol, or fined. Though lack of data prevents too confident a finding, it is likely that 72 per cent of these convicts had formerly been in trouble, and, assuming the almost impossible—that all men whose records have nothing concerning former offences had never been previously convicted—still 43 per cent of them had been in the hands of the law before. It would be idle to list comprehensively the types of former offences, but 'three months for a waistcoat', or some such object, or a similar period in prison for fighting, or 'a row', or simply 'before in prison', typifies the former offences of the men transported for 'other larcenies'.

Cunningham's comment about the juries not making mistakes is very likely true. For instance, that voice of criminal enterprise, J. H. Vaux, said that officers of the courts recognized a familiar face, and let the judge know.[14] Vaux was speaking of the Old Bailey, and there was less chance of being known in London

than in the country, where justices must have recognized some
of the men brought before them. Certainly some gaol officials
knew a good deal about their prisoners, which gives some ground
for laying more than a little importance on the gaol reports. The
prisoners, said the governor of Bury St Edmund's gaol, were
usually local inhabitants, and their character and disposition easily
discovered.[15] In Dublin, boys when brought to trial for the second
time were transported;[16] in London, it was not so much the offence
as the record that brought malefactors to Australia,[17] and in Warwickshire, a second offence was enough to bring transportation.[18]
In Yorkshire, the third time young felons came forward they were
sentenced to transportation at Leeds,[19] and in Manchester one
magistrate transported prisoners when housebreakers secured
plunder, even if it was their first offence.[20]

In short, then, there is evidence that transportation was not a
sentence passed lightly or for the first offence, unless it was a
serious one. Nor were the men sentenced to transportation auto-
matically sent off to Australia. For instance, Vaux was convicted
with a confederate named Bromley, and when they met again
after Vaux's return from New South Wales, Vaux was informed
that his former confederate had served his seven years on board
the hulks.[21] This was prior to 1812, at which time transportees
were selected, when the hulks were full, from all males under
fifty years of age who were sentenced to transportation for life
or fourteen years, and the number completed from the unruly or
those convicted of the worst crimes among the seven-year men.[22]
It is important to grasp that, as early as this, before the flood of
convicts began in 1815, English selection of prisoners did not
favour the country of reception. At 1833 the position was the
same, the men of the worst character, and those previously convicted for serious offences, being sent first. The main criteria
were previous convictions and bad character. However, after 1833
the position changed, and by 1835 it had been ordered that all
the men on the hulks be transported.[23]

How effective this selection was it is difficult to establish, but
here is the brief life story of one man who qualified for transportation. He was wild and disobedient as a youth, and committed
his first offence at thirteen years of age, when he robbed his
mother. Then he went to Canterbury, fell in with thieves and
prostitutes, and travelled up to London, where he became acquainted with a gang of criminals in Ratcliffe Highway. He be-

came adept at picking pockets under their expert tuition, and then branched out into housebreaking. After stealing jewellery worth £2,000 in 1848, he was apprehended, tried, and sentenced to transportation for life. 'I have returned from one of the penal settlements about a year ago and have since led an honest life.'[24]

It should be noticed how young this man was when he commenced his life of crime. This is typical of the men transported for 'other larcenies', for a relatively large number were under twenty years of age. Thus there is an association between youth and this sort of offence as well as between youth and urban areas.

A good deal of attention must be given to the young criminal and accounts of him, for although the average age of all the male convicts was in the mid-twenties, who will doubt that a substantial number of them, especially the town thieves, had been engaged in law-breaking for years? In 1834, for instance, the metropolitan police estimated that there were in London over 5,000 common thieves and 1,000 habitual depredators tried annually, and stated that thieves operated with impunity for six years on the average before they were finally caught.[25]

Such boys, aged under fifteen, were transported for stealing a saw, money, bread, a necklace, eight pounds of pork, knives and forks, two caps, a pistol and a book, kettles, and a watch. John Halfpenny, a bootmaker's boy of the ripe age of twelve, was convicted at Staffordshire in 1833 for stealing money, and sent to New South Wales. He was four feet two inches in height. Charles Kenny of Dublin was aged fourteen, and sent to Australia for seven years for stealing shoes; he was an errand boy, and previously convicted three times. Other eleven-year-old convicts included George Welch, who was tried in London in 1839 for theft, and who had formerly been imprisoned for two months for stealing sugar. He was tried with another boy of the same age who said, 'It was getting over a wall and taking two pairs of shoes etc.' Frederick John Slough was also eleven years when transported. He was tried at the Old Bailey for stealing three silver spoons in Upper Thames Street, and had previously been in the House of Correction for seven days for stealing a watch. And for picking pockets James Harris was sent from Bristol City to Van Diemen's Land in 1839; he had previously been gaoled for one month, and flogged for stealing a pistol.

One of the youngest convicts was Sylvester Carthy from Co. Carlow, who was an errand boy sent to New South Wales for

stealing money. He was ten. In 1837, two children of nine and
eleven years were sentenced to ten years' transportation, and one
child of eight, two of nine and eight of ten years, were sentenced
to transportation for a period of seven years.[26]

Nevertheless, it was unusual to permit transportation of youths
under fifteen years of age. As a rule they were only transported
when they reached that age.[27] It should also be noted that a few
ships contained lads only, so that the story is not so horrifying as
it appears. Yet it is fundamentally a gloomy one, reflecting the
brutality associated with the eighteenth and early nineteenth centuries. One may admire a Gainsborough but recognize the truth of
Hogarth's 'Gin Lane'.

Certainly the genteel world was a long way from the experience
of one candidate for transportation. It is instructive to compare
the description of this pickpocket with Dickens's sketch of Jack
Dawkins in *Oliver Twist:*

'He wore a ragged, dirty, and very thin great coat, of some
dark jean or linen, under which another thin coat, so arranged
that what appeared rents—and, indeed, were rents, but designedly
made—in the outer garments, were slits through which the hand
readily reached the pockets of the inner garment, and could there
deposit any booty.

"I have been in prison three times in the Compter, three times
in Brixton, three times in the Old Horse (Bridewell), once in the
Steel, and once in Maidstone—thirteen times in all . . . Every
time I came out harder than I went in. I saw Manning and his
wife hung . . . I did 4s. 6d. at the hanging—two handkerchiefs
and a purse with 2s. in it . . . I've lived a great deal in lodging
houses, and knows the ways of them. They are very bad places
for a boy to be in."

'He answered readily as to my enquiry, as what he thought
would become of him? "Transportation. If a boy has great luck
he may carry on for eight years . . . but transportation is what
he's sure to come to in the end." '[28]

There seems no doubt that young thieves were generally the
most troublesome to the authorities in both Britain and Australia.
A witness before a committee of enquiry in 1837 noted that some
boys were as young as twelve, and that many of them had been
tried three or four times, and put in prison innumerable times.[29]
This is correct as far as the convicts are concerned, and so is
another observer's view that most boys had been in gaol, and that

all were connected with loose women. His society had followed up 2,000 cases of juvenile delinquents, and in all but 200 or 300 instances those boys had been confined. They were addicted to pilfering of every description.[30] Another witness agreed:[31] the boys were principally 'on the cross'.*

At the same time, another thoughtful observer considered that juvenile offenders fell into three classes: (a) those not in gangs but in service; (b) pickpockets and those who stole from shop-windows and doorways, frequented coffee-houses, and formed gangs with boys of their own age; (c) desperate characters who had advanced from the other classes, and committed burglaries and highway robberies. These boys were rewarded by transportation, and all thieved under the gallows at executions, particularly just at the time when the culprit was 'turned off'. If a criminal died game, they would speak of him with respect, and call him a good fellow.[32] Some of the boys were marshalled for commission of crime: some would only pick the pockets of men, others steal only provisions, and others join in this division of labour by restricting themselves to rifling tills, or 'drawing the damper' as it was called in the manufacturing districts.[33]

Yet all prisoners in the group transported for 'other larcenies' were not young; though their numbers were relatively few, some were over fifty years of age, and some as old as seventy. For instance, Samuel Bratt, transported from London to Van Diemen's Land in 1835 for stealing three paint pots, was sixty years old. Another of the same age was Peter Tassiker, found guilty by Lancashire (Salford) General Sessions in 1841 of stealing iron. His trade was that of brewer, and he had previously been imprisoned seven times, including one month for the curious offence of being concealed in an oven. One of the oldest men transported was aged seventy, and tried at Leicester in 1838. This was William Sandlant, a woolcomber who was sent to Van Diemen's Land for stealing sugar and wool. The surgeon-superintendent had a good word for him: 'A well-disposed old man'. An account of his trial stated that he was convicted of stealing one hundred pounds weight of wool and a cask of gin, and that there had been several other cases against the prisoner, who had formerly been convicted in 1815. He admitted in Van Diemen's Land that he had been imprisoned for six weeks for stealing wool.

Few convicts were as old as sixty years, and men transported

* 'On the cross': dishonest, illegal, fraudulent.

for 'other larcenies' were not only young but included a relatively large number of single men. The offences committed by the married men were also various. Two examples show this. The first is James Marginson, transported from Yorkshire in 1835 for stealing a gun, an iron key, and a lantern. The nature of this theft becomes more meaningful when the gaol report is noticed: 'He was for several years an honest industrious farm labourer, but could not desist from night poaching.' The second case is quite different. Charged with larceny in a dwelling-house, Henry Hinks of London admitted to stealing £1,000 in money and jewellery from a 'Viscountess T. Dagahy of 95, Piccadilly', with whom he once lived. He claimed that he was taken to the house by a young man whose name was unknown to the prisoner. This mysterious stranger, according to Hinks, had been in the service of Don Pedro in Portugal. The surgeon's report noted that the prisoner was employed as a teacher on board the vessel which brought him to Van Diemen's Land.

Few prisoners were capable of acting as schoolmasters, and the trade of the men transported for 'other larcenies' was usually that of labourer. Nevertheless, transport workers appeared in large numbers, and so did metal workers. Farm workers were numerically many but relatively few. These workers in transport and communications were often errand boys* and stable hands. Offences committed were typified by the theft of a handkerchief, a box and 3s. 6d., two quires of emery paper, a watch key and chains, and sixteen pounds of lead fixed to a building. Other cases were those of a seaman transported for picking pockets, a stable boy for larceny, a waterman for stealing a watch from the person, an errand boy for picking pockets, a groom for stealing forks, a carter for larceny, a stableman for lead, a stableboy for butter from a shop, and a waterman for larceny.

There is nothing to be gained from instancing further occupations, and the types of things stolen have already been listed in some profusion. However, some of the numerically minor occupations were unusual for men transported on charges of 'other larcenies'. In these categories were prisoners engaged in commercial and financial affairs, and in technical occupations. Clerks were also prisoners who formed a distinctive group. All these cate-

* Probably the most famous messenger boy to be transported was John (Jack) Donahue per *Ann and Amelia* in 1824. The record of his occupation is overlooked by his biographer John Meredith in *The Wild Colonial Boy*. Donahue was transported for 'intent to commit felony'.

gories of occupation totalled only 3 per cent of the total transported for 'other larcenies', and two-thirds of the number were men following commercial and financial occupations. These callings were not as skilled as might appear, for under this head were noticed a hawker transported for larceny (undefined), a fish-monger for the theft of some handkerchiefs, a pedlar for larceny from the person, as well as a fish-boy, a 'huxter', and a hawker. But 'other larcenies' were also the cause of transportation of a linen draper named Joseph Wood, sent from Wales in 1824 for picking pockets; Robert Thomas Capps, a thirty-year-old ship and insurance broker, transported to New South Wales from London in 1828 for stealing spoons; a tobacconist named Isaac Sampson, transported in 1819 for larceny above the value of 40s. in a dwelling-house; and a woollen draper called George Biggs, sent out to New South Wales in 1823 for robbing his master. A few men were jewellers, such as Solomon Banks, transported from London to New South Wales in 1817 for burglary from a counting house; Moses Joseph convicted by Warwick Assizes in 1826 for stealing jewellery; and John Walsh transported from Co. Limerick in 1825 for a breach of trust. Some surgeons were also transported, among them being Charles Thompson, who was convicted before Middlesex Gaol Delivery in 1825 for stealing a gold seal and other goods.

Concerning the clerks, among the educated convicts whose disposal in the colonies was such a vexed question to the administrators on the spot, there is little information in most cases, convict records noting simply 'clerk'. There were, however, an attorney's clerk, two merchant's clerks, and a clerk in the customs house. One of these, Henry King, was transported in 1830 for thieving watches, and was tattooed with an optimistic 'J'ai bonne esperence' [sic].

As to the period for which men convicted of 'other larcenies' were transported, evidence shows that relatively many were transported for the minimum period and relatively few for fourteen years or life, no doubt because of the petty nature of many offences. The proportion of convicts sent to Australia on charges of 'other larcenies' was relatively high until the 1820s; however, a number of convicts transported before 1805 have no information on their records concerning offences, so this conclusion must remain tentative, although the large number of London-tried men transported in the early period suggests that 'other larceny' cases predominated, as they did throughout the whole period of transportation when compared with other offences, to which attention will now be directed.

Men transported for *burglary and housebreaking* formed 16 per cent of the convicts, and the main counties of trial were London, Lancashire, Yorkshire, Warwickshire and Somerset. Only one man out of every ten was tried in Ireland.

The offences were typically urban ones, and the circumstances surrounding these crimes can be gathered from one or two case studies. In London, for instance, William Dickens was convicted for a burglary committed 'through the greatest distress', but with no particulars of the distress recorded, and another London-tried man attempted an old dodge when he broke into a dwelling by luring away the lady of the house on a wild-goose chase, having convinced her that her husband had been admitted to hospital because of an accident. This trick was attempted by Thomas Chandler, transported in 1818 to New South Wales.

In Somerset, a farm labourer named William Webb was also convicted of burglary, and said when he arrived in Van Diemen's Land in 1828 that he had broken into a baker's shop and stolen 400 pence in coppers, that he had been two months in prison in Ilchester for assault, that he kept the wool-packs for a farmer, and that his wife and five children were on the parish. Another Somerset man was Benjamin Ashford, tried in 1846 for burglary, who said in Van Diemen's Land that he took silver plate valued at £11, and was prosecuted by a Mr Lear, at Ditchett. A newspaper report stated that he had been indicted with another man for entering the house of Robert Lees [*sic*] in Ditchett, and stealing a large quantity of plate, some of which Ashford sold the next morning, and some of which he arranged to sell the following week. The two were arrested and found with the stolen plate secreted on them. Former convictions were proved against both men.

Another Somerset man said that 'cheese etc.' was stolen, but that he knew nothing about it, and that his brother-in-law was on board with him. The brother-in-law supported his story. The man concerned was Thomas Speed, transported in 1841 to Hobart Town, and, according to the *Taunton Courier,* indicted with John

Dustin and Richard Stacey for burglary in the house of Mary Searle; Dustin (with a former conviction against him) was sentenced to fifteen years' transportation, the others to ten years each.

Among witnesses called in the case was Mary Searle, a shopkeeper, who said she had been awakened by smoke at five o'clock in the morning. When the fire was put out by neighbours, she went to the kitchen, where she missed bacon, lard, money from the till, handkerchiefs, six pounds of tobacco, and some cigars. A man named Brigstock then told the court that he saw a large hole in the bank of a field, and found concealed in it some tobacco. He replaced the tobacco and kept watch. He then observed Stacey come and take out the bag of tobacco and put it under his smock. The witness followed him, and found the bag in the house of Speed's mother, and Stacey in one of the bedrooms. Dustin and Speed entered the house and ran away when the tobacco was found.

Was Speed innocent? Perhaps he was, but lest it be thought that justice often miscarried, his was one of the very few cases in which the convict concerned protested that he was not guilty.

There can be little doubt of guilt in most cases. For example, James Everitt alias Everard was tried in 1801 in London for burglary from a barge. It was revealed in court that he had used the barge to get to the window of a dwelling-house backing on to the Thames. A ladder had been leant from the vessel to a window. William Allman was sent to New South Wales in 1800 for breaking and entering and stealing a pair of stays, and Robert Dean was charged with burglary and theft; when pursued, he tried to disguise himself by wearing his trousers and jacket inside out. Tried in 1830 for burglary, John Adams had been sentenced to transportation previously. He was tattooed with 'Nancy Lovely, yes my dear', an anchor and some obscene marks, and 'Agnes Griffin EE'. Warehouse-breaking and the theft of fifty pounds of worsted yarn brought transportation to another prisoner. This was Thomas Armitage, transported to New South Wales in 1833. A bricklayer ('tolerable') from Yorkshire, this man lived near Wakefield, and was connected with a gang of thieves, of whom several had recently been transported for poaching.

A relatively large number of Scottish prisoners were sent to Australia for burglary or housebreaking, and most of them were tried in Edinburgh or Glasgow. John Flynn, transported to Van Diemen's Land in 1843, stated that he stole a watch, and com-

mitted a burglary while an escapee from gaol for two days; and
James Reid alias John Terry was a labouring boy aged sixteen,
who said he had been apprenticed to a glass manufacturer. His
gaol report noted that he was, despite his tender years, an old
offender, but had behaved well in refusing to take an oath of
secrecy in a plan to escape from prison. He had not, however,
given information about his confederates. He had been previously
imprisoned in Edinburgh, and had once tried to escape.

The few Irish transported for burglary and housebreaking
made away with such items as kitchen utensils, meal, bacon, and
so on. Theft of meal was a peculiarly Irish offence; at any rate,
only Irish took it. They had done this as early as 1791, when
people gathered on the quay at Limerick, broke open a sloop
laden with meal, and afterwards forced open several shops from
which they removed more.[34] It is of passing interest to note that
the notorious bushranger, Martin Cash, was among those transported for housebreaking. In his autobiography, however, Cash
claims a more romantic reason for his journey to Australia: in a
moment of jealousy he fired a gun at a man through the window
while the other was making love to Cash's intended wife.[35]

Also among those sent out for housebreaking was a soldier
named Thomas McGaverin alias McGoverin alias McGavan. He
was handed over to the civil power in Scotland for trial on a
charge of taking £3.10s. He said that the offence occurred at a
toll-gate, and that he was tried with two other soldiers. McGaverin
had been in the 88th regiment for three years, and had received
150 lashes for selling his kit.

Such were the circumstances surrounding the transportation of
a cross-section of burglars and housebreakers. They formed
about one-sixth of each year's intake of convicts, about half
their number was transported for life, and there were many
young men among them.

Some of these youths were not held in high regard by persons
who noticed them. William Newton, for example, transported in
1838 to Van Diemen's Land, was 'a reputed thief', and a published report of his trial stated that Newton was thirteen years
old, and tried with two other boys, aged fifteen and thirteen, for
stealing a gold brooch and other articles. Another lad named
David Harley was 'a notorious thief', whose parents resided in
the Gorbals; he had been last working, he claimed, at herding
cows and sheep. A third youth was John Booth, who had been

imprisoned for running away from the work-house. All were fourteen years old, as was Thomas Dyster, tried at Colchester in Essex in 1826. He was convicted with three other youths, and had broken into a house; one boy named Eley was sixteen, and two named Kidd were fifteen and seventeen. All were charged with taking clothes in the daylight from James Wakefield's house. Eley and the two Kidd boys had all been convicted previously, and all had sentence of death passed upon them. Dyster had his sentence commuted to life transportation. On board the transport he continued to get into trouble, and received twenty-four stripes with the birch for striking another boy.

Many burglars and housebreakers had formerly been convicted, and the governor of Coldbath Fields prison in London went so far as to claim that three-quarters of the housebreakers who passed through his hands were returned transportees.[36] One fits the governor's bill perfectly. Born in St Giles's of Irish parents, this man said that two of his sisters had been sentenced to transportation, and another only recently released from prison. At the age of fourteen, he was sent out into the streets to get his living by selling oranges, and was soon in bad company, and playing pitch and toss. Often remaining out all night, sleeping under the dark arches of the Adelphi with other boys, he learnt to pick pockets, was caught and convicted, and received six months in prison. When he came out, he took to shop-lifting, but was again gaoled. After this he cohabited with a prostitute, 'a fair girl, about five feet three inches in height, inclined to be stout', and engaged with two other persons in an attempt to break into a counting-house. He was sent to prison yet again when a policeman saw his shadow on the roof, and gave the alarm. Other enterprises followed when he moved to live at Shoreditch. The *modus operandi* in one of these crimes was very ingenious: a ceiling was entered from above, a folded umbrella thrust down through a hole made by a knife, and then opened out to hold the falling wood and plaster as the hole was enlarged. Later he was injured when jumping out of a window, his expenses while laid up being paid by his 'pals'. A confederate was then taken, and transported for life, and another friend transported for seven years. Finally, after garrotting a soldier whom he and a companion befriended by pretending to take the Queen's shilling and enlist, he was transported for picking pockets. Returning from transportation,

he burgled the house of a surgeon by befriending a girl who was
in service next door. He had been in prison seven times.[37]

The second case study of a convict transported for burglary
concerns Thomas Gordon or Cordon or Condon, sent out to Van
Diemen's Land in 1852. He was apparently apprehended because
a girl with whom he had been living turned informer. Police
stated at Gordon's trial that nothing had been known of thieves
who took a watch and other articles valued at £30 from a house
at Westbourne Terrace in London, until a girl named Murphy,
who had been living with Gordon, came to them, and said that
Gordon and two other men in the dock gave her only a few
trifling articles of jewellery from the robbery, though the men
divided a large sum of money. The remainder of Miss Murphy's
evidence, and that of the police, 'proved that the prisoners belonged to as desperate and successful a gang as there is in the
metropolis'. Gordon had previously been in gaol for felony, and
was transported for seven years; the other two each received
twelve months' hard labour.

The offence of *animal theft* caused the transportation to Australia of 14 per cent of the convicts, among whom was a relatively
large number of Irish. Animal thieves sent to Australia had, as
a rule, been tried in rural areas, and large numbers originated
in Essex, Norfolk, Tipperary and Worcestershire, as well as Co.
Cork. Few men were from Lancashire and Dublin, and not many
from London in relation to the total numbers tried in the metropolis. Among them, however, was George Gibson, a ploughman
and shepherd born in Holbeach, Lincolnshire, and transported
to Van Diemen's Land in 1843 for stealing a horse; John Crittle,
a groom from Allington, Kent, also transported for horse-stealing;
a clerk named John Hutchinson, sent out in 1844 for taking a horse
('it was a horse and a chaise cart'); and a butcher transported
for sheep-stealing, and also tried in London.

The prisoner concerned in this last-mentioned offence was
Charles Edward Wilson, transported to Van Diemen's Land in
1842. When he arrived he said that he had stolen fifteen sheep,
that his prosecutor was a man named Mayville, that a boy named
Beardsmore, tried with him, was on board, and also that Archibald
Pretty was on board for the same offence. The boy stated that
his master took the sheep from near Leatherhead, Surrey, and

employed Beardsmore to drive them. This person was noted as having been in trouble with the law twice previously. The case was well-reported, and shows how far afield animal thieves operated. Extensive evidence was given at the trial that the prisoners had stolen the sheep from a farm at Ashstead, in Surrey, and the governor of Ilford gaol then told the court that one of his officers had intercepted a letter from one of the prisoners, written in blood drawn from a cut finger. This letter read, 'Dear Father and Mother', and begged for three or four persons to come forward at the trial and swear an alibi. Witnesses gave some of the sheep-stealers a good character, but both Wilson and Beardsmore were transported for fifteen years. The judge declared that there was no doubt of their guilt, and that it was necessary to make a severe example.

In another case John Davis was transported in 1818 for seven years for stealing two sows. He was arrested when unable to give a good account of how he came to be driving pigs down Tottenham Court Road towards St Giles's, London, at three o'clock in the morning. William Holden or Holder was transported the same year for stealing two live geese, although he pleaded distress, and occasionally there are signs that men were stealing animals with some provocation. John Teysum, for instance, a Monmouthshire coalminer transported in 1842 for sheep-stealing, said that '1,300 men were out of employment for three months; I did it through the greatest distress'; a Somerset farmer named James Humphries protested in 1834 that another man committed the sheep theft for which he was found guilty; and Thomas Pevett, tried in London in 1801 for stealing a ewe valued at 21s., and killing it with intent, was overheard saying of the person from whom he stole the animal, 'You are rich and I am poor, when this is gone I'll come for more'.*

There is not much evidence, however, that men had immediate excuses for breaking the law, though very often it is impossible to attribute motive. Little is known of Edward Million, transported in 1791 for abstracting six hens valued at half-a-crown, nor of Charles Davis, sent to New South Wales in 1798 for stealing a ewe valued at 10s., and killing it with intent to steal the carcase. What cases are available for study in detail show that in England anyway, the 'village Hampden' is not easily identified. For in-

---

* This sentence is printed in the trial report as prose, but is probably a rhyme.

stance, John Sowden, aged twenty-one, was charged with stealing a wether belonging to William Chambers, and it was alleged
that the sheep was taken at an inn near Leeds from a flock of
sixty on the way to Manchester. The son of the prosecutor gave
evidence that he saw the skin of the animal and its head in Mr
Lawton's butcher's shop in Leeds. Lawton stated that on the night
in question the prisoner had come into his shop, told him that he
was in the service of a person and that a coach had run over
and broken the leg of one of the sheep. Would the butcher dispose
of it? The prisoner then fetched the sheep on his back and received
37s. for it, and a receipt. He was apprehended the following
morning by a policeman and Lawton in Kirkgate. He tried to
escape but was caught. When told of the charge, he replied, 'It's
all right.' He was transported for life. The gaol report on this
prisoner stated that he was idle and profligate and lived by
plunder, and that he had been previously in prison. Sowden said
upon arrival at the Derwent that he had served three months in
gaol 'for leeches [?]; discharged for a shirt'.

This offence of animal stealing[38] usually involved the theft
of domestic animals such as horses and sheep, but included
also the theft of livestock such as pigs, cows and barn-yard
poultry. A handful of men purloined other animals, e.g. a grey-
hound and a game cock. As the case of the sheep-stealers Wilson
and Beardsmore suggests, marauders from towns stole animals
from the countryside. Besides the classes who travelled from fair
to fair and town to town in search of plunder, there were many
persons who made incursions from provincial towns into the
country, where it was thought that the more serious offences were
committed by migrants, though in Worcestershire (one of the
main counties sending out animal thieves to Australia) the sheep-
stealer was usually a local labourer. Nevertheless, there is reason
to believe that some horse and cattle thefts were committed by
strangers.[39]

In Ireland theft of pigs and horned cattle was by far the most
common offence, and only in rare cases was any other sort of
animal taken. Men sent to Van Diemen's Land did not give any
other information about the circumstances of these thefts, other
than the name of the prosecutor, though one man charged with
stealing a cow stated the offence and then said he had bought
the cow. This was Thomas Reilly, transported from Co. Leitrim.
There is no evidence that Irish were silent because some could

speak only Irish, though one convict, Michael Tierney from Co. Galway, sent out to Van Diemen's Land for stealing four lambs and four ewes, was not able to speak English.

Sheep-stealing in 1819 prevailed to such an extent that estates were almost laid waste, and people afraid to put their sheep out at all, they were stolen so fast,[40] but descriptive evidence concerning Irish crime has few details of animal theft; it is mainly concerned with the incidence of agrarian outrages, bloodshed following transmission of threatening letters, and the activities of the Whiteboys.

Such are some cases of transportation caused by animal theft, an offence which caused the despatch to Australia for life of a relatively large number of men, for the crime was always severely punished. The animal thieves also contained a relatively large number of men who were aged over forty years, and married, but few who had been previously in the hands of the police. Most of these prisoners were labourers, and many were farm labourers. This group of offenders baffles easy description as much as any other group of people, though it seems that animal thieves were not so accustomed to crime as were some other groups of convicts. No doubt this is partly explained by the numbers of Irish among them, for as the Lord-Lieutenant of Ireland stated in 1850: 'It is to be observed also, that his Excellency would wish to call the attention of Earl Grey particularly to the fact that the general character of the Irish convicts differs widely from that of the English. Their crimes for the most part are not the result of habitual profligacy and vicious contamination. They are not hardened offenders . . . nor are they usually found associated in gangs under experienced leaders for the commission of great and well-planned crimes. The offences of the Irish convicts are usually thefts to which they are often driven by distress.'[41]

The question of motive is very difficult to establish in a single case, let alone thousands, and though it appears that most theft was for the purpose of selling the animal, some stolen sheep were salted down for eating later, and buried with a large stone over them. But gangs operated also, as well as the individual labourer desperately putting by some salted meat against the winter. There were, in the 1830s, several such lawless bands around Broxton, Cheshire, including one, the Tattenhall gang, which had been depleted by transportation. Some were bred in the hills as thieves, and trained their children to be the same, and many were transported from around Frodsham, where there was a very bad set of men.[42] In Norfolk, about three miles from Norwich, three of the most notorious poachers and thieves of that city stole fifty ducks, and were transported for seven years for it; they had been in prison twenty times.[43] And in Cambridge, fowl-stealing was a common offence, the birds being sold in the open market, or to the cooks of the university colleges.[44]

Though the Fellows might be dining on stolen chickens, men did not steal horses for food, nor to salt down and bury. Robert Jones, transported in 1791, was charged with the theft of horses, and it was shown at the trial that not only had he taken two mares valued at £40, but the coach they were drawing as well; and John Ruffler, transported on the First Fleet, was sent to Sydney for stealing a gelding.

There is evidence of how men stole the horses. One method involved the employment of vagabonds, who were induced by professional thieves to lead horses out of paddocks to where the receivers lurked. The instrument of the theft then received 20s., and the animals were disposed of to horse-dealers. There were regular depots for the reception of stolen horses, and one man under sentence of transportation in 1828 had been concerned in several hundred such thefts.[45] Some horses were also stolen by Londoners, who, dressed as grooms or stablemen, loitered about the Old Kent Road. The stolen animal was then trimmed up and altered in appearance prior to being sold at Smithfield market.[46]

Seven per cent of male prisoners were transported for *robbery*. A relatively large number were Irish, and life sentences were common. Individual cases give an idea of the origin and character of these prisoners. Joseph Lacey, for instance, was transported for life in 1827 for highway robbery, and noted as 'a vicious bad fellow' by the compiler of his gaol report. The man Lacey was aged twenty-two, his father and mother were dead, and he admitted having been in gaol for two months for breaking windows.

Of quite a different background was William Stevenson, transported in 1841 for robbing a bank. He was noted as a grocer, and convicted of taking money from the Maidstone bank in Kent. Stevenson disclosed to the interrogators at Hobart Town that he had stolen £500, and that his master had been concerned with him in the offence. The trial of this man excited the greatest of interest in Maidstone, and the court first heard how Mr Mercer (apparently the bank manager) had written up to London for the delivery of £1,500 in gold and £500 in silver, which was sent in a box by coach to the town. Mercer became suspicious the morning after the specie arrived, and found that £500 was missing. He could discover no clue either in London or Maidstone. He subsequently dismissed Stevenson, but for another reason altogether. There followed a great deal more evidence, and the jury returned a verdict of guilty almost instantly. The report of the trial is not adequate for the reader to understand the ins and outs of the case properly, and there are sly references to women, including one named Donna Maria, and veiled allusions to 'electors', that suggest there was much more to this affair than meets the eye. It seems the prisoner was guilty, but it is not clear what became of the £500, or who his 'master' was. The prisoner is also a puzzling figure for he appeared to be following several occupations at once.

A second case illustrates a different form of robbery, George Webb declaring when he arrived in Van Diemen's Land, 'It was Mr. Floyd of Effington; he was knocked on the head; Thomas Laskin and William Maunder are on board; each received 15 years; George Dawton, a soldier in the Rifles, committed the assault and absconded.' A press report on this case noted that the participants included a twenty-five-year-old woman who was apparently a confederate of the group. There was no mention of a George Dawton.

Another example of robbery was the case of Thomas Tinan, tried in Lancashire, who took '4s. 6d. from Mr. Nelton at Thomas Street, Manchester, at the riots' in 1842; Henry Hope, convicted in 1841 of robbing in company with others, stated that seventeen sovereigns were taken from their victim ('we pushed him down'); and Joseph Webb, transported to New South Wales in 1833, was charged with robbing the post office, though an alternative account of him stated that the offence was embezzlement of money which came into his possession as a letter carrier.

In the case of the Irish, 'robbery' appears to have been rather 'larceny' in some cases, e.g. Thomas Rorke, from Co. Longford, was convicted of robbery, but said he had stolen two hundred and fifty eggs. James Kelly of Londonderry said his offence was stealing £3.10s. which he claimed to have won at thimble-rigging, the loser protesting that he had been robbed. A report on Kelly

stated that he had lived for four or five years on the proceeds of
thimble-rigging. Robert McAllister, from Co. Antrim, was charged
with highway robbery, and he stated that he had knocked down a
drunken man, and taken his shoes and hat. A fourth Irishman,
William Campion, was also transported for relieving a man of
his hat in a highway robbery: 'It was rioting. There was a fight
and I had another man's hat; prosecutor Mr. Dearby, Kilkenny.'
Although deep analysis of the Irish cases of robbery is difficult,
there appeared to be an element of factionalism, though such
feuds usually manifested themselves in the form of simple assault.

The men transported for *theft of wearing apparel* included
many young and persistent offenders transported for seven years,
and the characteristics of the group were the same in general as
those transported for 'other larcenies'. For instance, James Purcell, tried in 1827, explained that he had stolen a coat from his
father-in-law, and that he had been in the watch-house several
times; David Henry Donney, tried in 1845, and convicted for
making off with a box of clothes, claimed that he had been ten
months in the metropolitan police force, and had been imprisoned
for three months for the theft of a constable's staff; and Reuben
Winstanley, who stole two dozen pairs of stockings, had also been
previously in trouble ('four months for shoes, three months for
clothes, one month for a handkerchief, two others I don't recollect').
The group had been in trouble with the law more often than
not, but an extreme case was that of Luke Marshall, tried in
Yorkshire, who had been put in gaol for three months for stealing
a watch, three months for leaving his master, three weeks for
stealing clothes, and three months for vagrancy. As well, he had
been given nineteen lashes at the hulk for being absent without
leave, and on the way to Van Diemen's Land made himself
conspicuous in stealing wine on board. Another case of a man
often in previous trouble was James McCallum, tried in Perth for
stealing a pair of boots and a coat. He had been summarily convicted fourteen times, his gaol report noted, but McCallum said
that he had been punished twenty times for drunkenness and dis-
orderliness, and had been in prison for nine months on a charge
of stealing boots. Finally, a man in this group of convicts was the
only resurrection man noticed: 'an idle, disorderly, drunken vaga-
bond; has supported himself by theft and stealing dead bodies'.

The subject of this comment was George Barker, who had been convicted twice previously, but who perished on the way out to New South Wales.

Another aspect of the group was its youth. For instance, Charles Downes, aged fifteen, was transported for the theft of a coat from his mother; he had been away among thieves for three years, he stated. Another boy of the same age, tried in Preston, was John Holt, who said that velveteen trousers were stolen from a pawn-broker, and that 'my father was robbed and murdered before I was born'. Some prisoners were younger: Denis Finn, junior, was aged twelve. An errand boy tried in Wexford, he was sent to New South Wales for stealing a cloak. His father was on board for the same offence, his brother on another transport, and his mother convicted of the same crime.

On the other hand, William Button was evidently the bane of his family's life. He was fourteen years old, and sent to Van Diemen's Land for stealing a pair of shoes at Ipswich. A report of his trial disclosed that he stole a pair of children's shoes from a cart, and then sent them to a pawnbroker to be pledged in the name of Smith. He had twice previously been convicted of felony, and had been in prison seven times. This lad was transported for seven years, with a recommendation that he be sent to the peniten-tiary, where the Recorder hoped that he would be made an honest man, his respectable friends having asked that, if convicted, the prisoner be sent there to effect his reformation, all means to that end having failed at home. A report noted that he was 'connected with the most depraved thieves'.

Occupations of the group followed the usual pattern: there was a predominance of labourers, farm labourers, and transport workers, though the number of rural workers was relatively few. Of those employed in the manufacture of wearing apparel, all were, with one exception, tailors.

One unusual trade, however, was that of grocer. The man con-cerned was Carl Leopold Saurien, transported to Van Diemen's Land in 1833 for stealing clothes. He said that his father-in-law was a tailor at Tilsit in Prussia, and a note on his record stated that, according to the certificates he had, his previous character had been good. A newspaper noted briefly that a Prussian was tried for burglary at Ramsgate, and the report follows two others describing theft of wearing apparel from the landlord of the 'Star' public-house in Sandwich.

Though a large number of offences remain for discussion, they concern less than one-quarter of the convicts. Of this group, 4 per cent were sent to Australia for offences of a public nature, and 3 per cent for assaults on the person. (See Appendix 4.)

Half of the men despatched to the penal colonies for *offences of a public nature* were convicted for coining, or for passing counterfeit money. That is to say, palpable 'political' offenders were few in number, though some 'miscellaneous' offences committed by the Irish could be regarded as political in character, and will be examined later in this chapter. Charges which brought conviction to coiners, and offenders associated with the manufacture and uttering of spurious money, were typified by entries on the records such as 'forged notes' and 'uttering counterfeit coin'. Joseph Crighton, tried in Lancashire in 1842, was transported for having in his possession a mould for making coins, and said upon arrival at Hobart Town that it was for creating half-crowns and shillings. A few variations on the theme were accomplished by Stephen Evans, who was transported for fourteen years for the forgery or coining of a bank token, Jophet White, who came to New South Wales in 1816 from Ireland, for possessing improperly counterfeit stamp dies, and Patrick Smith, sent from Dublin City in 1817 for vending cards with a forged stamp.

Most coiners, however, were tried in England, and particularly London, where the practice of coining money generally engaged two people, usually a man and a woman. One such couple was arrested in 1845, though their guardian bulldog hampered the police by holding one officer by the trousers for twenty-five minutes. Four galvanic batteries in full play, and 500 counterfeit coins, were found, and the coiner received fifteen years' transportation. Passing such coin was accomplished by offering a shopkeeper a good coin first, getting back the coin by pretending to have change, discovering there was none, and then palming off the false coin.[47]

Over half the coiners transported were sentenced for fourteen years, and many came during the years 1815-24, when there was a drive on such offenders. But no matter when they were transported, coiners were likely to have unusual occupations for convicts for among them were an attorney's clerk, a shopkeeper and land surveyor, a merchant's clerk and travelling agent, a barber, a captain of marines, a land surveyor and draughtsman, a hawker, and a cattle dealer.

The shopkeeper who doubled as land surveyor was Patrick

Fallon, convicted in Lancashire in 1834, and he was tried with two other men for having made and counterfeited twenty pieces of coin resembling shillings. A report of the trial noted that John Healy, in the employ of the police, engaged a man named Sowerby to detect coiners, and introduced him to a woman who guided Sowerby to a house at Oak Place, Liverpool, where the prisoners were casting shillings from a plaster of paris mould. He spoke with them, and then went to the police, who took the coiners into custody. Sowerby admitted in court that he was employed to entrap people to make coins in order to procure their conviction. His unsavoury occupation brought results, for the jury found the three men guilty. The judge declared them to be common pests of society no longer fit to stay in England, and ordered their transportation for life.[48]

The remainder of the group of men tried for offences of a public nature was dominated by Irishmen transported for riots, routs and affrays. Such persons were on the *Minerva* in 1799, after the 1798 uprising, others were convicted in 1817 for administering unlawful oaths, and a batch came in the 1820s for offences under the Insurrection Act. Patrick Crehan and Patrick Green, for example, were transported for being improperly absent from their residences,[49] and Patrick McDonald was sent out in 1841 for Ribbonism,* an offence which was connected with the Whiteboys,[50] who terrorized different parts of Ireland, attacked houses and people to prevent new tenants replacing old ones, and in general resisted evictions by the landlords and their agents. Other riotous offences included attacking Shanagolden post office, robbing yeomen of their arms, seizing arms, and insurrection and firing at the King's troops.

When the land was as hopelessly sub-divided as it was in parts of Ireland, people became obsessed with hanging on to the few miserable acres from which they grubbed a living, existing

---

* One convict (T.S.A. 2/78, p. 45) made the following statement in Van Diemen's Land about the Ribbon men: 'Ribbon sects are illegal combinations, sworn to obey their chief, to take the arms of the Protestants and turn them out of the country. County delegates travel over Ireland giving the Ribbon men new signs and making appointments to meet at certain times. They also travel through England and Scotland. The members of the Society choose their delegates by a polling. They assemble every quarter. The oldest delegate is appointed chairman and has the general superintendence of the delegates. Parish masters are under the delegates and under the parish masters are Guardians who have the power to dismiss delegates. Each guardian is over twelve men. One parish master is over them and one delegate over all the parishes in the country.'

at a level scarcely above that of their pigs in an atmosphere of violence where ancient feuds served as an outlet for a desperate kind of pugnacity.* It was therefore no wonder that the Whiteboys thrived. All conditions favoured the organization, which had existed since mid-eighteenth century under a wide variety of names such as Peep-o'-Day-Boys, Thrashers, Righters, Carders, Caravats, Rockites, Ribbonmen, the Lady Clares, the Terry Alts and Blackfeet, and in Co. Clare in 1830 almost the whole peasantry was in a Whiteboy association.[51] However, Tipperary was the principal seat of riot, and an officer of the Irish constabulary could only account for this by remarking helplessly that, throughout all the ages, the county had been remarkable for the lawlessness of its peasantry.[52]

English rioters, on the other hand, were all tried between 1830 and 1832 during the agricultural disturbances,[53] and came almost entirely from certain southern districts. In Dorset, for instance, Richard Bleathman was transported in 1832 for assembling with others in the town of Blandford, and beginning to pull down the house and premises of George Moore.

Treason and sedition also brought a handful of men to Australia. Most of them were Irish, a typical charge being that brought against John Moroney, tried in Co. Tipperary in 1815 for being 'a seditious and disorderly person'.

There was also a number of less desperate offences, such as bigamy. William Gale was a case in point. He made a practice of marrying, and observed that not one of his wives came against him at his trial. He had some grounds for pride: he had had four wives, three of whom were alive when he was charged, and had married first at the age of seventeen. Another bigamist was Stephen Aldhouse, who was tried in 1842. His was an unusual case because he was a clergyman. He stated that he had believed

* Although poverty, high rents and evictions were all too evident, it was not unknown for comparatively wealthy Irish to live in squalor rather than reveal their assets, and thus have their rent increased. Wakefield (cited in Maxwell, *Ireland under the Georges,* p. 139) wrote in 1812 of visiting a farmer who lived in miserable circumstances: 'I asked him why he did not get a better house. His reply was that he should break his shins going upstairs.' This man was relatively wealthy. Cunningham (*Two Years in N.S.W.,* vol. 2, p. 241) asked the Irish convicts on a transport who would be their captain on the voyage out to Australia, and they at once referred to the mythical leader of the Ribbon men: 'and one of them exclaimed in a laughing good-humoured Irish way, "Och, your honour, we have got a captain already—that is *Captain Rock,* as he sits there, and a very good captain he is!"' Cunningham notes that this name was given to many individuals in Ireland.

his former wife dead, and remarried after eighteen years. Another Londoner was John Major Hallett, transported in 1852 to Van Diemen's Land. He was a coach painter, aged thirty-three, who represented himself as single, and won the affection of Sarah Turner, who had saved up £100 while in service. After he had been married to her for a month, Hallett absconded with all his bride's property. It was submitted in evidence, that he had paid his passage on board a vessel bound for America.

Finally, there were four other types of crimes listed as offences of a public nature. The first was perjury, for which only Irish were transported,* Patrick Donohue, for example, swearing falsely that he saw someone making pikes, and Patrick Hughes stating untruthfully that a certain woman had burnt down a house. The second offence was that of smuggling, and the third of aiding prisoners. William Pocock, for example, harboured a felon, and thereby got himself transported for ten years. He remarked in Van Diemen's Land that he had rescued a man charged with picking pockets. Richard Shead also was punished for unwise loyalty, and was transported to New South Wales in 1832 for taking instruments into the Cambridge gaol to help two inmates escape. Shead was employed by the keeper of the gaol, where he had been earlier a prisoner, to work in the garden, and had given the two prisoners material with which to make keys. Fourthly, some men committed sacrilege. One of these was Thomas Chetwode, who broke into the parish church at Condover, Shropshire, and took two silver flagons, two silver cups, and one silver plate valued at £30. The vicar found the chest in which the articles were kept had been forced open with an iron palisade, part of the fence around the burial yard. Chetwode had been seen enquiring for work on the morning preceding the robbery, and had attended evening service that day. About twelve months after the robbery, the prisoner offered part of the plate for sale to a watchmaker of Bridgnorth, whose suspicions were aroused when the prisoner said he could bring enough to make it up to twelve pounds weight.

Various sorts of *assault on the person* caused the transportation of 3 per cent of the convicts to Australia. Over half these men

---

* That is, only Irish were selected in the sample. Probably a few prisoners of other nationality were also transported for the offence, but their numbers are unlikely to be very large.

were tried in Ireland, and some tried elsewhere were Irish by birth. For instance, Michael O'Grady was convicted in Lower Canada for murder, and gave the following unattractive explanation: 'It was Mary Moore; she was a rambling woman and used to live at my house sometimes; I was drunk, I don't know what happened, it was with a pair of scissors.' Another Irish-born prisoner of the Crown, tried in Scotland, spoke at some length of the offence which landed him on the shores of Van Diemen's Land. This was James Hickie, who said that 'John Green was the murdered man; two men killed him and I was part concerned. Death was commuted to life transportation. Dennis Doolen and Pat Riddon were hanged. He was struck on the head with a poker and some iron. The murder was devised in my house; I took no means to prevent its accomplishment; our intention was to beat him till he was sufficiently bruised to go to hospital'.

A report of this offence is headed 'The Bishopsbridge Murder', and stated that the prisoners were charged with having, on a bridge over the Edinburgh-Glasgow railway line, assaulted John Green, a ganger, with an iron poker, bar or rod, felled him to the ground, and jumped on him, and kicked him repeatedly. Evidence was given by the men's landlady that the kitchen poker was missing, and that, the night before the murder, James Hickie had taken up the poker and put it to his forehead, saying that that was the spot to give a man a blow. Evidence was also given that Hickie was fifteen yards away when the beating was inflicted. This probably saved him from the gallows, for he was recommended to mercy by the jury. His two companions were hanged.

The Irish who were tried for murder or manslaughter came from the rural areas as a rule, and especially the south and west. For instance, James Dwyer was sent to Van Diemen's Land from Tipperary for manslaughter. He admitted to the offence, and stated that his brother was on board and that their victim was beaten when he applied twice for the rent. Dwyer's brother remarked when questioned that they had neglected to give the rent-collector his money. Other statements included the following:

'It was Cornelius Cameron. I know nothing about it.'

'He was struck on the head with a stone.'

'I struck him on the head five times and broke his skull. I did not intend to kill him. My brother Daniel escaped.'

'John Baring was killed through family affairs. He was struck on
the head with a stone and died the next day.'
'It was a riot between two factions . . . We were coming from a
fair.'
'He was struck with a stone.'

Such offences were principally motivated by family quarrels
and vendettas against tenants who replaced the old ones, for
crimes of violence in Ireland were almost always connected with
the possession of land, which was regarded as the first necessity
of life, or with feuds.[54] In King's Co. such a local state of war
existed between the Darrags and Cummins in the 1820s. These
two families attacked each other all the time, at fairs, funerals,
markets and such gatherings, without any preceding quarrel that
was apparent to the observer. Their weapons were stones and
loaded sticks about two feet long with a lump of lead at one end.
These weapons were carried concealed in coat sleeves. But the
most usual weapon was stones, with which they were extremely
accurate. They gave cruel blows with these and, if a man fell,
his head was pounded with more stones till he appeared dead or
senseless.

Possession of land was the second of the two principal causes
of violence and outrage, and if land was taken, a tenant evicted,
or a labourer dismissed, the manner of vengeance was again
murderous. Over and above these two causes of bloodshed was
another which arose when a man gave information to the police,
or evidence in a court case. The offending parties then laid in
wait and attacked, generally when the victim was returning home
from a fair or market. If he recovered from one of these assaults,
he was never the same man again.[55]

This was the position in the 1820s, and by 1844 the conditions
had not altered for the better, the long history of lawless violence,
especially in Tipperary, being remarked upon by the Devon
Commissioners who enquired at great length into the land question.
They confirmed that if a man were removed from a holding
which he had neglected or misused, he was looked upon in certain
districts as an injured man, and his friends wreaked terrible vengeance: 'At times a large numerical proportion of the neighbourhood look with indifference upon the most atrocious acts of violence, and by screening the criminal, abet and encourage the
crime. Murders are perpetrated at noonday on a public highway,

and whilst the assassin coolly retires, the people look on, and evince no horror at the bloody deed'.[56]

On the other hand, the offences of English prisoners give little evidence of violence endemic in society. William Weyman, tried in Gloucester in 1841, was transported as a result of bad luck (according to him), for when he and another person were firing pistols in turn at a candle, trying to snuff out the flame with a ball, his pistol burst and the swivel struck his friend in the right jaw, as a result of which he died. But another Gloucestershire case reflected an ugly incident, John Thomas (2) explaining his case thus: 'It was Constable Charles Pearce of Bristol. I was rescuing a man whom he had in custody for apples; he lived three weeks. He struck my son on the head with his staff and me on the arm. I did not strike him with any weapon. I then closed and we fell down. My son is on board.' His son's version was 'a police constable was hit with a fist of stones. It was my brother whom the constable had in charge, having seen him in the garden.' The third report is from a newspaper, which noted that apples were stolen from an orchard by the son, and that Pearce, a night-watchman, was attacked by the elder prisoner and another man, stones in hand. Many witnesses were called, and several gave the prisoners a good character, but all were transported for life for manslaughter.

Some more examples of the English prisoners' accounts of offences illustrate their nature:

'I and another young man went into a public house to drink and fell in with some more; one challenged me to fight; we went into the fields. The man who died struck the young man who was with me and I returned it. I struck the man with my fist and he died in five days after. My father was entirely innocent of it. He came up and I had struck him.'

'I was drunk in a public house with a young woman, she aggravated me and I struck her with my fist; she staggered across the room, fell against a sofa and died in half an hour afterwards.'

'It was through a quarrel between me and my wife; when another man interfered I struck him with my fist and he fell down dead.'

'Simon Levi was out shooting with me; I had a quarrel with someone else and in firing at him I shot Levi. I was drunk at the time.'

'I met a man on the road as I was going home from work; he was drunk and was found dead next morning. The man who had been working with me swore that I struck him with my fist.'

'I was going to strike one of the children: [my wife] prevented me and I struck her over the head with a plank.'

'My mother was living with me: I struck her because she wanted to go to my niece; I did not intend to hurt her, I merely wished to prevent her . . . she was eighty-five and had been very ill.'

The man concerned in this last-mentioned case was Thomas Breckenridge, transported in 1836, who had, his gaol report noted, a certificate signed by 125 persons as to his character. A press report of his trial noted that the deceased, an old woman of eighty-four, had left the house of the prisoner, and gone to live with her granddaughter. The prisoner, on the evening of the day when the offence occurred, came to the house and attempted to take the old lady back to his premises by force, and for that purpose took her up in his arms. His mother resisted and they struggled on the floor. The neighbours then interceded, and he left. The old lady was much agitated, and was unable to sit upright, and after two days in that state, she died. Breckenridge's employers, called in exculpation, gave him an excellent character for sobriety, steadiness and peaceful behaviour. The jury unanimously returned that the panel was guilty of culpable homicide, but strongly recommended him for mercy. The judge thereupon instantly sentenced him to life transportation, remarking that he could not understand why the jury had recommended mercy.

Other forms of assault, apart from homicide, sent men to Australia, and again the Irish form a disproportionately large element among the felons transported for such offences as assault, cutting and wounding, and malicious assault. The Irish gave evidence of their crimes in such statements as the following:

'Assaulting Dr. Hobbs with a stick . . .'

'Firing at Pat Ryan; he was shot in the belly with a pistol at Co. Tipperary.'

'Throwing a stone at William Fogherty, for spite.'

'Assaulting the police with firearms; they were ejecting a tenant and we resisted.'

'Grievous assault on a girl. She was a bad girl. She was struck with a stone. I was drunk.'

'Aggravated assault on Neil and James McNee. I owed them

money and there was a dispute about it. I knocked them down
with a spade. They struck me first.'
'I did not commit the offence, but was suspected, being at enmity
with him.'
'Assaulting a man about some land.'

There is, therefore, evidence that jealousy and spite, as well
as land troubles, lay behind Irish offences of assault, but eviction
and replacement of tenants was the cause of such bloodshed as
a rule, in one case two men being transported for firing at and
wounding a man placed on another's land. This man was then
murdered on his way to Mass, and when the priest ran out, some
of the country people murmured against him, and openly declared that it was a pity the priest himself was not struck down.
This was a general feeling, it was thought, among the common
people in Co. Tipperary: 'When turned out of the land, they get
demoralized, and frantic, and savage, and wild; and they go idle
about, and congregate together, and meet at wakes, and combine,
and then such and such a person's destruction is determined on;
and they prosper by degrees, two or three times, and any man
who considers himself aggrieved will join them, and they will meet
in the town, and speak of such a person, and say, it is a pity not
to do so and so to him, and they will watch him till they have
revenge on some party. I recollect a summer or two ago, I could
scarce go to my door that I did not hear of one person or the
other being shot. I have met a quantity of them, all armed, in the
open day, when I was going to take a walk—they never said
anything to me; they will never attack any one for money, but for
this revenge about the ground . . . touch the farm, and turn them
out, and they get frantic and wild,—the mind gets changed, and
there is sure some misfortune to follow from that'.[57]

Why the peasants sometimes became 'frantic and wild' is
suggested by the fact that arrears of rent were collected by taking
cattle. Corn was also seized, and even cabbages growing in the
garden; the very beds were taken from tenants and the saddles
from off the horses. Some people were stripped bare of everything
but their clothes, and in one notorious eviction the people had
their homes ruthlessly destroyed. This was in the village of Bal-
linglass, where the inhabitants were not in arrears with their
rent, and had in fact reclaimed 400 acres of bog. A detachment
of infantry, at the instigation of a Mrs Gerrard, carried out the

eviction, during which houses were ripped down and roofs torn off. Women and children ran about screaming with fear, or clung to door-posts from which they had to be forcibly removed. That night these people slept in the ruins, but next day the wreckage of their dwellings was burnt, and no neighbours permitted to take them in.[58]

Such shocking scenes are not reflected in the offences for which English prisoners were sent out to New South Wales and Van Diemen's Land, as the following explanations show:

'Wounding a gamekeeper whilst poaching.'

'Tried with my brother William for shooting and wounding a gamekeeper. I was poaching at the time.'

'Cutting and wounding French, a farmer's son.'

'He never was shot at; a man with me had a gun. Bennett and a lot more attacked us with sticks.'

'I cut my wife's throat because she cohabited with other men.'

'Poaching, shooting two pheasants and assaulting Samuel Stucklin, gamekeeper to Sir Walter Wigmore.'

'Stabbing a man in the side in a street row.'

'Maliciously wounding John Lucas in a street row.'

'Shooting with intent to kill; prosecutor Lord Kensington; I was shot in the head and my hand was cut.'

'Cutting and wounding William Jolly with a hoe.'

'Cutting and wounding a police constable in the Farm House inn at Lambeth; I had been there two hours before the row commenced, and was in bed when apprehended.'

The last-mentioned case was that of John McShane, and a report of his trial in *The Times* supports his statement made in Van Diemen's Land. The newspaper recorded that McPhane [*sic*], Richard Popham and William Donogue were charged with cutting and wounding police-constable Whatmow. The constable said in evidence that when about ten yards from the door of a beer-shop called the 'Farmhouse' he was struck a violent blow by Popham, who then tried to get to the beer-shop, and inflicted more blows on Whatmow. During the struggle, McPhane came out of the 'Farmhouse', and also struck the constable, who was thus forced to let go of Popham. When trying to deal with McPhane, Whatmow was kicked several times by the third prisoner, Donogue, who also appeared from the beer-shop. Donogue was finally secured in the tap-room of the inn, and McPhane found in bed at his lodgings. He at once said, 'I knew I should be nailed for this, but I shall only be fined, and if it should be £5 or even £10, I shall pay it.'

The judge remarked that the prisoners had committed a very serious and aggravated assault. The fact of their carrying such dangerous weapons as that produced (Popham's 'life preserver') was a circumstance of considerable aggravation. Donogue was then acquitted, and a sentence of fifteen years' transportation passed on the other two.

The crime of rape was another offence which sent a few men to Australia. Typical statements were:

'Assault with intent to ravish; prosecutrix Sarah Burley, 19 years, Doncaster.'

'Assault to ravish; a child eight years old. I was in liquor at the time.'

'Rape; on Bridget O'Donnell, twenty-five years old, on a fair night; prosecutrix at Tipperary.'

'Rape; on Mary Carey, aged twenty, on the road.'

One man was transported from India for this offence. This was William Haines, who was tried by a court-martial at Bombay in 1850 for carnally knowing a girl under the age of eight years.

Another offence of violence against the person was that of assault and robbery. Nearly all men tried for this offence were English, and the Irish were conspicuous by their absence. A man transported in 1791 took advantage of his victim when he was hustled by a mob outside Somerset House; and William Parish, transported for assault with a pistol with intent to rob, was alleged to have said, 'Your money or your life, you buggerer, or I will blow your bloody brains out.' His prospective victim, however, attacked Parish, who was presenting a pistol at him. There was a scuffle in which the robber got the worst of it, pleading finally (according to the triumphant victim), 'For God's sake give me a good licking and let me go.' He was tried as early as 1784, and was transported for seven years on the First Fleet.

Some other examples of assault and robbery brought forth the following statements:

'I used violence. I took his hat and handkerchief.'

'Stealing two half-crowns; they were won from a man with thimbles. He wanted them back and I assaulted him.'

'Prosecutrix Miss Ovendale, Tapsfield. It was nearly dark; I used abusive language and stole her reticule containing 30s.'

A press report on the reticule-stealer's enterprise noted that

Frederick Wood, a twenty-two-year-old shoemaker, was charged with assaulting Susannah Holingdale [*sic*] and Harriet Faulkner. Susannah Holingdale was seized, shaken, and knocked down, and then gave the prisoner her purse. Police-constable Puddeford said the prisoner was the son of respectable parents at Westerham. He had known him for eleven years, and he had not always borne a good character and had been in custody.

Offences of a different character were abduction and kidnapping, for which a few men were sent to Australia. Convict records give no reasons for the abductions, though in the case of Edward Murray, from Co. Roscommon, six men were concerned with the sixty-year-old prisoner. In remote parts of Ireland, abduction was not unknown until well into the nineteenth century. Girls, and sometimes middle-aged women, would be fixed upon by some enterprising fellow who, with the aid of friends, would drag the woman concerned out of her bed at night, throw her on to a horse, and carry her far away, where a so-called marriage would be performed.[59]

There are three other groups of offences: offences against property other than those already examined, miscellaneous offences, and military offences. Included in *offences against property* was receiving, an offence much resembling 'other larcenies' in the character of the convicts concerned. The nature of the offences is typified by illegal reception of two stolen guns, a gold ring, eight sovereigns 'stolen from a sailor', a hinge from a gate, three boxes of plate-glass, shirts, and plate valued at £50. The following case demonstrates the resemblance of receiving to 'other larcenies'.

It concerned Joshua Simmons, who was tried in London. According to police evidence, the prisoner, who kept a second-hand clothes shop in Field Lane, and who was well known to the police, was seen carrying a bag along Holborn Hill. When he was accosted, he said that the bag contained trousering stuff which he had bought an hour previously from a stranger in Oxford Street. He then tried to bribe the officers, whereupon they took him into custody. He broke free, fled down Farringdon Street and, when he was caught, commenced to attack one officer, and poked him in the eye with his umbrella. Judah Solomons gave evidence supporting the prisoner, saying that he, too, had been offered a piece of similar material. Fifteen witnesses gave the prisoner

Simmons a character, but it appeared that only one of them knew where he lived. The jury was out four and a half hours, and then returned a verdict of guilty of receiving, the second count in the indictment. Passing of sentence was postponed because the police intended to speak of the prisoner's career, and they subsequently recounted that his premises were open at all hours of the night, and that thieves were calling continually; the house was the resort of thieves and returned transportees, declared Inspector Brennan. The prisoner was transported for ten years.

Three other numerically minor offences were embezzlement, forgery, and stealing by a trick. Robert Spencer, a brewer who was employed as a schoolmaster on the way out to Van Diemen's Land, disclosed that his offence was forging a bill of exchange on Sampson Hanbury for £405. His forgery had been discovered by the bankers.[60] Thomas Heucher, transported from London also, in 1840, and convicted of forging and uttering a bill of £25, blamed his unhappy fate on the pernicious influence of bad company, and added that his father was an East India Company owner. A third forger, George Haig, came out to Australia in 1827 for uttering forged cheques, signed in the name of the second son of the Earl of Harrington. Haig's mother, said her son, lived on her means. Also convicted of forgery was a gentleman's servant, Robert Abercromby McKay, from Aberdeen, who said with no other explanation, 'I was A.W.L. and hearing that I was enquired for, I absconded'. There was also a master mariner named Constantine Asquith transported for forging a bill of lading, and Thomas Moore, a bookbinder, explained that 'It was forging a false entry in a ledger for the order of some marble paper; prosecutor John Wright; I was his traveller . . . I did it for the commission of £2. 15s. My salary was £150 p.a.'

A few surgeons were transported for forgery. Robert Lews said that his offence was forgery on his trustee, the clerk of the peace for Dorset, and William Hay Gibson was sent to Australia for ten years for delivering an order of £30 knowing it to be forged. The case of Gibson is either that of a fool or a very clever confidence trickster. He claimed to have a diploma when he arrived in Australia, but a note on his record stated that the home authorities had their doubts about his bona fides, and believed certificates he had concerning his former civil condition were false. To further confuse the issue, the prisoner stated that he was on leave from his regiment when taken up, that he was commissioned a captain in the 41st and 16th regiments, that his wife Catherine was now with her father Sir Thomas Neane at Blackheath, and that his brother was with (or identical with—the entry is ambiguous) Sir William Henry Gordorin, in the 17th Lancers. There were other facts of his career that Gibson did not divulge to the colonial interrogators.

In the press account of his trial it was noted that he was a married man with three children who had represented himself as single, gaining the affection of Thomas Wright's daughter whilst in Scarborough. He then presented himself to Wright as the husband of his daughter, whom he had deceived into believing she was married to him by special licence, and as being in the army with agents residing in Pall Mall. He then obtained £30 from Wright by forging an order. The prisoner told the court that he pleaded guilty to the charge, and appealed for the sentence of death to be passed upon him, as everybody he held dear now wished him dead. He was not gratified with his wish, but transported for ten years.

A few cases of embezzlement included that of a man on the first vessel to take convicts from Britain to Van Diemen's Land. He was an attorney's clerk named Jeremiah Emblin who was convicted of embezzling £400. Robert Turner embezzled £27 while a clerk of the county court at Deal, and Richard Green said that he dishonestly obtained £28 from the Midland Railway Company. The most spectacular case, in terms of money involved, was that of Henry Routh, who was tried in India. He said that the cause of his transportation was embezzlement of £40,000. He had been captain and paymaster in the 15th regiment for seven years.

A handful of convicts was transported for stealing by a trick or by fraud. For example, Thomas Littler, a London clerk, stated that he had delivered letters, and improperly received the postage as postman. James Burns (1) obtained enlistment money by enlisting for a second time, and John King secured the sum of 7s. 6d. when a person gave him that for repairing his watch, whereupon the prisoner spent it instead of giving it to the watch-repairer. Among other offences were those of William Kinsila, who fraudulently obtained subsistence when he was a deserter, and John Coin, who impersonated a seaman to gain prize money during the Napoleonic Wars, Jordan Wain, who conducted his own defence very ably, earned an income by pretending to women that

he had enough influence at the Home Office to secure pardons
for husbands who were lodged in gaol.

Two other offences among those grouped as crimes against
property were wilful destruction and poaching. Most of the few
men transported for the former offence were English, and sent
out in the year 1831 for machine-breaking during the agricultural
disturbances. Counties of trial were Buckinghamshire, Hampshire,
Huntingdonshire, Wiltshire, Sussex, Norfolk, Gloucestershire, Kent
and Berkshire. Nearly all these prisoners were farm workers.[61]

Other wilful destruction was in the form of arson, John Hobbs,
for instance, stating that the stack of hay he burnt was valued at
£200, and that he was drunk at the time of the blaze. Others
were convicted of arson in Dorset, where a stack of wheat was
burnt, and in Somerset, where three stacks of wheat were similarly
destroyed. Men also burnt hay in Essex and Cork, as well as in
Nottinghamshire, Cambridgeshire, Longford, Waterford, Limerick
and Edinburgh. No reason was given by any of these prisoners
for their activities, but some were doubtless caused by agricultural
distress, and a feeling of revenge on the part of some who were
suffering because of low wages or unemployment; other fires may
have been the result of quarrels about other matters. In Ireland
in 1846, some of the supposed causes of incendiary fires were:
dispossession of some tenants, sale of con-acre potatoes, a dispute
about land, and a rise in the price of potatoes.[62]

A few convicts killed or maimed animals.[63] Martin Donohue
of Galway, for instance, was transported for houghing sheep,
and his father and brother came out with him for the same
offence. Men who were charged with killing animals generally
declared that they had stolen the livestock concerned. Sheep were
the animals usually killed, though Edward Cassidy of Co. Fermanagh was transported for killing a horse. Revenge was possibly
the motive for this offence, and demolition of houses by John
Dwyer of Tipperary, and Edward Purcell of King's Co., may
have also been caused by similar feelings.

Finally, among those prisoners transported to New South Wales
and Van Diemen's Land for wilful destruction were a few men
convicted for cutting down trees, for scuttling a vessel, and for
destroying stocking-frames. The last-mentioned case concerned
George Green, sent to Van Diemen's Land in 1812, and such
was the interest excited in the fate of Green and other persons
accused of rioting and frame-breaking that the court and avenues

at Nottingham Assizes were crowded to suffocation on each day of the trial. Green and two others were charged, at Sutton in Ashfield, with breaking frames. No age was noted in the case of Green, but his two companions were sixteen and seventeen years old respectively. They had probably taken part in the Luddite riots.

Only a handful of men was transported for poaching. Offenders included James Scholes, tried in Yorkshire in 1828 for being found armed at night with intent to kill game, and a report on this case noted that the man concerned was a notorious poacher convicted of a very aggravated assault made far worse by the death of a keeper. Though very few men were sent to Australia for poaching, some transported on other charges had formerly been punished by imprisonment for offences against the game laws, which led to the commission of other offences, because they became acquainted with dissolute characters.[64]

None of the offences listed in Appendix 4 as *Miscellaneous* accounted for the transportation of many men to Australia. Some of them, however, are more dramatic crimes than the typical cases of larceny. Vagrancy, or being disorderly or idle, was one such charge. It brought about the transportation of Irishmen only, and their records give no hint of the actual circumstances under which a vagrant was transported, though James Buckley, condemned for vagrancy in 1841, admitted to having been four or five times in prison for being insane from drink. According to a report he had indications of madness.

Only Irish were transported for 'fire-arms' and 'making pike-heads'. Most of these men came to New South Wales in the 1830s, and were probably found illegally in possession of guns, or were trying to obtain them. 'Appearing armed', for instance, was an agrarian offence, in one case 'to intimidate his employer to let the land to the former tenants'; and a case of 'being in arms' was reported as follows. As a man named Ryan was driving cows from Newport to a farm belonging to Mr Cornelius Hogan, he was met by a person armed with a blunderbuss, who cautioned him not to come there again with strange cattle, and to tell his master not in future to send cattle to Tiermoyle but to give the neighbours preference.[65]

The offence of sending or posting threatening letters, and compelling to quit, was also associated with rural Ireland, although some English were concerned. A few gave an indication of their offences. For example, Anthony Ryan was charged with posting a threatening notice, and added that he had also been detected assaulting a habitation and shooting outside the house; and Denis Kilmartin, transported for compelling to quit, said upon arrival at the Derwent that 'it was with firearms compelling Hoolan to leave his premises'.

Such threats sometimes had bloodcurdling results. For instance, one farmer in Ireland decided to improve his property, on which he had fifty sub-tenants, by calling in an agricultural expert on drainage. The expert, named Powell, then received a threatening letter which mentioned that he would require police protection, and that a collection had been taken up to send his assassin to America, 'and if you don't take my advice, be God you will be killed'. He was. Men came to his house, dragged him out, and shot him dead in front of his daughter.[66] Gangs of four to eight men usually attacked houses, though threatening notices were sent by one person, and the outrages which followed usually showed confederacy. The following notice was found tied to a gate in Co. Dublin: 'We rite these few lines to warn you of the sword that does continue to tremble over you, for the takeing too acres of land that was in possession of a widow; and if you take land that was forceably taken, mark what will follow: land taken against a tenants will must remain by with the landlord or be commons for fourteen years. Moll Doyle's sons awoke from their slumber.'

A further type of threat, illustrating the state of parts of Ireland during the period of transportation to Australia, was that made to a Roman Catholic who was in treaty for land held by a Protestant in Co. Tyrone. This message mentioned that if the recipient took the house in question, 'the hammer and the sledge will be your fate . . . flames will be your bed . . . and you yourself will be hammered to death . . . No surrender. God save the Queen'.[67]

Other convicts were transported for being at large under sentence, or for returning from transportation. A sentence of transportation did not necessarily mean that a man was sent out of the country, and this is illustrated in the statement made by Charles Yeates: "I was tried for burglary in 1822 and received life; I escaped from the *Bellerophon* at Sheerness after two or three months. Once since for stealing paint for which I received three months in the House of Correction, and while under sentence I was identified as a Return Convict from the *Bellerophon*.'

Piracy was a charge which brought some men out to Australia from St Kitts in the West Indies. For instance, Richard Howlett was charged with piracy, but it was not piracy on the high seas; according to him, a wreck had been robbed.

The offence of theft, habit and repute also caused the transportation of some men. Abraham Samuels, for example, convicted of larceny and former convictions, said that he had stolen a cart, and that the prosecutor had come to the hulk and tried to get him off. All members of this group of offenders had, of course, been convicted previously, and Charles Plunkett stated that he had been gaoled for one month for fighting, one month for being a disorderly apprentice, one month for throwing at a policeman, and three months for robbery; and Thomas Coulson had been concerned in twenty-nine misdemeanours, it was noted.

The final group of offenders distinguished is that transported for *military offences*. Principal places of trial were England, India and Burma, North America, Ireland and the Mediterranean area (including France). Other places were the West Indies, Scotland, Mauritius, the Cape of Good Hope and New Zealand. There was a relatively large number of Irish-born among these soldiers. Offences were, as a rule, those of desertion and insubordination, such as might be covered by 'drunk and assaulting the guard'. For example, John Haydon was court-martialled in Quebec for disobedience and mutinous conduct, and admitted to striking his sergeant. This officer was also a prospective victim of Terence O'Neill, tried at Nova Scotia for drawing a bayonet on his sergeant. Statements of charge and admissions included the following:

'Disobedience and mutinous conduct when before the court martial for disobedience.'
'Desertion and making away with my clothes.'
'Maliciously wounding a corporal with a ginger beer bottle.'
'Drunk on parade and striking a superior officer,'
'Desertion because my brother William of the same Regiment did not agree with me; I was absent two months.'

Another soldier was Charles Simfield, tried at King William's Town at the Cape of Good Hope for insubordination. He explained that the cause of his punishment was 'breaking my rifle and insubordinate conduct; we were out on the border of the Caffres and had no rations for fourteen days'.

These military offenders had previously been in trouble more than any other group of convicts. Desertion was often the former offence, and many were branded with the letter 'D'. This mark was impressed on the left arm. Former offences had been severely punished, because not only had some of these men been marked but severely flogged as well. One had received 250 lashes for striking a sergeant, and another a punishment of 150 lashes for insolence. Yet another soldier stated that he had been flogged with 500 lashes for desertion ('this time I was absent seven months'), and a man transported in 1831 for mutiny observed that he had received more than 700 lashes. An Irish soldier had previously been flogged with 250 lashes, and another prisoner had been incarcerated six months, eighteen months, three months, and had received 1,100 lashes.

4

The Female Convicts

It is a melancholy fact, but not the less true, that far the greater proportion are utterly irreclaimable, being the most worthless and abandoned of human beings.[1]

The total number of female convicts sent to New South Wales and Van Diemen's Land was 24,960, which is 15 per cent of the total number of prisoners. The mortality rate *en route* was 2·3 per cent during the whole transportation period, and one-quarter of the 577 women who died were lost when the *Neva* was shipwrecked on King Island in Bass Strait in 1835; 145 women out of 151 perished.

Female convicts landed on Australian soil throughout the transportation era: there were women on the First Fleet, and women were transported until 1852, when the *Duchess of Northumberland* left England on 11 November of that year. The 1830s was the single decade during which most left Britain, and in the years between 1830 and 1849, 58 per cent of all women convicts left for Australia.[2]

Fifty-five per cent of the women were tried in England and 33 per cent in Ireland (see Appendix 4), but if native place is accepted as an indication of nationality, then the number of Irish women is increased markedly. On this basis, 43 per cent were English, 47 per cent Irish, and 9 per cent Scottish.

These Irish-born were in England for a fairly obvious reason, for it would be a commonplace observation to indicate effects of the Great Famine, and consequent wholesale migration from a prostrate Ireland, but there had been Irish 'colonies' in England for centuries. Nevertheless, periodic Irish famines undoubtedly increased the movement of population. As one Irish woman commented, 'Distress and want, and hunger and poverty—nothing else—druv us to this counthry. It was the will of God—glory be to His holy and blessed name! to fail the taties. To be sure, I couldn't dig one out of the ground fit to ate!'[3] Not all women had moved as far from their native home as this one, but 46 per cent of all the female prisoners had been tried in a county outside their birthplace. This figure, however, gives a false impression of the Irish, because relatively large numbers of them had not moved from their county of birth. When the Irish did move, they tended to go to England or Scotland, and particularly to London and Lancashire. Irish-born women tried in England totalled 14 per cent of the females sent to Australia from there.

The table in Appendix 4 shows that ten counties tried 54 per cent of the total number of women; with the exception of Limerick, all these counties were predominantly urban in character throughout the main period of transportation. London stands out, because 39 per cent of women transported prior to 1810 were tried in the metropolis, and 21 per cent of women transported during the whole period were convicted in the capital. In the formative years of New South Wales, therefore, every third convict woman sent to the colony had been tried in London, and most of them reared in the same districts around the City as were the men, e.g. Gray's Inn Lane, Bishopsgate and Clerkenwell. Eliza Glasgow, 'tried with a young man whom I do not know', stated that she had been born in the Aldgate workhouse.

The women were one year older than the men on the average, and their mean age was twenty-seven years. Most were single, and approximately 34 per cent were married or widowed. One-third of this latter group were noted as widows, but this figure may reflect lying, because comments made often included such statements of suspiciously recent and convenient deaths of partners as 'my husband died six months since', 'I have heard that my husband is dead', or 'my husband died since I was convicted'. Such statements were probably caused in some cases by a desire to get married in Australia, and this desire was so strong that some tried to secure admission to the widows' list by having forged letters posted in England, purporting to notice the death of a husband.[4] Hesitancies and contradictions on the question of marital status were also caused by the fact that women had lived with various men, but had never been legally married. Looseness of morality was a characteristic of some of the poorer parts of London, and licentiousness was fostered by the poor lodging-houses frequented by boys and girls, who rapidly formed attachments in these places of childish profligacy. A young prostitute spoke of coming up to London, falling in with three Irish girls and four men, and going haymaking with them: 'I had a fortnight of haymaking. I had a mate at haymaking and in a few days he ruined me. He told the master that I belonged to him. He did not say I was his wife. They don't call us their wives.'[5]

It was to be expected that such women would get into trouble with the police, and many convicts had a similar background. Six out of every ten had formerly been convicted, but Scottish and English-tried women were more likely than the Irish to have been punished previously. If, then, it were decided to consider the number of previous convictions as a criterion of criminality, the Scottish women were the most abandoned, followed by the English, and then the Irish. Nearly half of the women who had previously been punished more than four times were Scottish, and those convicted by the Glasgow Court of Justiciary were the worst of a bad lot. Elizabeth McGuire, for instance, had been convicted twenty or thirty times for drunkenness, and Elizabeth Semple, transported in 1846, stated that she had been in gaol for sixty days for the theft of a shirt, eight months again for a shirt, six months for stealing a glass, and six months for the theft of a watch.

There is a further factor of profound significance recorded in the case of some women who were made to come to Australia: they were noted as being 'on the town' at the time of their apprehension. Observations by exasperated officials, who perhaps had never had to deal with fallen women *en masse,* should not be regarded as anything but subjective, but it is seldom that much more than criticism of the female convicts and their standard of morals has been recorded. One surgeon-superintendent went so far as to favour concubinage of women with the sailors on the transport vessels, because he considered the women then became accustomed to personal attachment, a sentiment unknown to them previously. He recognized his charges as prostitutes and persistent petty criminals, and noted that he had on one vessel a woman nearly seventy years of age who had spent forty years of her life in and out of prisons. She became so well known that she was often trusted with the warrant for her own commital.[6]

Tales abound of the misbehaviour of women convicts. One officer, while on the way out to Australia, was three times obliged to gag some of his female charges for continually using violent and abusive language,[7] and at the Parramatta female factory, hundreds of women, described as the most abandoned in the British empire, threw everything over the walls of the prison yard. Such women were seldom sent out to Australia while there was a hope of reforming them in England,[8] and at the factory 'the atmosphere was polluted with the fumes of tobacco smoked by the women, and the walls echoed with the shrieks of passion, the peals of foolish laughter, and oaths of common converse'.[9] At the Hobart Town factory when the Rev. Bedford attempted to address the prisoners, they reacted by drawing up their gowns and, in unison, smacking their buttocks.[10] Some colonists considered women prisoners were all prostitutes[11] who, far from feeling their lowly state, flounced off the ships dressed in silks and satins and every frill they could afford.[12] In short, once they had recovered from sea-sickness, they looked forward to a fresh life in Australia, and were certainly not downcast or miserable at leaving Britain.[13]

Comments by gaolers and other officials on the character and disposition of the female felonry also include some damning estimates. Women falling under notice were commented upon in such terms as these:

'Punished five times on board; constantly trying to form an intimacy with one of the crew.'

'*Very very* bad indeed.'

'Troublesome, hankering after the sailors.'

'Free with the crew.'

'Has led a most abandoned life these last four years, tramping the country with different men. Her husband of the present, a capital convict, the worst character the gaoler ever knew.'

'Artful and deceitful.'

'In the Institution of the Guardian Society; one of Clancy Mullins and Norman's Gang of She-Devils; often and often in irons in the coal-hold.'

'She got her living in a bad way.'

'An immoral prostitute from an early age.'

'Drunken, dissipated and of bad disposition. Kept a disorderly house at Leeds harbouring numbers of males and females for improper connexion.'

'Four years on the town, off and on.'

'Impudent, vicious, sullen and violent temper.'

How common was the prostitute among the convict women? Thirteen per cent could be so described from their indent records, but this includes only the females sent to Van Diemen's Land.[14] It is possible that all the worst females were sent to the southern colony, but up to the early 1820s New South Wales received all women, and after 1840 the island received all convicted females.

These two facts suggest that probably at least one convict out of every five was a full- or part-time prostitute. Most of them confessed this in such words as 'on the town six years,' or 'on the town', or, as Elizabeth Martin described her situation with some modesty, 'I have latterly been on the town'.

Of the women who were noted as being 'on the town', two-thirds were tried in England; half of that two-thirds was from Lancashire and London, and the former had a slight edge over the capital. The great majority of the remainder were tried in Yorkshire, Warwickshire, Gloucestershire, Staffordshire, Kent, Cheshire and Surrey. One London prostitute described her life in London, where she walked the streets in the neighbourhood of the Seven Dials: 'I never picked pockets as other girls did; I was not nimble enough with my hands . . . I would like best to go to Australia. I could take a service in Sydney. I could get rid of my swearing.'[15] Her life story suggested that conditions had not altered greatly from the eighteenth century, when the path of such country girls coming to the metropolis had been fraught with danger. They were frequently met by procuresses, 'delusive snares . . . laid daily by the agents of Hell for the ruin of innocence'.[16]

In Ireland the counties of trial of the prostitutes were principally Dublin, Cork, Down, Antrim and Kildare, and in Scotland Glasgow and Edinburgh supplied most of the Scottish streetwalkers to Australia. Many of the Scottish prostitutes, unlike the Irish, had been on the streets for lengthy periods, up to fifteen years in some cases.

Women were not, however, transported for prostitution as such, and Appendix 4 shows that 52 per cent of females were sent out for 'other larcenies'. Two-thirds were tried in England and nearly one-third in Ireland, and the three main counties of trial were London, Lancashire and Dublin.

London thus demands close attention, and some idea of the circumstances of offences and the type of person committing them, can be gathered from the accounts of trials. Articles from a house were stolen by Esther Spencer, transported in 1795; she had entered a dwelling at Spitalfields, snatched up salt-holders and valuables, and then ran for it. No reason for the theft is apparent. Elizabeth Mandeville, nineteen years of age, was transported in 1808 to New South Wales for seven years for stealing money at Dyot Street (W.C.1) in mid-afternoon. At her trial at the Old Bailey it was stated that Mandeville, a black girl, had made it difficult for the prosecutor to give her in charge because she was strong and bit his wrist, cut his head, tore his shirt, and blacked one of his eyes. A third case concerned Mary Fincham, also aged nineteen, who stole a watch from the pocket of a drunken sailor in the street. Mary Arnold, transported in 1789, stole from the person by luring her victim into bed with her, and then making away with his money. In 1809 Mary Preston abstracted a counterpane ('the devil possessed me'); and stealing from an intoxicated man brought transportation to Charlotte Smith, who relieved her victim of his watch and money while he was vomiting.

So a list of cases could be prolonged, and include details of Mary Chambers, who stole three carpets and who was then chased into the unsavoury St Giles's Rookery. That some of these London women were living by doubtful means is quite certain from the trials. For example, Ann Baker was charged with stealing a watch and money, which theft, the prosecutor alleged, had occurred at night while he was in bed with the prisoner. He had missed her about four or five a.m., and also missed his money and watch, despite the fact that he had put them securely into his trousers and placed the trousers under his pillow.

In another case, Elizabeth Joiner stole a pair of sheets and four lbs. of roast beef. She had attempted to get the sheets out of the house from where they were stolen by pinning them round her body under her gown. Distress was not pleaded by Joiner but Elizabeth Taylor's situation was probably desperate when she stole valuables from a dwelling-house, for it was revealed that she was a pauper, had been discharged from St Clement's workhouse, and begged a lodging from the woman whom she subsequently robbed. Mary Butler, however, engaged in a different sort of offence when she stole, with a friend, a basket and some beans. This, said the prosecutor, had occurred in Covent Garden; the prisoners had plotted in Irish but, unfortunately for them, he understood the language and caught them trying to get vegetables for nothing. Another woman tried to increase her gains from prostitution by stealing a watch valued at 30s. The theft had occurred in the following way, stated the prosectuor: he had been in liquor, and spent the night with the prisoner, who took the opportunity to rifle his pockets while he was sleeping off his passion.

These, then, are some cases of London-tried women transported to Australia, and the conclusion that the females concerned were of indifferent character receives some support from an observer on a convict vessel sent to Australia in 1789. They were principally street-walkers, he thought, though there were such persons as a Mrs Barnsley, a sharper and shop-lifter whose family had been swindlers and highwaymen for a century, a Mrs Davis, who had swindled people of great quantities of goods under false names, and a Mary Williams, who was transported for receiving stolen goods. She and eight companions had been supported in Newgate by Lord George Gordon. Another London-tried girl had been visited by her people on this convict ship, and she had fainted on the spot as the sorrowful parents wept at her fate. When she recovered she told her mother and father that she had been ruined shortly after her arrival in the capital by a villain who had not protected her. She was thus forced upon the streets, taken up as a disorderly girl and transported.[17] (In fact, the trial of this girl reveals that she was not sent out to Australia for being disorderly but for stealing, with the help of her sister, a coat valued at 20s. It is not clear why she left home, nor whether she was quite the innocent and unfortunate victim of her weakness that we might think.)

Another woman for whom some sympathy might be spared was tattooed with the pathetic lines:

> William Jessie when this you see
> Remember me and bear me in your mind
> Let all the world say what they will
> Speak of me as you find.

On Mary Ann Brennan's left arm was evidence, however, of another attachment ('Alfred Whitfield I love to the heart'), and she admitted to having been 'on the town' for four years.

Not all London prisoners were prostitutes and thieves, however. No doubt there are some cases not reported, or reported inadequately, of females committing offences through immediate want and in pitiful circumstances. Yet one is left with the impression of an indifferent class of women, living in the squalid parts of London such as St Giles's, where, in 1817, a constable apprehended more than forty women of ill-fame within twenty minutes. Speaking of a house in Charlotte Street owned by a clerk of the Bedford Chapel, the officer said there had been a robbery at this brothel, and a gentleman had been left naked. The girl who had stripped him was stopped with his clothes in her arms. Four men had also been concerned in the enterprise, and one was transported for seven years.[18]

Offences earning transportation to Australia from Lancashire were very similar to the 'other larcenies' perpetrated in London, and in Dublin the picture was the same. In that city were tried 25 per cent of the Irish women transported for 'other larcenies', and it would be tedious to list cases when there is every reason to believe them identical with those outlined for London.

In the provinces, the general picture of the origin of the women convicts was the same. For example, Sarah Allen, a Sussex housemaid, was transported for larceny in 1843, and stated that it was highway robbery on a man, that £16 had been taken, and that a man named Taylor, with whom she had lived for twelve months, had received fifteen years' transportation for the same offence. She had been three years 'on the town'. Secondly, Charlotte Watts, a house servant from Oxford, was transported for stealing money, and noted as having formerly been convicted of a felony; she stated that she had received seven weeks in prison for stealing a pair of stockings. Thirdly, Elizabeth Mayo was tried in Hereford and convicted of stealing ribbon in a shop; and Ann Gardner of Oxford was transported for stealing money on its way through the post office.

Cases in provincial Ireland included that of a woman transported from Co. Mayo for larceny, Honor Mugan admitting to the theft of £2. 17s. 6d. from a man; Mary Reilly was transported from Fermanagh for picking 30s. from a pocket ('two years on the town'), Mary O'Neill of Cavan for stealing money, and Abigail Mahony was sent to New South Wales for shop-lifting. In Scotland, most of the group was tried at Glasgow for larceny from the person, and a few convicted of stealing blankets.

The other chief form of larceny was that of theft of wearing apparel, for which 18 per cent of the women were transported. In England, most of these people were tried in London and Lancashire: Ann Clapton stole two muslin aprons valued at 10s., Bridget Madden was tried in Lancashire for taking clothes from a jerry-shop in Blackburn; Jane Holbrook filched wearing apparel from two children in the street; Sarah Ann Traill took a cloak from a man; and Jane Dixon stole a shawl. A few other cases include those of Maria Nodes, who, charged with stealing wearing apparel in a dwelling-house, had stripped a fellow lodger's room.

Agnes Davison stole the clothes from a man who was asleep with her in bed, and became so drunk the next day that she told an officer of the law about her exploit. Catherine Forbes stole clothes from a house, and then pawned them; she was found to have seventy-one pawn duplicates in her possession.

There is no point in going into details of all other offences because they accounted for the transportation of so few women. But a few crimes deserve a comment or two. For instance, 'robbery' (so described) was the cause of transportation of a number of females sent to New South Wales or Van Diemen's Land for 'man robbery'. This offence was similar to some of those mentioned above under other headings, in that the woman concerned took her victim to a bedroom and, when he was asleep, made off with his watch and money or whatever valuables she could lay her hands on. If her partner for the moment was unlucky, he could lose all his clothes as well as his other possessions.

Those women transported for a current offence and a previous one (or ill-repute) had among their number a large proportion of Scottish women. An example is Margaret McLeod alias Fleming, who was tried in Edinburgh in 1835 for theft, habit, repute and previous conviction. She was a house servant, aged sixty-four, and a note on her record stated that she had been sentenced for fourteen years in 1826, but subsequently pardoned. McLeod herself said that she had been transported about thirteen years previously, had been sentenced to seven years in gaol for receiving, and that her daughter had been transported for seven years. A report on her trial stated that she pleaded guilty to a charge of theft, for the first of which, in 1826, sentence of transportation was awarded but afterwards remitted by the Crown. In awarding punishment, it was remarked from the bench that, finding the prisoner utterly irreclaimable, the only sentence the court could propose was that of transportation beyond the seas for life, which was accordingly pronounced.

Some of the other crimes for which women were transported to Australia diverge sharply from the typical offence. For example, nearly all the women transported for stealing an animal were tried in Ireland in the 1830s and 1840s, were convicted outside Dublin, and had no previous offences. Women stole the same sort of domestic animals that men did. A case in point was the theft of a sheep by Mary McMahon of Co. Clare, whose two nephews were also transported. Isabella Johnston of Fermanagh was sent to Australia with her sister for stealing a horse, Ellen Becket from Cork was convicted in 1848 of taking a goat that was not hers, Mary Clogherty of Galway was transported for the theft of a cow, and Bridget Lawlor or McGarry from Kilkenny was transported for stealing two fowls ('I had seven years for a book [?], for which four years and discharged; twelve months and two months for fowls').

Another offence which was different from the majority of crimes was that of wilful destruction. Most of the women sent to Australia for this offence were transported for arson. Such incendiarism was mainly the burning down of houses, though some haystacks also suffered. There were a few English arson cases, which were typified by that of a London woman convicted of maliciously setting fire to a house. A long account of the trial was in the newspapers, and it appeared that Mary Jane Fitzgerald, the prisoner, had been the creature of another woman who offered her money to set a house alight so that insurance money could be claimed. The attempt was bungled, and the London Insurance Company prosecuted both women. The evil genius of the affair, ironically enough, had made lavish and probably false promises to Fitzgerald that she would take her out to Australia if the money was forthcoming. Both came to Australia but not in the circumstances Fitzgerald had imagined.

A number of other offences can only be touched on. Receiving, for instance, was usually the reception of stolen wearing apparel. Mary Hayes was charged with this for receiving a trunk which contained valuables and other goods valued at £1,000. Another prisoner was Mary Barr, who stated she had received a dress and a shawl, and that her husband was tried and convicted with her.

Assaults on the person were few in number, though spectacular. Ann Killick, for instance, was transported for cutting and wounding a man, and Maria Le Noble, tried at St Helier in the Channel Islands, was said to be the keeper of a brothel on the island of Jersey. Another case of a violent offence concerned a woman transported for stabbing, Ann Sinner alias Ruffey alias Hedges stating in Van Diemen's Land that 'a man named Crawley took some liberties; I was tipsy and stabbed him in the side'. Elizabeth Cleveland, who was charged with throwing burning liquid over a person, announced that 'I threw vitriol over George Day. I did this in a passion. He struck me first.' Catherine McCormack, tried in Dublin in 1829, was transported for being an accessory to rape.

Not commented upon or described in this outline of the offences for which women prisoners were transported, are hundreds of cases that are curious, pathetic, dull and vicious. Some cases are not recorded at all, and others so sketchily that it would be impossible to establish the circumstances. It is seldom, however, that women protested their innocence, or that accounts of trials suggest that they were blameless, and there is no reason to suppose that miscarriages of justice often occurred.

Almost all female convicts were listed as domestic servants of one sort or another, though there were a number of street-walkers who probably had no other source of income than prostitution, but who may have acted as domestic servants occasionally. Form of occupation listed on the records was generally that of housemaid, kitchen-maid or cook. As well, there were nurse-maids, laundresses, and servants of all work. A few women were more skilled. For instance, there were bonnet-makers, needle-women and sempstresses, cap-makers, stay-makers and boot-closers. But some of these callings were probably invented on the spur of the moment: one woman recorded as a domestic servant warned the interrogators at Hobart Town that 'I have never been brought up to housework'. She was Phillis Perry, a prostitute.

A tiny proportion of convicts had unusual callings: Elizabeth Rowley, who was born in Burslem, was a pottery girl; Margaret Martin was a factory girl from Liverpool, but did not say what sort of factory it was (she did say she had been 'on the town nine months'); and Ann Edwards was a silk weaver from Spitalfields, noted as 'an unfortunate girl, on the town four years'.

There were occasional examples of higher callings, for a few women were governesses. Susan Whitburn, for example, was a nursery governess transported for abstracting silver spoons from a dwelling-house, but she said (giving the lie to her apparently high civil condition) that she had previously been sentenced to seven years' transportation, which had been mitigated to twelve months in gaol by the intervention of Lord Palmerston. Sarah Slow was sent out of the country for forging a cheque, and said that her husband, George, was a clerk at Bread Street, Cheapside, on £160 a year. She was married with one child. Hannah Augusta Hipsley was sent to Australia for improperly pledging a shawl, and was competent to teach drawing, music, singing, fancy needle-work, and French. Her father was a colonel in the Dragoons, she stated, her brother Gustavus a lieutenant-colonel in the American service, another a lieutenant in the navy, and a third brother, Edward, on an East Indiaman vessel. If all this were true, she was the black sheep of the family, because she admitted she had previously been sent to prison for two years for forging a bill, and had served eleven months of that sentence.

Apart from such people listed above, there were a few silk weavers, women who worked in cotton factories and factories whose nature was not revealed, a frame-worker, a huckster, a victualler, and a nailer. One woman's calling was down as simply 'hard work', another's as 'none', one as 'gipsy', and one as 'good for nothing'.

> Macbeth a harvest of applause will reap,
> For some of us, I fear, have murdered sleep;
> His lady, too, with grace will sleep and talk,
> Our females have been used at night to walk.[19]

This part of the prologue to a play staged in early New South Wales suggests that the Australian convict women were not of the highest quality, but though nearly all commentators agree on the bad character of many of the female prisoners, it would not do to over-emphasize their worst aspects. Doubtless there were many circumstances that are not known, and can now never be known, which might modify the general picture of the character of the women convicts. Yet the concentration of women convicts tried in the cities, the accounts of trials, and the type of objects stolen, strongly suggest that the female prisoners were an indifferent batch of settlers. How they and the male convicts fared in Australia must now be considered.

CONVICTS IN AUSTRALIA

5

The Male Convicts in Australia

Two posts standant, one beam crossant,
One rope pendant, one knave on the end on't.
—suggested coat of arms for Van Diemen's Land.[1]

No distinctions have so far been drawn between the men who were despatched to the two colonies: all have been regarded as going to Australia. But there were some differences in the origin of the New South Wales and Van Diemen's Land convicts, and the most remarkable of these is that of nationality. In the years prior to 1840 when transportation to New South Wales was discontinued and stepped up in the southern colony, no convicts tried in Ireland were sent directly to Van Diemen's Land. New South Wales, on the other hand, had sent to it 20,480 Irish out of a total number of 67,980 convicts.[2]

This almost certainly reflects a policy decision, but there is no reason at once apparent for it, nor has any document found solved the problem. The evidence of Alexander McLeay, New South Wales colonial secretary, bears upon the question, and implies that he knew nothing of the reason in 1838: 'It is well-known that all convicts transported from Ireland are, without exception, sent direct to this colony, and that since Van Diemen's Land was made a separate government, no Irish convicts have been transferred from hence to that Island, as was before the practice.'[3]

That New South Wales alone was favoured for the reception of the Irish did not escape the attention of another observer, J. D. Lang, who noted that the Irish were sent only to New South Wales and who went on to observe that no less than one-third of the total population of the colony of New South Wales in 1837 was composed of Irish Roman Catholics, of whom nineteen-twentieths were convicts or emancipated convicts.[4]

Lang gave no reasons for the direction of Irish to the mother colony, but twenty years after transportation had ceased, one writer did venture an opinion: 'By an arrangement, the reason of which has never been satisfactorily explained, nearly all convicts transported from Ireland were sent to the penal settlement of

New South Wales—none, or at most very few, to that of Tasmania. It has been alleged that this arose by accident; by others from a design of forming the smaller island of Tasmania into a Protestant colony.'[5]

Yet another view had it that all was due to the machinations of Governor Arthur of Van Diemen's Land: 'Probably owing to the influence which Sir George Arthur possessed in Downing Street, a very large proportion of the best inland and agricultural labourers have been forwarded to Hobart Town, while Irish offenders and London pickpockets have constituted the aggregate of the number sent to Sydney.'[6]

In 1837 Arthur himself recorded evidence about transportation and, when questioned on this subject, answered that the colony of destination of the convicts was adjusted in England; he added that it was regulated, as far as he knew, in the office of the Secretary of State for the Home Department.[7] Arthur's answer could, of course, be regarded as evasive, but if there was any truth in the charge that he succeeded in keeping the Irish out of his colony, another governor apparently knew nothing of it, for Darling observed: 'I have understood . . . that no convicts of either Sex are ever sent from Ireland to Van Diemen's Land. I have not been informed of the reason, but unless it is one of importance, I would beg to suggest that this Colony may be relieved of a portion of the Irish convicts, particularly the women sent here.'[8] The answer he received advances knowledge very little: 'The statement . . . respecting the alleged practice of sending all Irish convicts to New South Wales, shall be communicated to Mr. Secretary Peel',[9] and evidently Peel did not take any effective action, for no change in policy occurred until only Van Diemen's Land and Norfolk Island remained as penal colonies on the eastern seaboard of Australia.

The allegation that Arthur was at the bottom of the decision may possibly have some truth in it; in 1837 he was defending himself and his twelve-year administration in Van Diemen's Land, and may have thought that admission of manipulation before he left England for the colony might tell against him.

Perhaps the matter was decided almost accidentally, a series of Irish ships sent to New South Wales convincing someone in Britain that it would be best, for purposes of administration, to continue sending the Irish to New South Wales. Or perhaps the Irish authorities had never heard of Van Diemen's Land as a separate colony, and thus continued to direct all ships to 'New South Wales', not realizing that the two colonies were administratively separated in 1825.[10] Whatever the reason, the fact remains that it is intriguing to speculate on the course of the history of New South Wales and Tasmania if Irish had been sent to Van Diemen's Land as well as to New South Wales in the period prior to 1840.

Another difference between the two colonies lies in the years of departure of the convict settlers because Van Diemen's Land was not settled until 1803, fifteen years after the first convicts had set foot on the soil of Australia. The island was an outstation of New South Wales until 1825, though prisoners were sent directly to the island from Britain in 1803, 1812 and in greater frequency after 1818. Nevertheless, the settlement at the Derwent was little more than an appendage of the mother colony and a place of secondary punishment for mainland prisoners until the administration of Lieut.-Governor Sorell (1817-24) when, with an increase in the number of respectable settlers, the demand was heard for assigned servants.

Such assigned servants were remarkably different in one respect from those in New South Wales, because the number of formerly convicted prisoners sent to Van Diemen's Land was very high. It seems likely that the more persistent offenders were deliberately shipped to the southern colony, and, because the Irish were less likely to have been previous offenders, a policy that had determined to make Van Diemen's Land a 'sink' would therefore keep them out.

The life of the convicts in the parent colony is difficult to follow because of lack of comprehensive documentation, and conclusions must be drawn from descriptive evidence and from analogies with Van Diemen's Land, where there is still in existence a particularly valuable set of records. These are the conduct registers,[11] which record in dossier form the offences and punishments of convicts, as well as other data. Certain points may be established from the records of conduct. For instance, what was the frequency and nature of offences and punishments? What proportion of the prisoners remained under supervision to the end of their days? What number were freed, and when?

There were two systems of discipline during the transportation era. The years from the establishment of European settlement to 1840 were the period of the assignment system,[12] and the twelve subsequent years cover the period of the probation system.[13] The former, as its name implies, provided that convicts upon arrival were assigned either to the government or to free settlers. Van Diemen's Land colonists seeking labour sent in to the central administration their requests for labourers, or carpenters, or whatever sort of tradesmen they needed, and, according to certain conditions, their wishes were granted as far as the supply permitted. The master was in a position to charge any of his servants with insubordination or misconduct, or bring other charges against them. Though he could not punish the convict himself, the master could and did send the man to the nearest magistrate, who heard the case and decided punishment. As for men assigned to the government, their position was much the same, except that their master was the overseer of the moment. Grave offences were tried before Quarter Sessions or the Supreme Court, first established in Van Diemen's Land in 1824. The New South Wales court had made a circuit prior to that date, but one of the great grievances of the Van Diemen's Land settlers before the island's separation from the government of the mother colony was that they were obliged, at great expense and trouble, to take cases to Sydney for trial. Minor cases were heard by local magistrates, however, from the earliest days.

The probation system, instituted in 1840, replaced the method of assignment, and provided for the settlement of prisoners at a number of probation stations throughout the island. Upon arrival, men were marched to these stations where they advanced through different stages of probation according to their behaviour. Convicts were permitted more freedom if they continued to conduct themselves well and could work for settlers, but they were subject to convict discipline at all times.

Some men were never punished by colonial authorities, but others committed offences serious enough to have themselves brought before superior courts, and, in some cases, hanged. These two extremes of convict careers will be examined in turn.

Approximately 10 per cent of prisoners were in the hands of the administration until freed, and were never punished. A striking point concerning this group is that very many more of them were transported during the probation period than prior to it, although approximately the same number of men were sent to the colony during these two periods. There are a number of possible reasons for the change in frequency of punishment and, indeed, it is conceivable that the convict administration did not change greatly but that it was the character of the prisoners which changed. Large numbers of Irish came, not previous offenders in many cases and not inured to crime to the extent of the London pickpocket, and no doubt these men were less likely to offend than were the hardened city convicts. But there is evidence that the probation system was not administered as severely as it might have been and that punishments were thus handed out less frequently, with the result that probationers' records indicate not a change in the sort of person being sent out, but in the system of discipline.

It is more important to note that the convicts were not continually under the eyes of a master who had a close interest in their work. In addition, flogging was rarely used after 1840, and therefore men were less likely to become hardened to, and careless of, punishment. Finally, the prevalence of seven-year sentences after the late 1830s meant that relatively more men claimed tickets-of-leave than in earlier years, because the seven-year man came up for consideration as a ticket-of-leave holder much sooner than did the 'lifer', who had to serve eight years of his sentence before being considered for the indulgence.[14]

Another aspect of this group of men, never punished while in Van Diemen's Land, concerns their nationality, for the Irish formed a higher proportion than overall numbers indicated it would, thus suggesting that convicts tried in Ireland were perhaps less criminal than the English. The group under consideration also contained relatively many married men, but relatively few prisoners tried in London and Lancashire. That is to say, men from these areas appeared to live up to their bad reputations.

This means, then, that men who appeared to have committed offences at home in circumstances of distress and upheaval of society were not punished in Van Diemen's Land; but the factors of shorter sentences, and a probation system which aimed at encouraging reformation by classification of prisoners, makes it impossible to establish the point with certainty. All that can be said is that the men who came to Van Diemen's Land after 1840 were less likely to be punished than the men who arrived in the years of the assignment system.

The second group of prisoners here examined forms the other extreme, and are those convicted before superior courts. They also numbered about one out of every ten convicts transported, and include a few men (slightly less than one per cent of all transportees) who were hanged. Most were executed for murder, though Samuel O'Hara was executed for cutting out a vessel in 1821, and another prisoner suffered the extreme penalty of the law for breaking and entering. He was Martin Higgins, born in Co. Sligo, and tried in Lancashire in 1822, when aged nineteen, for stealing caps. His record to the time of his trial by the Supreme Court noted that he had been punished for insubordination and rioting (twenty-five lashes), absence without leave (admonition and hard labour), neglect of duty (admonition), an attack on another person (twenty-five lashes), and malingering (labour in chains). These offences occurred during a period of five years.

The Supreme Court which tried this prisoner had been sitting for nearly two years from July 1825, and during that time 700 prisoners had been brought before it. The day on which Higgins was found guilty, a much affected judge passed sentence of death upon eighteen men. The *Hobart Town Gazette* reported the hanging of this group, and gave its readers a description that is a grim monument to the foundation of Van Diemen's Land. Its reporter wrote that, when the prisoners were un-ironed to have their arms pinioned for the gibbet, he had never before seen men so resigned to death. Higgins's turn came: 'Martin Higgins, a short thick man aged twenty-six . . . had the rope next put about his neck. This man had been a servant about Pitt Water. On the night previous to his execution he sent for a little boy in the penitentiary, named Riley, purposely that he might take warning by his miserable end . . . "Do not do", said he, "as they do in the penitentiary. There are many that I should have sent for, but I wanted you to see the situation I am in." '

The *Gazette's* prose was lucid, and among the lines written describing the scene as the prisoners spent their last few minutes of life were:

'He had screwed up his courage, as it were, to the last, to meet the rage of the short and stormy passage he was about to take . . .

'His father is now in the prisoners' barracks, a prisoner for life, for returning from transportation . . . His family and connections were numerous and most have been either executed or transported, having been long the dread of Yorkshire, noted as Snowden Dunhill's gang . . . As his father left the cell, the prisoner laid his head against the wall and wept bitterly.

'He was remarkably fervent and sung the hymn on the scaffold with great loudness.

'Henry Oakley, aged twenty-four, was the last . . . He was lamentably insensible to the awfulness of his situation.'[15]

Another man who ended his days upon the scaffold was John Somers, tried in Gloucester in 1827 at the age of fifteen for stealing from the person. He said upon arrival in the colony that he was 'a natural child', and that he had been in gaol twice before. His record prior to the offence which caused his execution was singularly good; he had been in trouble only once for misconduct, for which he was admonished. After serving three years of his seven-year transportation sentence thus satisfactorily, he was charged with the rape of a nine-year-old child and found guilty, the judge advising him to look upon his life in this world as closed. Though Somers pleaded his innocence, the Governor of Van Diemen's Land could find no extenuating circumstances, and 'at twenty minutes past nine he was launched into eternity'.

The third case illustrating the end of some of the convicts was that of a man transported in 1852 for stealing at Preston a watch, a key and some money. He had his ticket-of-leave at the time he was charged with assault and robbery on James Rowland at Hobart Town in 1856. Rowland gave evidence that he went into Wright's public house in Macquarie Street, and there changed a £10 note. He observed the prisoner O'Neill, and as he was going back to his ship, on which he was second mate, Rowland reached within thirty yards of Constitution Dock when he was seized from behind by his neckcloth, and half-strangled. He saw that his assailant was the man in the public-house, and as soon as he could speak, asked O'Neill why he had been attacked. 'He then struck me on the forehead and I became senseless.' Rowland was able to reach his ship, and later recognized the prisoner on board a little craft named the *River Chief* in the Derwent. The police then apprehended the prisoner and his wife. O'Neill made no defence at all, and the judge, stating that robbery and violence stalked the land, passed the sentence of death. The prisoner's wife, who was in the court, uttered shrieks, and had to be removed.

The great proportion of men tried before superior courts were not executed, however, but sentenced to penal settlements for such offences as cutting and wounding, stealing money, burglary, and so on. A few cases show the types of offences considered serious enough to be brought before Quarter Sessions or the Supreme Court. One was that of Samuel Turner, transported in 1826 for stealing ducks. He had six offences recorded against his name during five years, including his discovery playing bagatelle at an inn, for which he was ordered to leave the district. In general, he had not committed offences of a serious nature, at one point with superb indifference 'hunting the kangaroo in Dulverton Parish on Saturday and Sunday last and publicly announcing his determination to abscond from Mr. Notman's road party'. For this resolution Turner was ordered to labour in chains. However, in 1829 he was convicted of theft, and had his sentence extended for three years. Two years later he was in trouble again, and for stealing a pig was sentenced to fourteen years in gaol.

It transpired in a lengthy account of the case that Turner was concerned in the pig-theft by implication rather than execution, for fellow-prisoners had crossed the Derwent one Saturday night in a boat from their road party camp, and killed and brought back someone else's pig. The animal was then scalded, according to a convict who informed on his companions, and its entrails buried. Evidence was given about the use of the boat, and boot-marks near it identified with the pattern on one of the convict's boots. No reason was advanced for the theft, though circumstances point strongly to the conclusion that the pig was stolen for extra food, and not for revenge.

A second case not only documents in some small way the fate of the 10 per cent of prisoners who were punished by superior courts, but also gives an insight into the activities of men under convict discipline in Van Diemen's Land. William Coles was sentenced at Somerset Assizes in 1838 to fourteen years' transportation for stealing a mare. He had been in prison twice previously (seven months for a felony and fourteen days for apple-stealing), and was a farm labourer aged nineteen years. In Van Diemen's Land he was before the magistrates thirty times in twelve years, and was finally indicted on a charge of robbery under arms. His previous offences had ranged from taking eggs out of a nest belonging to the government to attempting an unnatural crime by enticing. The offence which landed him before the Supreme Court occurred on 29 June 1845 when, with another runaway, he stopped people in a road, robbed one of his watch and money and marched them at gunpoint into James Evans's 'Wheatsheaf' inn on the Richmond Road. All the residents but one were bailed up, and that one escaped and went for reinforcements. These were brought up, and the two bushrangers captured after shots had been fired. The men were found guilty, without hesitation, by the jury, the prisoners pleading that they had used no violence, and that they had been tipsy. The death sentence was commuted to transportation to Norfolk Island. How long the men had been outlaws, or why they absconded, was not stated, but in a third case, some details were given.

This third case shows what the convict system could accomplish when its victim refused to knuckle under. The man concerned was transported from London for fourteen years for larceny from the person in 1825, and stated that he had committed highway robbery by stealing a book from a child. This prisoner, William Driscoll, was born in St Giles's, London, and had previously been gaoled for a month for stealing a handkerchief. He had been flogged on the way out to Van Diemen's Land, the first of a number of such punishments. He was fourteen years old, and heavily tattooed. Driscoll is therefore recognizable as a familiar type of city prisoner.

During his term in Van Diemen's Land he was punished no less than seventy different times, and received a total of 420 lashes, including one hundred for attempting to abscond in 1844. This was one of the rare instances of a man being flogged during the probation era. After such offences as bathing and thereby endangering himself (solitary confinement), and throwing stones at his overseer at Port Arthur (thirty lashes), Driscoll was convicted in 1847 for robbery under arms on Edward Dumaresq, and sent for eight years to Norfolk Island, having six months of that sentence remitted for his exertions in saving the captain and others in the *Waterwitch* from drowning. When he arrived back from Norfolk Island, he was sent straight to Port Arthur to work in chains. From that settlement he absconded in 1855, and remained at large until the end of the year as a bushranger with £100 reward on his head. The trial resulting from his capture was reported, and in it we hear a convict speak for himself.

Driscoll was charged, together with another prisoner named Flaherty, for assault and robbery on Thomas Watson, the chief district constable of Great Swanport, on the road to Bicheno. According to Watson's evidence, Flaherty had said to his companion when Watson fell into their hands, 'This is the fellow who on Sunday last had a party out after us, and I'll blow his bloody brains out.' Driscoll dissuaded him, however, and the witness Watson was marched off the road into the bush, where he found two men tied up to a peppermint gum. Watson was secured to the same tree, and had his watch and money removed. The prisoner Driscoll then mounted Watson's horse, and rode out on to the road, where he robbed a passer-by of bread, cheese and gin, breaking his gun while doing it, and then repairing the weapon with a kangaroo snare. After drinking some of the gin, he rode out again, and brought in another traveller named Carpenter, and tied him up too; shortly afterwards he bailed up yet another person on the road. The two bushrangers then set off along the road on horseback with Watson and one of the others until they met a Dr Storey and a Mrs Cotton riding in a gig. Just as they met, another party approached, but when he went up to them Driscoll was bucked off Watson's mare, Flaherty threatening to shoot Watson if he tried to interfere with the fallen man, who then got up. The captives were now in a large majority and, according to Watson's evidence he diverted Flaherty's attention, whereupon all non-bushrangers rushed the other convict and his companion, and secured them. The jury found the prisoners guilty, but brought in a strong recommendation for mercy because of the humanity shown by the two runaways.

Before the judge passed sentence, Driscoll spoke vigorously for some time. He outlined his career in the colony, and said that the punishment he had undergone since first setting foot on the island was indescribable. His life as a bushranger had been a fearful one, and he attributed his crimes to an undeserved sentence of life transportation, part of which he spent at Port Arthur. He claimed he had been an innocent man. Driscoll's reason for turning bushranger he ascribed to the fact that he was refused a ticket-of-leave, and was treated unkindly by his master. He denied being a companion of Whelan (a well-known bushranger). The judge then remarked favourably upon the prisoner's intelligence and determination of character, whereupon Driscoll twice interrupted His Honour, and swore that he would never again disobey regulations. He was then sentenced to five years' penal servitude at Port Arthur, but kept his word so well that he had only one subsequent offence recorded against him; he received a ticket-of-leave in 1857, and his conditional pardon the following year. His only lapse was a drinking bout a few weeks before his pardon was due. This premature celebration, for which he was fined, did not prevent him receiving the indulgence, and his record, so far as the Convict Department was concerned, ended. He was then forty-seven years old, and had spent thirty-three years under supervision.

Men like Driscoll, sentenced by superior courts, were generally sent to penal settlements. Of the horrors of these places of secondary punishment much is popularly known from Marcus Clarke's *For the Term of his Natural Life*. Clarke, however, was not an historian concerned with examining the convict system dispassionately, so it will be worthwhile to determine the extent of re-transportation to a penal settlement. The comprehensive nature of the Van Diemen's Land records permits this. In brief, 15 per cent of all convicts transported were sent to Port Arthur, or one of the other places of secondary punishment, such as Macquarie Harbour, the period varying from a week to several years.

Though one traveller noted that many educated convicts were sent to Port Arthur upon arrival, because they were considered to have abused their advantages more than the uneducated,[16] admission to the settlement in 1841 was limited to 'those who have been once or often convicted before the Supreme Court or Quarter Sessions; those who have been sentenced thither by the magistrates for being notoriously bad characters, and unfit for assignment or to remain in the settled districts'.[17] Because sentence to such a penal settlement was considered a very severe punishment, it will be necessary to inspect some particular cases, and the origins of the settlements.

The first such place of punishment for second offenders was at Macquarie Harbour, which was established in 1821 by Lieut.-Governor Sorell, acting under Macquarie's earlier instructions.[18] To this rain-soaked, isolated settlement men were sent for such offences as making a copper tea-kettle, wilful destruction, and attempting an unnatural crime, for which the convict concerned was ordered to be given one hundred lashes as well. During his term at Macquarie Harbour, Joseph Wright, the man sentenced to a hundred lashes, received a total of 386 stripes for misconduct, neglect of duty, theft, and illegal possession. James Robinson was also a prisoner sent to this settlement. He was so punished for making false representations to a hut-keeper. He had formerly been punished twenty-eight times, and awarded 400 lashes for such offences as leaving the hospital, he being a patient, and raising scandalous and false reports prejudicial to the character of his overseer. Robinson had been twice convicted by a superior court for theft. At the age of twenty-seven, having been eleven years in Van Diemen's Land, he died in 1831 at Macquarie Harbour, when it was being broken up in favour of Port Arthur.

Port Arthur was designated a penal settlement in 1830, and it was to this place on Tasman's Peninsula that the vast majority of men sentenced to severe punishment were sent. A case was that of Elias Goulder, transported in 1833 from Surrey, who was convicted for burglary by the Supreme Court of Van Diemen's Land in 1844. He was ordered to be transported for fifteen years, of which three were to be spent at Port Arthur. (It was not unknown for sentences of transportation to be pronounced upon transportees, who would then be sent off to Port Arthur or Norfolk Island.) Another convict was convicted for stealing by the Quarter Sessions at New Norfolk and sent to a penal settlement for four years, and a third offender was sent there for three years for breaking and entering. On the other hand, some men were directed to the Peninsula by magistrates' courts. For instance, for absconding, Titus Blacker was sent there, to labour in chains after eight previous offences for misconduct, drunkenness and neglect of duty as a police constable, and so was Alfred Stallard for misconduct after six earlier offences, which included selling water for the general station at Waterloo Point.

At Port Arthur itself, solitary confinement was a favourite punishment, though it was by no means the only one. There were other more insidious forms of punishment not prescribed by the regulations. Most notice in the colony was not taken of official punishments, but of the degradation caused by the confinement of so many men. Commission of unnatural offences caused great horror among free colonists, but no one could say whether such acts were common. Still no one can say, but the convicts' records do occasionally note punishments for homosexual acts, though they were very rarely recorded. In fact, to what extent the fears of respectable settlers were justified cannot be known, because although the records mention homosexuality they concern only the men apprehended.

Though some men were sent to the penal settlements, this sort of punishment was not common. What, then, were the principal

punishments and offences? How often were the convicts punished?
During the whole period, five offences was the average number
committed by the male prisoners in Van Diemen's Land. In the
assignment period this figure was six, and in the probation period,
four. This finding is consistent with a change in penal discipline
after 1840, but it must be remembered that the proportion of
'lifers' decreased greatly during the years after the late 1830s, so
that men were not under discipline for such lengthy periods and
therefore had far less prospect of building up a record. Except
for those men never in trouble in the colony, and those who were
in trouble so serious that some were hanged and others severely
punished by the superior courts, there remains the vast majority
of 80 per cent of prisoners whose careers fall between these two
extremes, some admonished once or twice for slight offences,
others suffering many punishments short of re-transportation
ordered by superior courts.

Most common offences were drunkenness, and absence without
leave, together with many other forms of misconduct, such as:
'Found rambling in the bush with two free women.'
'Sending a bribe to the overseer to exempt him from wheeling
barrows.'
'Disturbing the family at a late hour, and refusing to put out the
light.'
'Absent without leave from the Brickfields and found smoking in
Mr. Spode's kitchen. [Mr. Spode was the Superintendent of
Convicts.]'
'An attack on the person and stating that if he were returned to
Mr. S. Lord's service, he might look out.'
'Neglect of duty and going to bed in the middle of the day.'
'Suspicion of placing gunpowder in a chimney of the blacksmith's
forge with an intention of blowing it up.'
'Hooting and shouting at Mr. D. C. Watkins when sent down on
duty.'

So the list of offences could be extended for a long time,
offences which give a fascinating kaleidoscopic picture of life
among the convict rank and file in Van Diemen's Land. But
though such a list might be entertaining, it would not indicate
the general picture of the convict system. Admittedly any such
picture will be at a high level of generalization, but a calculation
of the average number of offences and inspection of some typical

cases will give a fairer and more objective estimate of the convict system than will examination of curious offences or second-hand opinions.

Drunkenness, absence without leave, and misconduct were the common offences committed by convicts, and these were typically punished by gaol sentences and labour in road gangs, together with flagellation prior to 1840. It would be commonplace to point out that a quick flogging was by far the most economical form of punishment from the point of view of the master, and it was generally administered prior to 1840 when the assignment system disappeared: 38 per cent of all prisoners were flogged at least once during the period up to 1840, but in the probation period, this figure was only 4 per cent.[19]

It is clear from the offences brought to light that the convict servant was at the mercy of master or overseer, and that a fancied insolent look or observation from a prisoner could be regarded as misconduct and punished as such.[20] Some of the offences for which the convicts were brought before magistrates were scarcely serious. What is to be made of the case of Alfred Watkins who was placed in gaol for fourteen days for stating in the presence of the work-gang that he was glad the potato crop had failed, of Henry Alexander who was given six months' hard labour for being in his master's garden with a female servant sitting on his lap, and insolence to his mistress, and of Michael Conean who was placed in gaol for seven days for refusing to tell his name when driving a cart on which no name was painted?

As a rule, however, trifling offences were not punished with severity but more often than not by admonition, though some petty breaches of the regulations were punished viciously on occasion, particularly in the 1820s when Governor Arthur was establishing his effective, all-seeing and predictable administration. In 1825 Benjamin Horton was awarded twenty-five lashes for giving a signal to a fellow prisoner, who was improperly employed, that the superintendent was approaching; and in 1822 John Callicott was sentenced to twenty-five lashes and sent to Macquarie Harbour for imitating an order. The offence of selling water earned another man twenty-five lashes in the same period, though in 1832 a prisoner was merely admonished for inducing the labourers to leave the harvest field, and another put to work on the tread-wheel for leaving his work and saying that he had not enough meat.

Some other offences show flashes of defiance and spirit. For instance, two men were punished for an offence against the office of the Governor, one being admonished for using the Lieut.-Governor's name in a disrespectful manner, and another gaoled for not saluting the Lieut.-Governor when passing. Other instances showing independence included one in which a boundary dispute may have been involved because a prisoner was charged with absence without leave, pulling down the fence of a paddock at New Town and turning in two horses to graze, for which determination the prisoner concerned was sentenced to hard labour. Another convict was given a sentence of two years' hard labour in chains when he left the district without a pass, obtained boots and shoes in the name of Mr Horne, circulated reports that he had sheep in Mr Horne's flock, and committed other acts of gross misconduct and fraud. Another, not intimidated by the forces of justice, was sent to labour in chains for insolence in the police office and for using threatening gestures to the district constable; while another's feelings towards his officers were such that he was ordered one hundred lashes for throwing a brick-bat at the assistant superintendent and striking him. Richard Jones was also aggrieved enough to throw a sickle at the overseer, for which action he was placed in solitary confinement, and James McInally, a lad at Point Puer, was punished by being placed in solitary confinement for throwing a stone at the school door during lessons.

Yet convict life had another side to it: encouragement was given to the convicts to make a good name for themselves in the eyes of the government by appointment to the police force as constables, but usually they were dismissed for misdemeanours. Thomas Chalkley was only a month in the police before being dismissed because of his suspicious conduct when he was disarmed by bushrangers. It was considered that he knew these men, and co-operated with them. John Attiwell was gaoled for obtaining the reward twice for apprehending a runaway, and later for suspected sheep-stealing; Thomas Cass, for lying down drunk on the road with his musket alongside him, was sentenced to hard labour; and a third man was dismissed for taking a female prisoner to the penitentiary in a state of intoxication and being intoxicated himself. This same individual had formerly been sent to Port Arthur for having in his possession three 'flash' bills of £500, and a knife with a saw in it.

Other prisoners entrusted with posts of responsibility were punished for permitting prisoners to get drunk and being incapable of proceeding to Launceston, allowing a female prisoner ordered to be placed in the stocks to conceal her person with a large shawl, and misconduct as watchman in not reporting singing in the cells during the night, by which means prisoners made their escape. One prisoner was made government flogger, but forfeited his salary because of drunkenness.

Setting thieves to catch thieves did not, therefore, always have the desired result, but praiseworthy acts by prisoners were rewarded. One policeman was favourably under notice for his good conduct in apprehending a desperate runaway, though presumably not for taking away another man's wife, for which assiduity he was transferred to another part of the island. One other prisoner was very handsomely rewarded for his exertions in catching Benjamin Ball, a desperate bushranger, for he was not only given one hundred sovereigns but a free pardon as well. Yet another prisoner demonstrated that, though the life of a convict was in general a hard one, the system was not as vicious as it could have been; he was John William Grundell, who was promised a ticket-of-leave for his zeal and meritorious conduct in protecting his master's flocks against the wild dogs, and the further indulgence of a conditional pardon was promised at no distant period provided his conduct continued equally praiseworthy. For preventing his mistress's house from being robbed, James Eyre was awarded his ticket-of-leave.

Some offences can only be described as curious. Among these was the case of a man who, for carelessly driving his goat-cart, was compelled to break stones on four Saturday afternoons, of another who defended his breach of the regulations by stating that his master had called him 'a damned lying scoundrel', and of another who was given thirty-six lashes for the offence of secreting two pounds of canary seed at Government House. James Askins also had access to the seat of government, for he was the gardener at Government House, and was noted with favour for giving up a gold seal he found in the government garden, but then he blotted his copy-book by taking milk from the government cow, for which he was sentenced to a term of hard labour.

Other offences included making a fire in the bush and exciting a strong suspicion that a piece of a goat lost by Mr Boyd was being cooked there; biting off portion of another man's nose; and being found in the chimney of his master's bedroom between 9 and 10 p.m. A sense of humour was exhibited by few convicts: George Fletcher had his period of probation extended for having the temerity to laugh in the ranks, and William Davis (2) was admonished for cutting a broad arrow upon another man's hair.

Here are some other infringements which give an idea of the sorts of offences recorded, and reflect the life of the prisoner in Van Diemen's Land:

'Refusing work and singing obscene songs in the lock-up during prayers.'

'Drunk and insulting the passers-by.'

'Conniving at the baker having bread in the oven improperly after the batch was drawn out.'

'Throwing a stone or missile during Divine Service and thereby creating a disturbance.'

'Improperly placing government trousers in the bake-house.'

'Leaving his work and running after the coach.'

'Skulking from his labour under pretence of being sick.'

'Enforcing his master's cart down a steep hill with one hundred bushels of oats on it and thereby killing one bullock and injuring another.'

'Applying his master's horse and cart to his own advantage and working half price.'

'Attempting to defraud Mr. Barclay by tendering him a Coronation Medal for a shilling.'

'Spending four days escorting female prisoners when two days would have sufficed.'

'Sleeping in Divine Service.'

The point is that, although some 10 per cent of prisoners committed serious offences which brought them before superior courts, and a similar number never offended during their time in the hands of masters these were not the typical cases; those that follow are.

Thomas Ankin, a labourer, was transported in 1833, and his history is representative of many. Tried by Cambridgeshire Quarter Sessions in the Isle of Ely, he was convicted of stealing goods from a carrier's wagon. He had been born at Ely, and stated that his offence was robbing a stage-wagon; Ankin had previously been in gaol for six months on a charge of receiving stolen goods. He was twenty years of age when convicted, and the surgeon-superintendent noted that he had participated or connived in theft during the voyage out. His first offence in the colony, that of being improperly in company with a woman at Perth, was punished with fifty lashes, but thereafter for four offences of misconduct, absence without leave, drunkenness, and being without a pass, he was admonished on each occasion. Ankin received a ticket-of-leave in 1838 and was freed in 1840, at the age of twenty-seven. Nothing more is known of him.

A second case that was typical in the number of times the offender was before magistrates, concerned Andrew Carr or Brady or Patrick Byrnes, tried in Co. Meath in 1841 for larceny. He stated that he had stolen harness, and had formerly been convicted and sentenced to three months in gaol for the theft of horse's winkers. He was twenty-seven, married, and a mason ('very indifferent') by trade. His period of transportation was seven years. Carr was punished five times in the colony for misconduct, absence without leave, receiving, and theft. He was admonished once for being absent without leave, but his other punishments were hard labour, solitary confinement, and cancellation of a ticket-of-leave awarded in 1847. No details of his release were noted.

A final case typifying the career of convicts in the colony was that of William Potter, tried by Devonshire Assizes in 1837 for burglary. He was single, aged twenty-two, and a gardener by occupation. He had been in prison previously. Potter's four offences in the colony were those of being absent without leave three times between 1838 and 1842 (for which he was gaoled and admonished on two occasions, and for which he had his period of probation extended on the third), and drunk once. For the last-mentioned offence he was given a sentence of hard labour. He received his ticket-of-leave in 1843, and a conditional pardon in 1848.

How does the preceding description of convict life in Van Diemen's Land square with accounts published by convicts? There are not many of these, and what there are generally reflect very unusual aspects of the convict system because the writers were men of higher education than the vast majority of prisoners. Such persons as clerks, for example, were placed where their talents could be of use to their masters, and so there is not much justification for talking about Australia's first novelist, the Van Diemen's Land convict Henry Savery, if it is wished to inspect convict life among the rank and file. It is not surprising, in view of the magnitude of his work, that Henry Mayhew interviewed returned convicts. What is more surprising is that one of them spoke of his life in Van Diemen's Land at some length, and because his is an account from someone who would surely have remained silent had he not met Mayhew and because it has the ring of authenticity, it will be quoted at some length.

This man's background was typical of the city convict. He was a Londoner, and as a young man fond of a roving life and the company of women. He ran away from home, and became acquainted with eight other youths at Bartlemy Fair (all of them were finally transported to Australia), after which, with a young woman also subsequently despatched to Van Diemen's Land, he picked pockets in Fleet Street for a living. He then started passing bad notes with a 'mate' who was also later transported, and although such uttering was a capital offence, the gallows held no terror for him, he said. The next step in his criminal career was a move out into the country on a gambling project which involved throwing loaded dice for prizes marked on a table. This table was erected at race meetings, and between races he and a confederate engaged in highway robbery.

Upon his return to London, he was arrested when he tried to palm off some spurious money on a person who did the same thing himself, and was tried at the Old Bailey. The result was a sentence of fourteen years' transportation to Van Diemen's Land. When he arrived there, this prisoner was sent to Launceston, where he had a severe master; later on he worked in a government potato field, in the charcoal-works and at the Marine Department. Several times punishments were inflicted—once it was twenty-five lashes because a bag of flour burst and he picked some up in a cap: 'The cats the convicts were then flogged with were each six feet long, made out of the log-line of a ship of 500 tons burden; nine over-end knots were in each tail, and nine tails whipped at each end with a wax-end. With this we had half-minute lashes; a quick lashing would have meant certain death . . . When I was first flogged, there was enquiry among my fellow-convicts, as "How did D—— (meaning me) stand it—did he sing?" The answer was, "He was like a pebble"; that is, I never once said "oh" or gave out any expression of the pain I suffered. I took my flogging like a stone. If I had sung, some of the convicts would have given me lush with a locust in it (laudanum hocussing), and when I was asleep would have given me a crack on the

head that would have laid me straight. That first flogging made
me ripe. I said to myself, "I can take it like a bullock". I could
have taken the flogger's life at the same time, I felt such revenge.
Flogging always gives me that feeling . . . In all I had eight
hundred and seventy-five lashes at my different punishments . . .
Seven years before my time was up I took to the bush. I could
stand it no longer, of course not.'[21] This convict finally absconded
from Van Diemen's Land, and there is no reason to dismiss his
story, though it must be questioned whether he received the
extraordinary number of lashes he said he had.

Absconding of this sort was not common, and about 80 per
cent of the convicts were emancipated or free by servitude in
1860, eighteen years after the last convicts left Britain for Van
Diemen's Land. Three per cent successfully absconded, and 12
per cent were not recorded as having been freed. Whether this
latter group of men got away from the island, or whether the
note of their being freed was omitted from their dossiers as a
result of clerical error, is unknown, but certainly very few prisoners
remained in the hands of the colonial authorities by the 1860s.
Thus, perhaps 15 per cent ran away, but the true figure is
probably much less.[22]

Van Diemen's Land proved a good gaol, and unless a fleeing
prisoner managed to escape in a boat leaving from an isolated
part of the coast, he was likely to be found when police searched
departing vessels. Thorough inspections were made, though sometimes the vigilance of the police was at fault: a female prisoner
absconded, packed and labelled in a pretended case of stuffed
birds.[23] There is no way of knowing precisely how many Van
Diemen's Land convicts thus absconded, though Governor Arthur
noted that drastic steps had been taken during his term of office
to find stowaways; vessels had even been fumigated if the absconder could not be found otherwise, for prisoners had placed
themselves in casks, and under packages, and suffered excruciating
pain to escape.[24]

It is difficult to establish the number of absconders, and also
difficult to calculate how many convicts stayed on in the island
and were not attracted across Bass Strait to the gold diggings;
once a convict was released his name seldom appeared again on
the records unless he became a backslider and committed another
offence. But some prisoners' deaths are recorded (over and above
deaths during the period of transportation), and this one per cent

form a group called locally the 'imperial paupers', that is, men who, after being transported, were reckoned to be a charge on imperial funds as they spent their declining years in institutions.

A few cases illustrate the fag-end of the convict system. Thomas Smith, tried at the age of eighteen in Cheshire for stealing three rabbits, is an example. Previously in prison twice, he was a labourer and was transported in 1845 for seven years. He became free by servitude in the colony in 1852, having been imprisoned twice for breaches of the regulations. He reappeared on the registers in 1861 when he was sentenced to hard labour in Launceston for idleness, and then in 1876 was sent to gaol again for the same reason. He appeared to lead an itinerant life in the colony, and his record closed with the notice of his death in Launceston gaol in 1886.

Some other prisoners, freed in mid-century, died at depots for invalids in the 1880s, and one convict appeared on the books for the last time in 1890 when he was recorded dead in Hobart, having been for many years in business in Elizabeth Street. He was, of course, free by servitude at this time. Another man, from Latrobe, was admitted to an invalid depot as late as 1892, when he was seventy years old. He had been freed forty-two years earlier, and was presumably thrown upon the State.

Yet another old man, William Fowler, who reappeared on the records after a lapse of many years, had been transported as early as 1823. Free by servitude in 1830, he was subsequently sent to gaol for fourteen years in 1837 for stealing money from the person, and conditionally pardoned in 1847. His career is worth noting in some detail, for his life spanned much of the transportation era. Convicted when twenty-two by Hereford Assizes for stealing five handkerchiefs, he had been a shoemaker, born in Bristol. His first recorded punishment in Van Diemen's Land, sixteen months after the arrival of his ship, when he was employed on the public works, was fifty lashes for misconduct. Between that time and 1837 he was punished ten times, receiving a total of 120 lashes. For thirty years after 1847, his record was silent, until in 1877 at Campbell Town he was sentenced to hard labour for being idle. A year later came the same punishment for the same offence, and a year later the identical thing happened at Longford, when he was seventy-eight years old. Nothing is noted of his death. Perhaps he perished in the bush—one man, an absconder from Port Arthur in 1866, was supposed to be living in a hollow log, and subsisting on native game.[25] The final lost and lonely years of such old men, who had drunk deeply at the bitter springs of 'the system', can only be described as solitary and poor, as they wandered the island, lodging in the open air or begging shelter, to end their days in gaol or a government home, or in unknown circumstances.

During the assignment period at least, the general picture of life for the convict in Van Diemen's Land was a dark one, though not as dark as it could have been. Yet on the island there existed one of the most amazing communities on the face of the nineteenth-century earth, importing some of the worst and most depraved criminals of Britain with which to increase the numbers of a society built on the rum traffic, to such an extent that under one of the early governors the whole colony was drunk together for weeks on end.[26] In a colony that was so constituted, it is not surprising to learn that 'near Perth (V.D.L.) we passed a gibbet, lately erected; on which the body of a prisoner who committed murder near the spot, was suspended, with a view of deterring from the crime'.[27] Within the space of fifty years there were packed into the savage history of Van Diemen's Land so many terrible events that to later generations it appeared that the convict era had passed at some distant and barbaric time.

There can be no easy answer to the question of why convicts committed the offences they did in Van Diemen's Land, but though some were the result of the blind hitting out of desperate men driven to near madness by an inflexible system of discipline in the penal settlements, most offences were not of a vicious character. The most fruitful parallel is with an army and its administration. Convicts tended to regard their masters as other ranks regarded their officers in the armed services. There is no direct evidence of smouldering warfare between convict and master, but the idea that convicts were the aggrieved parties was impressed industriously upon newcomers in the penitentiary.[28]

Convict discipline was severe and attempts to abscond were common, though whether men tried to escape because of desperation it is imposible to say. The number who were apprehended in Hobart Town suggests that absconding was less a determined effort to leave the colony than a yearning for the flesh-pots of the raw capital. But certainly a few men complained of bad food, and the lack of adequate rations was one cause of men taking to the bush.[29]

Incidence and type of offences can be explained by the character and origins of many of the convicts, as well as the character of master and overseers and 'the system' under Arthur. Prisoners from the towns of Britain had been accustomed to a St Giles-like existence in which the most important features were idleness, a battle of wits with those robbed, and a lack of any sort of supervision. It is revealing to note, particularly among youthful convicts, the reaction to penal discipline. They appeared unable to comprehend a system which ruthlessly enforced regulations, which could not be bought off, and which was as emotionless as the cold, just and hard eye of George Arthur himself.

How far transportation succeeded in reforming convicts cannot be known, nor anything but a general estimate be made of the extent to which it deterred potential law-breakers in Britain. In the early years of Van Diemen's Land, any reformation would have been in spite of the administration rather than because of it, for profligacy and drunkenness pervaded all society.[30] Yet numbers of prisoners who had been brought up in vice and idleness improved in the colony in assigned service, and cases of spectacular reformation did occur.[31] There is no evidence that most convicts sank into constant breaches of the law and the assignment regulations, though certainly some did. However, nothing is known of prisoners' careers once convicts were out of the hands of the administration, and so it cannot be definitely assumed that these men did not backslide.

Sobriety was not a characteristic of the convicts. They no doubt had a taste for drink prior to their conviction in Britain, and the system of convict discipline drove them to seek solace in the bottle when they could, and when they could not. At Hobart Town in the late 1820s prisoners spent more money at inns than did house-owners or mechanics: where a man who was not a convict spent a shilling, the prisoner spent ten shillings. Where they got the money, no one knew.[32]

The most profound factor preventing reformation, and perhaps driving men to persistent offence, was the lash. Its advantages of cheapness and speed are obvious, and it was a means of enforcing discipline in the armed forces, the officers of which filled many posts in early Australia. It would be difficult to find a more effective means of hardening the heart of the convict than by flogging him. Degrading to all concerned, the cat-o'-nine-tails was feared until its first use, after which a marked deterioration of the convict's character set in. A similar effect followed the placing of men into the brutalizing chain gangs, as indeed did sentences to penal settlements such as Port Arthur,[33] where prisoners were able to mix with the most depraved and vicious criminals thrown up by the jungle-like cities of early nineteenth-century Britain.

The proportion of men severely punished in Van Diemen's Land was not large. Arthur, indeed, was fully persuaded that in the colony a great majority of masters took pains with their assigned servants, admonished them, and advised them. Nevertheless, he thought that one-quarter of the Van Diemen's Land convicts were irreclaimable, and relapsed into crime very easily.[34] Arthur's figure was probably too high for the whole period of transportation to Van Diemen's Land.

In New South Wales there are no comprehensive records of convicts' conduct available. To analyse how convicts fared in the parent colony it is necessary to fall back on the musters, the census of 1828, and the few documents that are objective enough to be useful.

By no means all the convicts transported were on strength when the first apparently complete muster was held in 1806, because 50 per cent of prisoners were not mentioned. Mortality was high on some of the first ships, and no doubt certain prisoners left the colony when they were freed, or else escaped, but there are no reliable figures of departures in the early years, though there are a number of opinions by those on the spot which suggest that many convicts departed from New South Wales. Passages to Europe were procured with the greatest of ease,[35] and ex-convicts reappeared in London.[36] Others went into the South Seas[37] and spread far and wide as beachcombers and petty kings, some found their way to New Zealand,[38] others yet again appeared in India and drew unfavourable attention to themselves,[39] and more took passage on American ships.[40]

The number of prisoners who left is, however, impossible to establish with any accuracy, though useless adjectives such as 'many' are not lacking. For instance, by 1819 'many' convicts had returned to New South Wales a second time after their arrival back in Britain, and there were 'a great many' desertions from the colony.[41] Some of these deserters never reached civilization, no doubt, and men were lost in the bush, or at sea, and never heard of again. How many perished in the attempt to walk to

China, or some fabled settlement to the north of Sydney, is un-known, although it was reported that fifty skeletons were found along the route to the Orient.[42] It is a moot point which of all these reasons explain the disappearance of half the transported convicts, but probably all played a part. It is, however, significant that more than half of the missing men were transported on the Second and Third Fleets, on which mortality was high. It was also high in New South Wales, for 486 sick were landed from the Second Fleet, and, according to one source, of 122 Irish who arrived in 1791, only 50 were alive the following year.[43] If this sort of mortality occurred very often, then the population of con-victs must have added up to considerably less than that which left Britain.

Death as a result of ill-treatment on the voyage, the starvation time in early New South Wales, and successful attempts to leave what must have been a most unattractive colony for the London thief, probably accounted for most of the convicts missing at 1806, though an incomplete muster, and misspelt surnames, may have helped. After 1811, when Macquarie conducted the second com-prehensive muster of which there is a record, numbers of missing convicts fell sharply, and the totals which left Britain yearly were reduced only by mortality *en route*, by natural deaths in New South Wales, and by a few successful escapes.

An assignment system of convict management was adopted in New South Wales, and used throughout most of the transportation period. The general character of assignment need not be men-tioned again, because it was basically the same as that employed later in Van Diemen's Land. However, without the comprehensive records of conduct kept in Van Diemen's Land, there is little that can be done to assess the nature of convict discipline in New South Wales. The material for an objective study is meagre, and limited to a few documents and much rumour and slanted evidence. The documents must be discussed first, in order to compare the disci-pline in the two colonies.

One of these is a deposition book used by the Hunter River Bench in 1831 and 1832.[44] In this book are noted the details of cases tried summarily before the magistrates in that district, and there is nothing in it to suggest that forms of offences and punish-ment were any different from those in Van Diemen's Land, except that the ordering of floggings appeared more general. But perhaps the Bench was severe at the Hunter River. Three cases show the similarities to discipline enforced in Van Diemen's Land.

One of these concerned William Watkins, assigned servant to T. P. McQueen, who was charged with leaving his station without orders. The prisoner was tried before Francis Little, Esq., and heard his overseer charge that Watkins had driven sheep to another station without permission. The prisoner admitted this, and said that hunger drove him to leave his master because the beef was so bad he could not eat it. The overseer had refused to change it when Watkins complained of its quality. The overseer then produced a specimen of the offending meat, which the Bench pronounced to be perfectly good. Watkins had his ticket-of-leave put back for eighteen months.

John Jones, assigned servant to D. McIntyre, was charged with disobedience of orders. The overseer told the court that his master instructed him not to let the men leave off reaping for breakfast till nine o'clock. Jones and four other men had left, and when asked where they were going, had replied, ' "To breakfast". The prisoner then said that he would see me buggered first before he would stop till nine o'clock.' Jones admitted using the language, but said it was not addressed to the overseer. He was ordered fifty lashes for his impertinence.

A third man tried at the Hunter River was Ralph or Ralfe Rolands or Rawlins, who was charged with being drunk and with abstracting spirits from a cask under his charge. His master was H. Dangar, and the overseer gave evidence that he started three men, Rolands one of them, from Noelsfield to Dartbrook with a dray. They were instructed to get a keg of brandy. They had done this, and then come on as far as Colonel Dumaresq's fence where one of the men was accidentally killed when the dray passed over him. The bullocks had been turned loose, the harness lost, and there was a deficiency of spirits. The gardener at Colonel Dumaresq's stated to the court that he had heard a noise, and seen the prisoner on the ground, another sitting on a log, and a third man singing to them. They all appeared drunk. The bullocks had been tied up, and there was a keg of brandy on the ground between the shafts. Rolands, in his defence, said that they had been detained at the place from where they picked up the brandy, and had to stay the night at Dumaresq's. The bullocks had been brought in in the morning. When the accident occurred, he had been so bewildered that he had cast the bullocks loose without the harness on them, from which cause it was lost. He was ordered fifty lashes, and the prisoner identified as the man singing was given the same sentence.

These charges and punishments are typical of the cases in the deposition book, and though the cases were tried before one Bench only in the whole colony, is it likely that other magistrates were hearing dissimilar charges and awarding dissimilar punishments? That, in fact, charges and punishments were much like those so well documented in Van Diemen's Land, is confirmed by the dossiers of men transported to Van Diemen's Land after having been freed in New South Wales. Such men are noted in the records of the island colony with the offence causing their transportation to the island after 1840, and a record of conduct headed, typically, with 'police history from Sydney'. These records of careers are very similar to those of Van Diemen's Land men, and confirm to some extent that discipline, offences and punishments were very much the same in both colonies.

There is another small piece of evidence that the assignment system was administered and breaches of the regulations punished in the same way in the two colonies, for in one record[45] there appear the following offences and punishments: stealing a pair of shoes (25 lashes), neglect of duty (150 lashes), absence without leave and telling a falsity against his overseer (150 lashes). These few offences and punishments cannot safely be regarded as typical, but there is every reason to believe that the only difference between New South Wales and Van Diemen's Land administration of the assignment system is that the New South Wales records are unavailable.

There is, however, one noticeable difference between the two colonies. This is the part played in the growth of New South Wales by its emancipated convicts, for the mother colony was for a longer and earlier period dominated by a convict population which had time to become free and active in money-making prior to extensive free immigration. Few Van Diemen's Land convicts, so far as can be established, became much more than small farmers. Van Diemen's Land had no equivalent to the prominent and wealthy Simeon Lord or Samuel Terry, because this pair was in Australia and freed at a time when opportunities for commerce were great, and the scope of opportunity wider. Thus attention must be given to convicts' careers in New South Wales not in terms of discipline, but in terms of more general histories.

Although nothing is known of those New South Wales men who never broke a regulation, and nothing is known of those men (by analogy with Van Diemen's Land the majority of prisoners) who were punished a few times only, a little is known of the men tried by superior courts because some were sent to Norfolk Island and then on to Van Diemen's Land, and had their records transmitted with them. Of the total number of such men and their particulars there is no reliable evidence, but a few examples will serve to show in what circumstances these men were tried.

One of them was James King, who came out in 1818. He was tried at the age of twenty-seven by Somerset Assizes for larceny in a dwelling-house, and awarded life transportation for stealing a gold and silver watch-chain, seal and key from a person named A. Rich. King arrived in New South Wales on 31 December 1818; in 1821 he was employed by the government at Emu Plains, and by 1828 he had received the indulgence of a ticket-of-leave and had become a watchmaker at Parramatta. (His trade at home had been that of watch-finisher.) Then, according to his police history, in February 1831 he was sentenced to three months' labour in an ironed gang for embezzlement, his only offence noted in New South Wales. Some time between that date and 1838 he evidently relinquished watchmaking, because in 1838 he was a constable, and charged with shooting at William Henry Peacock.

According to Peacock, he (Peacock) was overseer to a Mrs Morris at the Vale of Clwydd, and he was going to her station with two drays when he camped for the night outside a public-house at Penrith on 15 June 1838. The prisoner King was a constable who, with some men under escort, had stopped at the same spot. During the night he came, very drunk, to Peacock's camp and said he must put Peacock's men on the chain. When told by the prosecutor that he would do well to look after the ones he already had, King informed Peacock that he was a magistrate as well as a policeman, and could put them all on the chain if he wanted to. Under this delusion of grandeur, he put a pistol to Peacock's head, stepped back, and fired at him. The pistol was loaded with slugs which did Peacock no great harm. King was found guilty and sentenced to death.

This sentence was subsequently commuted, and he arrived at Norfolk Island on 5 November of that year, where he was in trouble twice: for malingering he was admonished, and for attending the hospital under false pretences he was ordered to stay in gaol till the Sunday morning. It was seven years later that King left the island to be transferred to Van Diemen's Land, where he had no offences recorded. He received a ticket-of-leave in 1846, and a conditional pardon four years later. By this time he would have been fifty-nine years old. What became of him then is not known.

Another example of a man who hardly succeeded in his new colonial life was Thomas Galloway, who in 1825 was sentenced to seven years' transportation by Surrey Quarter Sessions for fraud. His calling was that of a sailor in the Royal Navy. Galloway's career in New South Wales included eleven offences, and eight of them were attempts to abscond. He was also given fifty lashes in 1830 for attempting to obtain money under false pretences. In 1832 he was free by servitude, but what he did after that for eleven years is not documented though by 1843 he was in Melbourne before the Supreme Court on a charge of larceny. He was found guilty and transported for seven years, of which two were to be passed at Norfolk Island. Galloway arrived there in 1844 for detention, and had no offences noted against his name. Transferred to Van Diemen's Land, he was granted a ticket-of-leave in 1846, but a year later died in the Bothwell district.

A final example of a convict who, by being despatched to Van Diemen's Land, gives a glimpse of convict life in New South Wales, was Robert Taylor, tried in London for housebreaking in 1833. His career in New South Wales is not well documented, but in 1838 he received twelve months in an ironed gang for the theft of some shingles. He must then have escaped, because a year later he was charged with five other convicts for stealing a gun and other articles from the dwelling-house of Henry Allen, at Piper's Creek, Port Macquarie, putting him in fear, and tying his hands and striking him. At the trial it was stated that the prisoners were runaways, and that when they robbed Allen, he struck at one of them with a poker. He was then beaten, and tied by his hands to a bedpost. Taylor was given fifteen years' transportation for this, and sent to Norfolk Island. Two pieces of information are recorded of his life there; he was, in 1840, admonished for possession of a stolen shirt, and, five years later, recommended for praiseworthy conduct in saving the life of a fellow prisoner who attempted to drown himself in the sea. Transferred to Van Diemen's Land, he committed no offences for which he was punished, and received a ticket-of-leave in 1847 and a conditional pardon in 1850.

Other men sent to Norfolk Island and then to Van Diemen's Land were nearly all bushrangers, and appear to have little to recommend them, though not all were typified by a gang of five who successively raped a mother of fifteen children. Four of this group were hanged, and the fifth one saved from the gallows by the evidence of the woman, who said he had restrained his companions and thus saved her life.[46]

There is little doubt that the discipline on Norfolk Island was severe in the extreme, but the convict dossiers are not full enough to test the truth of the horrifying pictures painted of that penal settlement. It has been said that when the trials were over at Norfolk Island, men were hung up like tassels on a blind.[47]

Of the numbers of convicts who were not punished at all, or who suffered little at the hands of magistrates, not even a guess can be made without invoking an analogy with Van Diemen's Land. However, by using other data (not available for the Van Diemen's Land prisoners) an analysis can be made of the men who did well in New South Wales. Such people set the other extreme of colonial careers.[48]

Typical of the few New South Wales convicts who flourished exceedingly in their new home was James Underwood, who arrived in the First Fleet after being convicted in Wiltshire in 1786 for killing sheep. Trained as a shipwright, in 1798 he began shipbuilding at the mouth of the Tank Stream, and was the first private shipbuilder in Australia. He was associated with Henry Kable and Simeon Lord, two prominent emancipists, in whaling and sealing ventures, and in 1813 he acquired a licence for an inn. In 1824 he established a distillery at Botany, but returned to England in 1844, where he died. His brother came out free to New South Wales, and also engaged in sealing and merchant enterprises. James Underwood married a currency girl about fifteen years after he arrived and, according to one record, had seven children.

Such is the nature of the records that there is only one possible yardstick with which to measure apparent success stories such as Underwood's, and that is to note men who were, at some point, landholders or business proprietors, or who had risen above the occupation of labourer. Unfortunately, it is impossible to go further than the 1828 census (later records are not complete lists of all inhabitants of New South Wales), and to permit men who were going up in the world a chance to be recorded at 1828, the period must be limited even more to that ending at approximately 1821. The principal difficulty in such analysis lies in the interpretation of 'landholder', because except for the 1806 and 1828 records, there is no full account of what areas of land were held.

Of the men transported prior to 1821 16 per cent became something more than labourers. Included in this 16 per cent are such persons as brewers, carpenters, tinsmiths, tailors, and harness-makers, as well as those who are noted as landholders or merchants. It is noteworthy that of the men on strength at 1810 50 per cent did well, to the extent of becoming landholders or merchants or tradesmen.

Such are the figures, and they can be illustrated by particular cases. One example of a minor success story was Paul Bushell, who was tried in Warwickshire in 1789 and transported for fourteen years at the age of about twenty-one. He was granted a conditional pardon twelve years later, and in 1802 he possessed a family of four, thirty acres and thirty hogs. In 1808 Bushell signed an address to William Paterson upon that officer's arrival from Van Diemen's Land after the overthrow of Governor Bligh, and the next year he is mentioned as the purchaser of cattle. He married a convict woman who was pardoned conditionally in 1798, but it is not clear when the marriage occurred. His wife died in 1820 and was buried at Wilberforce, where Bushell was a landholder in 1825, and where, with landholders and merchants, he protested against the system of dollar payments. At the age of fifty, in June 1822, Bushell married Isabella Brown, also of Wilberforce, who was born in the colony and who was twenty-one years old at the time of her marriage. They appear to have had four children, born between 1823 and 1829. Bushell held 190 acres in the Hawkesbury district in 1820, and the 1828 census records that he then had 310 acres at Wilberforce, where he was appointed to a sub-committee opposed to a system of national education. In 1834 he was at 'Pitt Town, Windsor'. He died at the age of eighty-four in 1853 and was buried at St John's, Wilberforce. His wife survived him till August 1883, when she died at the age of eighty.

Another convict materially successful in New South Wales was John Pye, sent out in 1791 for fourteen years on the ill-fated Third Fleet. Like Bushell, he was tried in Warwickshire. By 1802 Pye had acquired eighty acres of land (the first grant being made in 1796), forty of which were clear and thirty-nine in wheat and maize. He possessed eight sheep, fifteen goats, fifty-two hogs, and a family of nine. A list of grants made between 1800 and 1803 mentions that he acquired an additional seventy acres in 1802 at Toongabbe for cultivation, and describes him as being settled after his sentence of transportation had expired and as 'industrious'. According to the 1806 muster Pye had one hundred [sic] acres of land, and in a petition to the Colonial Secretary in 1810 concerning a land grant he stated that he had a wife and eight children, 200 sheep, fourteen head of horned cattle, and some horses. In 1818, Macquarie granted him 300 acres at Bathurst. In 1821 he was mustered as a landholder at Baulkham Hills. He held 400 acres by grant, and 400 by purchase, and a year later received a hotel licence for the 'Lamb and Lark' on the Windsor Road at Baulkham Hills. This hotel was apparently taken over by his son, John Pye junior, about 1828, by which time Pye senior held 1,210 acres of land at Seven Hills. He married a woman who apparently arrived free in 1790; it was possibly one of his sons who later tendered for the government domain at Parramatta, and who was a councillor there in 1847.

A third convict who apparently flourished in his new enforced home was Nathaniel Lawrence, a Somerset man who was transported in 1796 for life. He was granted a conditional pardon in 1804, an absolute pardon (later cancelled) in 1809, and a free pardon in 1813. By 1806 he had become a baker, and the following year married Margaret Doyle at St John's, Parramatta. Four years later he was granted a liquor licence in Pitt's Row, Sydney, 'the principal Brewers at Sydney having represented that it would be a great accommodation to the Labouring People and to the Lower Classes of the Inhabitants in general, to have plenty of good wholesome Beer brewed for their drinking', and was soon quite prosperous, as an advertisement in 1811 shows: 'That valuable and desirable Situation No. 34 Pitt-street, the present residence of Nathaniel Lawrence; comprising an excellent weather-boarded and brick-nogged Dwelling House, with a commodious Bake-house, large Granary with two floors, and a compleat stable for two horses . . . and every convenience fit for the

brewing and baking line.' Lawrence's home life may not have
gone so well: 'Nathaniel Lawrence of Pitt-street, hereby Cau-
tions Shopkeepers and others against giving Trust or Credit to his
Wife Margaret', he announced to the public in 1812.

Lawrence evidently continued to do well in business: he opened
a wholesale brewery at his Pitt Street premises in 1813, went to
England and returned in 1814-15, and was granted a wine and
spirit licence in 1816. Four years later, in a memorial addressed
to Justice Wylde, Lawrence stated that he had been a brewer for
fourteen years, and that he was the first person who commenced
that business in Sydney. He further noted how he had erected a
granary and drying house and malt-house at a cost of about
£1600, and prayed that his brewing licence be renewed. He added
that he was about to go to England for the express purpose of
purchasing hops and utensils for the establishment of a porter
brewery. He was away during 1820-21.

Lawrence died in January 1826 'of the Visitation of God'. It
was recorded in the press that for many years he had kept an
establishment commonly known as 'Natty's Brewery', 'which property is said to be of considerable value'. His remains were accompanied to the grave by a large crowd of friends and acquain-
tances.

Many more such little case studies could be cited, but they pose
more questions than can be answered from the documents available. For example, William Parr was transported in 1812 for
'forged bank notes etc.', after trial in Kent. He was a native of
Liverpool, aged thirty-nine, and a land surveyor and draughtsman
by profession. He received a ticket-of-leave in 1814, and a
conditional pardon was granted in October 1821. He was noted
as a ticket-of-leave draughtsman in 1819, and two years later
as a dealer in Sydney. In 1823 he was living in George Street,
Sydney, but he left the colony in January 1824.

This man may have accompanied Oxley on his exploring expedition in 1817, for a William Parr was acting mineralogist with
the party. He received £50 for his exertions on the expedition,
but there is only circumstantial evidence that the convict and the
explorer were the same person, though it may be significant that
the convict was a land-surveyor, if not a mineralogist.

Another example of enterprise was John Jobbins, transported in
1815 for stealing a coat. He was 'a notorious character', aged
twenty-one, and had been tried at Gloucester Assizes. In 1821

he was a householder in Sydney and free by servitude, and seven years later a butcher in Cambridge Street, owning four horses and 110 head of cattle. His business evidently thrived. He secured a land grant in St Lawrence parish in 1831, and was assigned convicts during the following two years, after which he applied to purchase land near Yass on the Murrambateman Creek, and to purchase further lands in the following years. He still owned his butcher's shop in 1834, however; he had land in Bathurst Street, and claimed an allotment in Pitt Street. His enterprises further afield suffered by an attack from bushrangers in 1839, when Jobbins was recorded as a grazier at Yass, and a few months later he wrote that an attack had been made by the blacks on his station at Towangah, near the head of the Ovens River. No other references to this remarkable example of the rise of a convict have been found, and though a note on the convict indent states that he was 'dead', it does not say when or in what circumstances.

Another convict who also disappears into the mists of history prior to his death is Thomas Henry Hart. He was transported in 1815 after being found guilty of burglary. An account of his trial noted that he was a baker at Kentish Town, London. Five years after his arrival he was granted a conditional pardon, which was shortly afterwards listed as a free pardon. In January 1817 Hart married Frances Shannon, twenty-four, in St Phillip's Church, Sydney. She was a convict who had arrived in the colony twelve months previously, having been convicted at Nottingham Assizes in 1815 and sentenced to fourteen years' transportation. She was by trade a dressmaker. They had five children in the following eight years.

On receiving his ticket-of-leave, Hart worked as a baker at 74 Pitt Street, and in 1819 was mustered as a servant to Dr Bromley. Two years later, however, he had become a merchant, and applied for and received a spirit licence. At this time his premises were at 36 Pitt Street, where he was able at the end of 1821 to offer the public tobacco, saddlery, salted salmon, butter, cheese, hams and various spirits, all imported. In the next few years his business evidently went from strength to strength as he supplied wheat and meat to the government stores. However, his fortunes took a turn for the worse in 1825, when he was committed to trial for receiving stolen goods.

His trial aroused much public interest, because one of the prisoners was 'rather in opulent and respectable circumstances'.

'A more just visitation of the law we have not had the opportunity of recording for some time past. The Justice of the British Court is not to be impeded or cut short either by the aid of wealth, or by the combination of influence—or even both . . . Not content with that liberality which the late Governor, in mercy, extended towards him, he yielded to the force of old and powerful habits, and thus re-subjected himself to the lash.' Hart was sentenced to fourteen years' transportation, and in 1825 was mustered at Port Macquarie.

Despite this setback to his fortunes, Hart somehow managed to secure a certificate of freedom in 1828, and the census of that year describes him as a merchant and trader who possessed 1,856 acres and 200 cattle. A year later he purchased a stock of printing materials, destined, it was reported, for Van Diemen's Land where he hoped to establish a newspaper, and in 1830 he was granted a licence for the 'George and Dragon', in Pitt Street. He also hired out a hackney coach from the premises, and later ran a coach daily between Sydney and Windsor.

Then he was again in trouble with the law, because in 1832 he was tried and convicted before the Supreme Court for stealing a watch and other articles from Andrew Syme, and sentenced to seven years' transportation. His wife died in 1839 at her residence in Pitt Street, and between 1842 and 1844 Hart was involved in insolvency proceedings, after which it is more difficult to trace his progress.

Another convict was tried at Dublin in 1824 for false pretences. He was Edward O'Shaughnessy, a goldsmith and jeweller who changed his occupation to journalism: in 1825 he was a government servant to Robert Howe (editor of the *Gazette*), in 1828 a reporter, and, in the course of time, editor of the paper. He later apparently brought a charge of libel against the Rev. Dr Lang. O'Shaughnessy died in May 1840.

Information concerning other convicts varies greatly. John Silverthorn, for instance, was transported on the First Fleet after his trial in 1784 in Wiltshire for highway robbery. He married Mary Wickham during his first year at Sydney, and in 1791 had forty acres of land at Prospect. He was still in the colony at 1811, and ten years later was a sawyer at Parramatta. There were three children.

Paul Bailey came out in 1791, after his conviction in London for stealing during a fire. In 1806 he was free by servitude, in

1811 still in the colony, and in 1819 noted as a landholder. Two years later, however, he was listed as a blind man living at Windsor, and in 1825 was a pauper at the same settlement.

David Roberts was transported in 1806 by Gloucester (City) Assizes. He was a labourer and shoemaker, aged twenty-four. By 1825 he was conditionally pardoned, and a landholder at Windsor, and three years later a shoemaker in Pitt Town where he had forty acres of land. He married a convict woman who came out in 1801, and they had two children by 1828.

There is little to be gained by continuing a list of such convicts, for the data do not permit much fruitful speculation. For instance, a butcher named William Chapman, aged twenty-one, was transported in 1816 for highway robbery in London. In 1819 he was listed as 'in the colony', in 1821 he was a government servant to H. Gasking, Sydney, and in 1828 he had his ticket-of-leave and was employed as a labourer to Thomas Huxley at Lower Portland Head. Whether this man remained a family retainer to the end of his life, worked up and down the country, set up in business, or went to sea, there is no way of knowing. But one convict who did go to sea, and who evidently led an adventurous if not criminal life, was Randle Oare, transported in 1810 for cattle-stealing. By 1814 a Randal Fore [*sic*] was listed in a proclamation by Macquarie directed against absconders in Van Diemen's Land, who had 'unlawfully absconded and fled from their usual Habitations and Employments . . . into the Woods and retired Places . . . with intent to support and maintain themselves by Rapine and Violence . . . Idleness and Debauchery'. This man was almost certainly Oare, because the following year there is a record of him as a sealer in Bass Strait.

It is difficult to know what became of Oare, and it is also difficult to learn much of Jonathan Cooper, transported for assault and robbery in 1818. He was stable-boy aged twenty-one, and sent out to New South Wales for life. A government labourer in 1819, Cooper was not noticed in the 1828 census, but in 1837 was at Penrith, where he held a ticket-of-leave.

A final case that illustrates the varied careers of New South Wales convicts concerns Christopher Robley, transported from Cumberland in 1810 for larceny. Five years later he married Mary Cummins, aged twenty, and free, in Sydney, and apparently worked as a ticket-of-leave blacksmith, the trade he followed in England. By 1821 he had been conditionally pardoned, and was a sawyer at Sydney, but in 1828 he had become a sheriff's officer, living at Clarence Street with his wife and five children.

Enough has been written to show how much and how little can be gleaned from records giving positive identification to convicts but some points can be established. One is that about half the men who can be traced to 1821 or thereabouts evidently did establish themselves as landholders, or, more often, as tradesmen. It was this convict class which was, no doubt, the backbone of emancipist agitation for legal rights, which felt it had a stake in the country, and which had contributed something to its advance.

Another factor which can be quantitatively estimated concerns marriage of convicts. It would be foolish to affirm that every convict who married is so noted in the documents consulted, but there are enough recorded to ask, and partly answer, the questions, how many convicts married in New South Wales, and whom did they marry?

Now after 1828, there does not exist any full list of the inhabitants of the colony, and thus it is necessary to close the gates of an enquiry into marriage rates and civil status, at 1821 or thereabouts, for many convicts transported after that date would not have served enough of their sentences to enable them to marry. By 1828 only 9 per cent of the men transported prior to 1822 had definitely married, but how many others were married and not so recorded is unknown, and therefore the figure of 9 per cent must be regarded as a minimum figure only. It ignores cohabitation. The civil condition of the women who married these convicts is as follows:

Convict women	53 per cent
Women born in the colony	19 per cent
Women of unknown origin	22 per cent
Women who came free	6 per cent

The information on which this table is based is so exiguous that little speculation is possible from it, except the obvious indication that convict men tended to marry convict women. One other factor is the age discrepancy between husbands and wives in the case of women born in the colony. The men were much older than their partners, as a rule, and where it is possible to make a comparison this difference in age ranges between seventeen and thirty-three years. Thus, because the women of their own age group were missing, men married into the next generation.

The opposite applied when men married convict women, because in about half the cases where comparison is possible, the women were older than their male partners. Presumably when the relatively few native-born girls were married, the prospective husband had to make do with what he could get. There is an indication that some women who came free, and later were noted as married to convicts, were the wives of those men; convict men who were married to such women nearly always did well, perhaps because their free wives brought out money. But the numbers are small.

The data do not permit much estimate of family-size of convict marriages. What information there is yields the following conclusions: those women who had come free by 1821, and married convict men, had three children each up to 1828; those who had no civil condition noted on the records also had three children each; and the women who were convicts had only one child each.

In conclusion, it might be said that convicts did establish themselves in New South Wales, and contributed to the economic welfare and development of the colony in the years prior to the 1820s, but the bakers and bootmakers and small landholders epitomized this emancipist class far more than did the great magnates such as Samuel Terry. There are few examples of men having land early in their careers, and then losing it, but we do not know how frequently this occurred during the first twelve or so years of settlement. Once a man had secured land, it was rare indeed, if it had been granted at or after 1806, that he was not still a landholder in 1821 or 1828, but the large number of men who do not appear on the muster records and who may have left the colony by 1806 could have sold up their land, or lost it to the rum traffickers. It was notorious that small farmers got themselves hopelessly into debt, and were compelled to sell out to men with wiser and stronger heads. Emancipists exhausted the ground because they knew little of farming, it was said, and it then fell by mortgage into the hands of the rum dealers: this was the history of probably three-quarters of the small emancipist class.[49] It may have been, but evidence suggests that this conclusion is an exaggeration for the period after 1806.

Convicts, then, did not do too badly during and immediately following Macquarie's governorship, but there is only descriptive evidence concerning the extent and effect of reformation of convicts in the colony. It was considered by some that at least a few prisoners were improved by transportation, although there were also individuals who chose to emphasize the worst aspects of what was certainly a most extraordinary society. One observer who was inclined to look on the bright side noted with satisfaction that two incorrigible Dublin thieves had been compelled to work at last, and finally came to take a pride in it.[50] Another person thought also that many convicts became reformed and 'really good men', particularly those sent out for a base crime and those men transported for political offences did especially well, it was considered by observers on the spot. Even town thieves became industrious, though they knew nothing when they landed except how to commit crimes. They soon mastered agricultural work, though the system would have been improved if the inexperienced criminals had been separated from the hardened.[51]

One factor which hampered reformation, and adoption of a respectable life by the prisoner, was the great discrepancy in the numbers of men and women transported. Those proportions being what they were, it was inevitable that a substantial number of men were compelled to remain bachelors, whether they cared for that state or not. It was this difference in the numbers of men and women, and their age when freed, that led to the archetype picture of old ex-convicts working all their lives for one landed proprietor, or as shearers, itinerant labourers, or bullock drivers, the ranks of which included many convicts because their knowledge of the country and their rough habits made them suited to long bullock hauls.[52] Such men developed eccentricities in their loneliness, and were known to fill their huts with parrots, possums and dogs for company.[53]

Not all had a good or sympathetic word for the emancipist, and the state of Australian society during the transportation period. Pitt Town was seen as a settlement of seven hundred people, many of whom had been convicts notorious for their drunkenness, profligacy and neglect of worship, and in Campbell and Appin were many 'low Irish'.[54] It was not surprising that standards of conduct in New South Wales were not always high for, as in Van Diemen's Land, the scenes before the eyes of the population were not calculated to edify. When a man was sentenced to receive one hundred lashes at the cart's tail in early New South Wales, and when there existed stocks which could accommodate eight or ten people at a time, when ticket-of-leave policemen had a pecuniary interest in the number of arrests they made, when 'bloody' was the common adjective, when it was said that under Governor King the colony consisted of those who sold rum and those who drank it,[55] and when the whole of society appeared to be in a state of constant motion to and from the courts, it would not do to apply civilized standards of conduct. There is no reason to suppose that the consumption of beer and spirits was at anything but world-record heights; indeed, drinking among the lower classes was thought to be prosecuted to an extent unknown anywhere else. The Rocks was notorious as the antipodean St Giles's, but the latter area was thought a paradise in comparison with the Sydney district.[56]

The impingement of the convict system on its subjects, both bond and free, is not readily amenable to quantitative analysis, but the picture was a dark one, regarded as such by the enlightened observers of the time. The system was not as bad as it might have been, but it was bad enough, though for the man who had enough intelligence to see that little would be gained if he persisted in breaking regulations when he could struggle along without doing so, the system was not hell on earth. Nevertheless, it was far from heaven for those unfortunate enough to suffer at the hands of vicious overseers and masters.

Yet what did James Underwood, Samuel Terry or Simeon Lord think of the convict system? Presumably those wealthy emancipists were shrewd enough to work out their time quietly, perhaps under a good master, by agreeing with those it paid to agree with, and then taking advantage of a small colony which needed the services they worked up by industry and enterprise. But during all the period convicts were aware of the existence, sometimes as masters, of ex-convicts whose success in money-making was more than they could have imagined in their wildest dreams. The presence in the society of successful ex-convicts, together with Macquarie's policy of encouragement to the emancipist class, must have been most favourable to the convict. When he went off the rails, therefore, he was either driven by a bad master to abscond or hit back in some way, or else he forgot the future prospects available, and acted upon impulse. Either these, or he was basically a stupid man, or so inured to crime that he scarcely knew how to refrain from it. Records do not enable these speculations to be tested with positive evidence, though it is known that, after Bigge's reports on the state of the colony at the end of Macquarie's régime, the prisoner's lot became a harder one.

New South Wales, however, did present an opportunity for a fresh start, because all convicts, whether good, bad or indifferent, had been through the courts, in gaol, and convicted of breaking the laws of their country; their prospects in Britain were not bright, but there must be balanced against this side of the story the heavy fact that many men were in virtual slavery.

For the man who behaved reasonably well, there were opportunities for rehabilitation in New South Wales, particularly if the prisoner was young when freed. In the case of the older man, more set in his ways, and with a family in Britain, doubtless transportation could be an agonizing punishment, especially if that man were not an habitual law-breaker—he had little chance of returning to England, and he would be old when released. Shortly, convicts could have made the best of a bad job, and for a very few it must have been the worst job, because as late as 1839, two men murdered another in an ironed gang in order to be brought to Sydney, and there tried and hanged.[57]

The Female Convicts in Australia

The wild buoyancy of their dispositions being bridled by the severe restraints imposed upon them, they were like wanton colts loosened from the stall when they landed, and . . . broke out into all manner of extravagancies.[1]

Almost the same number of women were sent to each of the two penal colonies: 12,460 to New South Wales and 12,500 to Van Diemen's Land. Most of the Van Diemen's Land women, however, were transported after 1840, and, until that year, the island had sent to it only 3,480, not quite a third of the number sent to the parent colony. Until transportation to New South Wales ceased, no woman tried in Ireland had been conveyed directly to Van Diemen's Land, compared with 5,040 sent to Sydney. Concentration of Irish women was therefore even more marked, prior to 1840, in New South Wales than was that of the men. After 1840 3,580 Irish women were sent to Van Diemen's Land.[2]

A large number of Scottish women were also sent to the southern colony, and, because Scottish women were indubitably the worst prisoners, it could be that Van Diemen's Land was selected for the worst convicts among the women as well as the men. There is no documentary proof of this, but there is some indication that Van Diemen's Land was fixed upon as a penal colony for the worst offenders in the early 1820s because a relatively large number of women who were former offenders were sent to the island, compared with the numbers despatched to New South Wales. This discrepancy could be due to chance, but this seems improbable.

(a) *Van Diemen's Land.* On the average, convict women committed between three and four punishable offences each. The range was from no offences at all to one prisoner who was punished eighty times. About one-fifth had no offences recorded, and only 4 per cent were convicted before the superior courts. No women were hanged.

Those who had no offences recorded against them had the characteristics of the men transported after 1840, i.e., relatively many were Irish, with no former offences, transported for the minimum period. The 4 per cent of women who were in serious trouble were not confined to any one group of convicts or to any particular period of time.

One of the serious offences tried by the Supreme Court was assault and robbery, for which Elizabeth Fagan or Gibbs received a sentence of fifteen years' transportation. Fagan was transported in 1841 for stealing clothes. She was aged nineteen, tried in Co. Down, and had previously been imprisoned two months in Ireland for the same type of theft, and was 'on the town'. In 1851 she was tried, with her husband, at Launceston for assaulting a man and robbing him of £ 1, four half-crowns and 4s.

In his evidence the prosecutor stated that he was met in the street by the prisoner, who invited him to her home. He accompanied her there, and then sent out for some drink. He later went to a public-house with the prisoner, and changed some money, after which they went back to her house. When he was leaving, she thrust her hand into his trouser pocket, tore out his money, and gave it to her husband, who had just arrived on the scene. The witness was then struck on the head with a ginger beer bottle held by Fagan, kicked by both parties, and dragged out of the house.

The prisoners were both found guilty, and the death sentence recorded. This woman had been before magistrates fifty times previously, mainly for absence without leave from her employment, for being drunk, and other forms of misconduct. In September 1854, three years after this conviction for assault and robbery, she was gazetted for absconding from the custody of a police constable while proceeding to the Cascades female factory. She was retaken and granted the indulgence of a ticket-of-leave seven years after the conviction at Launceston on the assault charge, but this was revoked in 1862 when she was listed as absent without leave. Nothing further of her career is thereafter noted, and presumably she escaped. Fagan had previously absconded thirteen times, and had been thirteen times recaptured, for which she was sentenced to solitary confinement, had her sentence of transportation extended, and was committed to prison with hard labour at the wash-tubs.

Other prisoners before the Supreme Court were given life imprisonment for theft, twelve months' gaol for assault and robbery, two years in prison at Oatlands with hard labour for stealing two pairs of stockings, and two years in the House of Correction in Launceston for perjury.

This last-mentioned case concerned Margaret Stevens alias McCarty, who committed more offences than any other female convict. She was tried by Middlesex Gaol Delivery in 1832 for stealing a gown and a cake of soap. Recorded as having been in trouble previously, she admitted to serving one month for shop-lifting. She was a house-servant, aged thirty-one, born in Somerset. Although listed on the indent as married, she was one of those who denied the truth of this, stating that her husband had died while she was in Newgate. She was transported for life, and her subsequent career indicates that perhaps this severe sentence was passed in the full knowledge that she was a chronic case.

As late as 1871 in Van Diemen's Land she was indicted at Launceston for perjury following an inquest into the death of Rheuben Morrell, who was killed when a loaded dray passed over him. Stevens had claimed that on the night of the accident, she left the 'Eagle's Return' at the same time as the deceased man and Thomas Rumpff, that she had walked by herself to a shep-herd's hut, the men bringing on their teams behind, and that she had had no conversation with them, nor ridden in the drays with them. The attorney-general stated that this was a pack of lies—in fact, Stevens had left with the men, Morrell being quite drunk, Rumpff not so intoxicated, and the defendant sober. The party had stopped at Mrs Hogg's house, and when Stevens had been refused a night's lodging, she had left with the men. Morrell had had an empty dray drawn by three horses, Rumpff a four-horse wagon loaded with bark. The defendant had ridden with Morrell in his dray. Rumpff gave evidence that this was so, and the jury found the woman Stevens guilty of perjury as charged.

She had started committing offences eight days after the ship on which she was transported arrived in the colony, receiving a sentence of solitary confinement for drunkenness. Thereafter her offences, committed with a dreary and monotonous regularity, were mainly drunkenness, absenteeism and misbehaviour of other kinds. In 1852 she was granted a ticket-of-leave which was revoked again after eight months. Marriage in 1838 had no ap-parent effect on her criminal career, and the final entry on her record was the two-year sentence for perjury, at which time she was sixty-nine years old. Her offences included those of 'being drunk and indecently exposing her person in holding connexion with a soldier' and 'absent without leave and throwing water on the watch-house keeper.' She was conditionally pardoned in

1858, perhaps as a gesture of despair on the part of the administration.

Another of the 4 per cent of women felons who appeared before the superior courts of Van Diemen's Land was one transported in 1830 for fourteen years. This was Ann Knott alias Carringdon or Mary Purdy, who was convicted in 1849 for illegally pledging at Hobart Town. She had pleaded distress on an earlier occasion because her husband was 'very bad', and a subscription had been taken up for her. She was fined 1s. on that occasion, but now had to go to prison for one month with hard labour.

Other females convicted before Quarter Sessions included one Catherine Burns, who had previously been convicted twenty times in the colony for misconduct and other offences. She was transported to Newcastle in 1821 for theft, placed in the stocks for neglect of duty, sent to the female factory for being found in a disorderly house, and to the same place with her two illegitimate children for living in adultery with a settler at the Lower Clyde. As well, she was apprehended absent without leave and drunk in the bush with a free man, for which she was gaoled. For not seeing her children at the orphan school, she was put in a solitary cell, and last appears on the records in 1835, when she was sentenced to seven years' imprisonment for theft. A free certificate was granted in 1843.

A third woman had her sentence of transportation extended for three years as a punishment for stealing a bottle of wine in 1836. She was Ann Herwick, who had formerly been punished four times, including hard labour for indecent conduct, and imprisonment for three months for concealing a police constable in her bedroom. She was originally transported from London for stealing a shirt from a shop.

Thus two extremes of convict life have been noted—those women who were never in trouble, and those who were in trouble serious enough for them to be tried before the superior courts. The usual offences, however, were absence without leave, drunkenness, and misconduct, which were typically punished by periods in gaol with hard labour (at the wash-tubs) or in the female factory, though prior to Governor Arthur's administration, an iron collar (with a long prong on each side of it) was placed around the neck of convict women who misbehaved. This gave them the appearance of horned cattle.[3] There was, of course, in the case of women, a restricted range of punishments available, and although the records of conduct do not notice punishments other than imprisonment for the most part, sometimes sophistications were worked up. One of these was cutting off all the hair on the head of the offender.

It was observed earlier that a certain number of women confessed to prostitution, and that some female prisoners, particularly those from the cities of Britain, were accustomed to loose living. Perusal of the record of offences committed by the female convicts in Van Diemen's Land shows that some of the female felons continued to lead immoral lives. Whether this was true of all or many of them can be established by using the records a little arbitrarily, though most records leave little doubt of the sort of lives being led by the women concerned. This is not to say that because a female was once apprehended in a disorderly house, she was a prostitute during all her period of imprisonment, but in context with other listed offences, it is practicable to come to some conclusion on the point.

One in eight of the women transported was punished for such forms of misconduct, which were particularly prevalent prior to 1840. There is unlikely to be a simple reason for this, but some factors are the severe and efficient administration of Arthur, whose officers seem to have overlooked few misdemeanours, the arrival of Irish (often not habitual offenders) only after 1840, and a generally less severe administration by the convict department and magistrates during the probation period. Perhaps an even more telling factor was the type of women sent to the colony prior to 1840, because the worst convicts were almost certainly singled out for transportation to Van Diemen's Land. Scottish prisoners were sent in relatively large numbers, and they were a more abandoned set of women than either English or Irish convicts.

It is noteworthy that those women who were charged with sexual misdemeanours committed, on the average, sixteen offences each, compared with approximately five over all. Wording of the charges was sometimes in the form 'drunk and found in a disorderly house', but more often was 'misconduct in being found in a brothel in bed with a man'. Some women were so apprehended many times.

Some examples of types of offences regarded as an indication of immoral living and punished with hard labour were as follows: 'misconduct in being in a brothel with her mistress's child'; 'being a common prostitute'; 'encouraging her master's daughter, a child of eleven, to have sexual connexion with a man'; 'living in a brothel, the worst in Hobart Town'; 'absent without leave and found in a brothel'; 'getting out of her room and sleeping with her master's men in the barn'; 'found in a brothel in bed with a man'; 'found in the yard of an inn in an indecent posture for an immoral purpose'; 'misconduct in having two men and two women in bed with her'; 'in bed with a man in a brothel in Goulburn Street'; 'disorderly conduct in having a police constable secreted in her house between nine and ten last night, her husband being in gaol and she being intoxicated'.

So the evidence of indiscriminate love-making could be extended, until life among the ranks of the convict women in Van Diemen's Land appeared as a constant game of cat and mouse with the police, women being apprehended with men under their beds as well as in them, and the police officers sometimes unconcerned about which side they were on.

One other record kept in Van Diemen's Land bears upon such misconduct as that mirrored in the offences described, for when women were delivered of children they were taken from employment to a lying-in hospital. The name of the child, and date of birth, were recorded, and so it is possible to note a piece of rare information which enables the conclusion to be made that 11 per cent of the women had illegitimate children. (This figure is in one respect higher because women who died on the way to the colony or in the hands of the administration, or absconded, were included in the calculation.) Some women had more than one child, and one had three. Approximately one-fifth of the 11 per cent were recorded as subsequently married.

Marriage rates over all were not high, considering the excess of males in Van Diemen's Land. Approximately 27 per cent of the women were recorded as having married, but there is no way of knowing whether all women who married whilst in the hands of the convict department were recorded and, of course, it is not known how many women were married after they were freed.*

That some convicts were depraved there is no doubt, though it must not be forgotten that one woman in every five transported was never before a magistrate at all. Yet the fact remains that

* There are registers of marriage in the Tasmanian State Archives. From these and Registrar-General's records it would be possible to trace a very large proportion of marriages taking place in Van Diemen's Land of freed convict women.

the average female prisoner was punished approximately five times, usually for some form of 'misconduct' or for being intoxicated, or absent without leave. One form of misconduct, that concerned with sexual misdemeanors, has been examined, but there remain a great many others which are most varied.

For example, one woman was gaoled for contracting marriage without permission, another for damaging the furniture in her husband's house whilst under the influence of liquor, and threatening to run a knife through him, and a third was sent off to the female factory for repeatedly wearing her mistress's clothes, disobedience of orders, and flatly refusing to continue in her service. Other offences were: throwing letters over a wall; refusing to attend court and sending an insolent message; repeated insolence, and threatening to split open her mistress's head, and further declaring that she would commit any enormity to get sent to the female factory; drunk and disorderly when in charge of a little child; concealing a policeman in her bedroom; wearing a chemise belonging to her mistress, and also a gown belonging to her fellow servant; inciting the prisoners to insubordination, and threatening to run one through with a knife; and refusing to be sworn in a case.

Other reflections of life in Van Diemen's Land, and the character of some of the island's inhabitants, appear in such offences as those of Margaret Fitzgerald, who came to a man's house and enticed away his servants; Sarah Slow, who was found in the street in men's clothes; and Ellen Marlin, who was discovered lying 'beastly drunk' in the road. Other women were before the courts for refusing to proceed when *en route*; placing her mistress's child in the hands of a common prostitute to nurse; being on a man's premises to incite a quarrel between him and his wife; attempting to introduce provisions and pipes and tobacco into the watch-house; conveying bread from one prisoner to another in exchange for a petticoat; concealing herself to avoid going to chapel; being found in an inn with a male prisoner, and improperly administering to him ale with snuff in it for the purpose of stupefying him; wearing an apron with the number inside, and challenging another woman to fight; cutting up and converting two government petticoats into one; using diabolical and threatening language; and secreting spirits and exciting bushrangers against her mistress upon the occasion of her master being robbed.

Any generalization about the behaviour of these women is, to some extent, untrue, because nothing is known of their activities outside the comprehension of the convict department; and a recital of offences emphasizes misbehaviour and improprieties. To balance the findings of the enquiry, a few cases will be recorded of women who conformed to the mean number of offences. These should be regarded as 'average' careers of women convicts in Van Diemen's Land.

Mary Crighton, for example, was tried in the Glasgow Court of Justiciary in 1851, and transported for theft. A housemaid aged eighteen, native place Glasgow, she was single, and stated that her offence was housebreaking. It was noted that she had been punished twice previously for theft, and she confessed she had been in gaol for two months for stealing trousers. Her ship arrived in the Derwent on 8 July 1852, fifteen months after her trial, and four months after leaving Britain. Her offences in Van Diemen's Land were three in number: three months after her arrival she was imprisoned for misconduct, and twice the following year she was gaoled again for attempting to abscond. No more offences followed, and fourteen months later she was permitted a ticket-of-leave. Her petition to marry a convict was granted after another two months, three weeks later she was married, and conditionally pardoned in September 1856.

The second typical case is that of Maria Farrell or Henry, an Irish woman aged twenty-three, transported for the theft of a child's frock in Dublin City. She was born in Co. Kildare, and recorded as being previously often in trouble. The prisoner confessed to 'twenty-five times for drunkenness', and stated she had been 'on the town' for four years. She was a housemaid, and unmarried. Tried at Dublin City in October 1848, she left Ireland in April the following year, and arrived in Van Diemen's Land on 23 July 1849, sentenced to a seven-year term of transportation. Four months later she was gaoled for misconduct, and after six months again imprisoned for being found in a disorderly house. After six months elapsed, in December 1850 Farrell was sentenced to hard labour for drunkenness, and then within two years given the same punishment three times for three different attempts to abscond. No more offences were recorded against her name; in November 1855 she was awarded her free certificate in Hobart Town, and recorded no more.

A third woman was Sarah Millican, sentenced to seven years'

transportation in July 1846 for stealing wearing apparel. She was tried by Ipswich Quarter Sessions; her native place was Bury St Edmunds. She had formerly been sentenced to three months' gaol for stealing a sheet, she was a needlewoman and dressmaker, and was married with one child. Her husband Thomas, she stated, was living in Ipswich. Millican committed, and was punished for, only one offence in the colony, when she was gaoled for being absent without leave and being found in a brothel. She was drowned in September 1849.

So more and more cases could be listed, all posing more questions than can be answered, for of the more complex circumstances of the many misdemeanours recorded nothing is known, and of the reaction of these women to their conviction and transportation there is descriptive evidence only, the general accuracy of which there is no way of checking. There is also no way of knowing the motive for the many offences set down in the records, but it would be foolish to suppose, in the light of the offences and the origin of these women in Britain, that they were so ill-treated in Van Diemen's Land that they succumbed to the bottle and the brothel. There is only too much evidence that some of them (precisely how many is not known) permitted conviction and transportation across the world to interfere but little with their way of life, and it can be understood how the ladies of Van Diemen's Land found an endless subject of conversation in the conduct of their female servants.

(b) *New South Wales.* Of the offences committed by convict women in New South Wales, nothing is known from documentary sources that can be used systematically and satisfactorily. What happened to the female convicts once they reached Port Jackson is a question that is answerable, in theory, from an inspection of the muster records, though their comprehensiveness is always questionable.[4] How many women were on strength in 1806, eighteen years after the arrival of the First Fleet? A count of the women transported prior to 1806 shows that seventy-five died *en route* and, if we make allowance for the *Lady Shore,* which was seized by the military guard in 1797 and sailed off to South America with sixty-six female prisoners who were never heard of again,[5] 37 per cent of the women are missing.

It is unlikely that mortality was quite as severe as this. The population of early New South Wales was not an unhealthy one in terms of diseases, though the severities of the early famine years were considerable. Some deaths can certainly be assumed, especially as a result of the 1791 voyages, and natural deaths must have accounted for some women. It is significant that all but a few of the women not mustered in 1806 were embarked prior to 1793.

Two other possibilities, other than mortality, remain to account for the disappearance of 37 per cent of the females. One is that they had left the colony, and the other is that they were recorded under the names of husbands. The second possibility is almost certainly to be discounted, because it was only in 1828 that women were first recorded under their married names. How many left the colony cannot be known, though we may be sure that some did, but there would have been no demand for them to work their passages home in the way the men did.

This 'wastage' in the early years did not continue; 85 per cent of those transported between 1811 and 1819 were on strength at the latter date, and of those sent to New South Wales between 1806 and 1819 79 per cent were still in the colony at 1819. This suggests that it was only during the first six or seven years of the colony's existence that substantial numbers of female transportees were lost. After that time the number of missing persons is small enough to be attributed to death, escapes and, perhaps, clerical errors in the muster records. In 1825 46 per cent of the women transported were on strength, but by this time natural deaths must have been carrying off some of the early arrivals.

It seems, therefore, that there was a relatively heavy loss of women in the years to 1793, whether principally because of deaths, escapes, or legal departures it is difficult to say. Secondly, after the beginning of the nineteenth century these losses were reduced, and most female felons stayed in the colony. However, their numbers were not so great as might have been gathered from total departures from Britain.

Information that illustrates the progress or decline of convicts in New South Wales is exiguous, as it is for male prisoners. Nevertheless, the history of particular prisoners gives a glimpse of convict life in the colony. For instance, Sarah Burdo, whose trial suggested she was a prostitute, and who was transported in 1787 for stealing three and a half guineas, was not mustered in 1806, but in 1811 appeared 'in the colony', and at 1819 as a midwife. By 1825 she was married, and dwelling at Parramatta, and in 1828 she was noted as seventy-three years of age, and married to an individual who came out free on the *Alexander,* also in 1787. This man, Isaac Archer, was seventy-five years old, and a householder at Parramatta; three years earlier he had been listed as a landholder. If Burdo had married between 1819 and 1825, as appears the case, then certainly there were no children. But both parties were on the First Fleet, and therefore it is possible that they had married early, and that this was omitted from the records scrutinized.

There is also something known of Mary Randall, convicted and sentenced to fourteen years' transportation by Middlesex Gaol Delivery in 1792 for receiving wearing apparel. She is recorded as London-born and married, and, if her age in the 1828 census is correct, she was forty-eight years old, and evidently transported under her married name. The facts as they stand are that she was recorded as married by 1806, as a housekeeper in 1819, employed by her husband in 1821, and as 'married' in 1825 and 1828. Her husband was Paul Randall, transported in 1791; he may have come down in the world, because he was a landholder in 1821, an innkeeper at Richmond in 1825, and a labourer in 1828, holding two acres of ground.

A third case is that of Susannah Williams, transported for seven years in 1801 for stealing earrings. She was a servant to a London jeweller, and aged twenty years. She had her ticket-of-leave by 1806, and was recorded as living with Thomas Sparks, transported in 1790. In 1811 she was still in the colony, in 1819 she was working as a housekeeper, and in 1825 she had married Sparks, and was living in Sydney. By 1828 she was forty-four years old, and her husband, a waterman, seventy-three. The couple lived in Cambridge Street, Sydney, and had had three children, whose ages ranged from fourteen to twenty-two years.

Other women of whom a little is known include Anne Griffith or Griffin, transported from Co. Meath in 1818 for having forged notes in her possession. She was a housekeeper, aged thirty-six years. In 1819 she was single, and living at Sydney, but in 1821 she was married to John Norris, transported in 1800, and living at Parramatta where he was a conditionally pardoned stonemason. In 1828 the couple was still at Parramatta, the husband holding twelve acres of land. No children were recorded. Though there is no apparent difference between the ages of these people, it is noticeable that they were relatively old when they married, and that the husband had been in the colony for twenty years.

Jane Meredith was tried in Devon in 1815, and sentenced to fourteen years' transportation for stealing in a dwelling-house. Her occupation was that of needleworker, and she was twenty-one. In 1819 she had evidently misbehaved because she was in the public factory at Parramatta, but two years later she is recorded as married to a Windsor surgeon Parment (or Parmeter or Parmeton), who had also arrived as a prisoner in 1815. By 1828 he was free by servitude, and held 720 acres of land at Patrick's Plains. There were four children, but no wife listed. Perhaps she had died, or run away, though her omission from the census may be due to clerical error. It is possible that this marriage was a Parramatta factory one; men came to the factory to select partners and this woman's marriage followed speedily from her incarceration.

One more case must suffice to show what material can be gathered by a systematic analysis of the convicts transported to New South Wales. This concerns Ann Haynes or Foss, transported in 1805 for passing counterfeit money. She was recorded as a needlewoman, aged twenty-eight. In 1818 she married a convict who had been transported in 1814. He was a shoemaker in Castlereagh Street, Sydney, where the couple lived in 1828.

There is another question upon which some light can also be thrown. This concerns marriage of female convicts. Now by 1825 36 per cent of the women transported prior to 1820 had married, and from 1793 (after which date nearly all women can be traced) to 1819 38 per cent were recorded as having married.

These figures must be considered low (even allowing for mortality) when the disproportion of the sexes in New South Wales is remembered, and a better test might be to establish marriage rates in a later period, such as 1811 to 1816. If the women who arrived during this period are noted at 1821, when they had been in the colony for four years at least the figures are still surprisingly low for only 42 per cent were married. By 1825 66 per cent of women transported between 1811 and 1816 had married.

It is difficult to conclude very much from the analysis, but there are no indications that convict women transported in the period up to 1825 all finally married in the colony, and though it appears that perhaps 60 per cent did, this must be regarded as a cautious estimate. It is fair to conclude that marriage rates were not as high as might confidently have been expected in a population so numerically dominated by males.

Whom did these convict women take as husbands? Of those transported prior to 1826, 42 per cent were married by 1828. Some records do not specify the civil condition of the husband, but the analysis suggests that convict married convict when they did take partners. There are too many doubtful factors, however, for anything more than a tentative conclusion.

Few of the men whom the convict women married appeared as well-to-do, though Mary Mullett, transported in 1795, married a jeweller named James Austin who was transported from Ireland in 1799; and Mary Page, who was sent to New South Wales in 1804, was recorded in 1828 as married to John Lyons, a land-holder with seventy-nine acres of land at Wilberforce. Other women were married at the date of the first census in 1828 to such men as bootmakers, policemen and small landholders, but in no case was there a convict woman married to a landed proprietor. Whether any later married well is unknown.*

Two impressions emerge from the analysis. One is that mar-riage was by no means universal among the convict women of early New South Wales, and the second is that when it did occur there was likely to be a wide discrepancy between the ages of the parties or, if not, it was likely that they were relatively old when married. The male convict, if desiring to marry, was more likely to marry a native-born girl, for he must have known that a con-vict woman was unlikely to make a satisfactory partner. Female convicts, especially those from London, were not the sort of women to attract men into marriage.

* Catherine Crowley, who, according to the *Australian Encyclopaedia,* was the mother of William Charles Wentworth, was transported for 'stealing clothes etc. from a dwelling house [with firearms?]'. This woman, a spinster of the parish of Newcastham in Staffordshire, was tried in Staffordshire on 30 July 1788, and transported for seven years on the *Neptune* in 1790. It is thought that D'Arcy Wentworth's association with her commenced during the voyage and continued on Norfolk Island, where W. C. Wentworth was born.

7

Conclusion

I think that many of those who have been sent out have been driven to commit the offence . . . through want.[1]

Drunkenness is the sole procuring cause of transportation in the case of a large proportion of the prison population of these colonies.[2]

It has been shown that approximately two-thirds of the convicts transported to New South Wales and Van Diemen's Land were tried in England, and approximately one-third in Ireland. Numbers tried in Scotland and abroad were relatively small, and if nationality is reckoned by country of birth rather than country of trial, these figures were not altered very much, except in the case of Irish-born women convicted in England.

Male convicts were transported in relatively small numbers prior to 1815, but thereafter the annual contingents sent out to Australia increased sharply, reaching a maximum figure in the 1830s. The prisoners transported for life formed approximately a quarter of these convicts, but it was far more common for a felon to receive a seven-year sentence, and every second convict was transported for that minimum period. Nor was the typical prisoner an 'old lag', because the mean age of the convicts was approximately twenty-six years. In other words, the convicts were young, and thus it was to be expected that well over 50 per cent were single. In addition, certainly half, and probably two-thirds or thereabouts, had formerly been punished by public justice, generally for forms of larceny.

It would be commonplace to point out the different economic and social backgrounds of England and Ireland during the transportation era, and this analysis has indicated that the Irish differed from the overall picture of the convicts presented in Appendix 4 in the form of tables: they were older than the average felon, included more married men, had not been in trouble with the police so often, were frequently sent out to Australia for shorter periods of transportation than the English, and included in their ranks many unskilled men. All convict ships, whether from England or Ireland, included men who had, for one reason or another, moved from their place of birth. In fact, one man in every three had been tried elsewhere than in the county of his upbringing.

In the same way as the Irish differed from the general run of convicts, so did the English men tried in rural counties, for they included a relatively large number of convicts transported for life, were slightly older than the average (though still nearly all under thirty years of age), and were mostly agricultural workers. Irish tried outside Dublin and Cork differed more sharply still from the general pattern, for they were older, and included more married men. In number of former offences there was a difference, too, because the Irish country convict was as likely as not to be innocent of former offences. Seven-year sentences were common, and the men concerned (farm labourers as a rule) had been born in their county of trial.

Although certain rural convicts differed in general characteristics from other convicts, the urban prisoner was nearer to the typical felon sent to Australia. Men from the cities, and especially from London, demand most attention. The London-tried men were particularly prominent in the early years of settlement, and formed 25 per cent of the men transported prior to 1810. Also, urban prisoners included a large number of very young men who had been offenders before transportation.

Not only were the urban prisoners typically younger than expected, but the great majority were transported for forms of larceny, though not all, by any means, for offences which could carry only a small fine today. The offence designated 'other larcenies' accounted for approximately one-third of all male prisoners, the great majority of whom were people tried in London, Lancashire, Yorkshire, Surrey and Warwickshire. They were relatively young, included many persons transported for picking pockets, and were particularly prominent in the early years of transportation before 1820. They sprang almost entirely from the industrial classes.

Other main offences were burglary and housebreaking, animal theft, robbery, and theft of wearing apparel. The burglars and housebreakers differed little from the general run of prisoners, measured in terms of age, marital status and so on, and the men transported for the theft of apparel appeared very similar types to those sent to Australia for 'other larcenies'. Men transported for animal stealing, however, included many Irish and English rural convicts, and these were punished severely by life sentences of transportation. They tended to be older than most convicts, and had among them a large number of men who had not been previously in trouble with the police. Men transported for robbery included more Irish than might have been expected from a general view of the convicts.

Individuals transported for coining predominated among those transported for offences of a public nature, and many arrived around the year 1820. Other convicts transported for offences against the state included a relatively large number of Irish transported for riots, routs and affrays. Assaults on the person accounted for transportation of a large number of Irish, too, and it has been observed how the conditions of life in Ireland led to such offences being committed.

Though the turbulence of Irish rural life during the transportation period is well documented and well known, the background of the urban offender, whether from Dublin or the City of Cork, or from the English cities, is more relevant to a general discussion of the origin and character of the convicts. An inadequate police-force, slums, and overcrowding, gave rise to city conditions nourishing a large criminal fringe of depredators. Though not all were confirmed criminals, the convicts sent to Australia from the cities included many persistent offenders who were thieves from an early age.

Women convicts comprise 15 per cent of the total number of prisoners transported to the colonies of New South Wales and Van Diemen's Land. They also were relatively young (though a little older than the men) and, in the majority of cases, had been in trouble with the law prior to their transportation. Also owning to a city background, they included probably at least 20 per cent who were prostitutes: accounts of their trials confirmed that many were 'on the town' when taken up. Nearly all were domestic servants, and transported for forms of larceny. One in every three had been tried in Ireland, and rather more had been born there. Approximately 10 per cent were tried in Scotland, principally for larceny and a former conviction.

The female prisoners had little to recommend them, and, in the early years especially, they included many Londoners who had led dissolute lives in an Hogarthian capital. The Irish women appeared to be the best of a bad lot. Careers of the women convicts in Australia confirmed the impression that, although not surrendering themselves to abandonment completely, they yet were an indifferent group of settlers. The marriage-rate does not appear to have been as high as the discrepancy between the sexes in Australia suggested it would be. However, the records do not permit much speculation, although in Van Diemen's Land convicts did not demonstrate that they were irreclaimable.

Nor could the lives of the convict men be followed as closely as might have been desired, but in Van Diemen's Land they were punished, on the average, five times each. One in ten was convicted for a serious offence before the superior courts of the colony, and another 10 per cent appeared never to have been punished at all. There is no reason to suppose the figures for New South Wales were much different, though this cannot be shown except by analogy. In the mother colony, the freed convicts settled to a trade in many cases, certainly in the years to the departure of Governor Macquarie, but the data do not permit close analysis. Spectacular success stories were very few.

Anyone who is bold enough to generalize about why 150,000 people committed crimes is asking for trouble, but the great object of drawing the sample was to base speculation firmly on facts, to show what in fact did occur, and not what someone said was supposed to occur, to set the record straight, and to reduce levels of generality as much as possible. But the complex questions remain—why did the convicts sent to Australia commit offences? How 'bad' were they?

It is tempting to stray into the field of psychiatry when considering why a certain felon committed the offence which landed him finally on Australian soil, though by a recital of the circumstances of the crime, enough can be shown in some cases to let the facts speak for themselves. There is no true general delinquency or criminal activity—each case is a different one, and motives are different in some respects. And though the man may say why he committed a certain offence, is he telling the truth, and does he, in fact, know why he stole a certain article or assaulted someone, or whatever it was he did? These are deep waters, and even if one wished to analyse particular cases in such a comprehensive way, the information is not available. The person is long dead, and cannot be cross-examined or interviewed.

What must be borne in mind, therefore, are the characteristics of the majority of the offenders sent to Australia, their age, place of trial, occupation, and their former offences. Then an examination can be made of the opinions of criminal law reformers and welfare workers and police, and from these sources and from the prisoners' statements, some common ground may be found. The gentlemen who gave evidence to parliamentary committees were of many kinds and, though generally amateurs, they were not overnight experts. The views of experienced magistrates, clerks of courts, and philanthropists have been quoted from reports of committees who turned to these people for the expert opinion they sought.

The crime for which most men were transported was 'other larcenies', and there were certain features of this offence which gave a good idea of the sort of person committing it, and getting himself transported to Australia. These features or characteristics of the offenders were three in number: they were youthful, came typically from London, Birmingham, Manchester, Dublin and Liverpool, and had formerly been punished. The question of why offences were committed now becomes more explicit, and concerns what is known of the conditions of life in those cities. They were not all the same, and varied throughout the transportation period, but they had in common the overcrowding, undermanned police force, exploding population, and professional body of criminals that was remarked upon by so many observers. Indeed, these characteristics of large cities still exist. It is likely, therefore, that comments made specifically about London criminals apply with equal relevance to the other cities mentioned.

Extent of former offences suggested that these offenders were not newcomers to crime, but there is no common reason given by independent observers for their misbehaviour. For example, one person interested in the welfare of the destitute of the London streets and in prison discipline said that the reason for young men taking up a life of crime was the influence of bad company, the evil effect of their connection with loose women, and of distress.[3] And a witness before a committee of parliament spoke sorrowfully of boys lodging in the open air under the green stalls in Covent Garden, because they dared not go home without money.[4] Another opinion was that they had generally lost one parent,[5] and therefore lacked that firm home control and affection without which the tendency to roam the streets and get into trouble was always present.

Apart from poor upbringing (for whatever reason) and distress, there were other factors upon which comment was passed. Among these was the problem of unspeakable gaols, which had no possible reformatory effect in most cases, and the question of the administration of the criminal law and its practice of condoning a kind of perjury when prosecutors and witnesses were permitted to undervalue stolen goods.

However, let the convicts transported for larceny speak for themselves. A man sentenced to seven years' transportation ascribed the ruin of youths in London to 'flash houses', low lodging-places, free concerts, and penny rooms. Another blamed his downfall on the fact that he was not favoured with God-fearing parents, and another said that he found himself on a convict vessel because, after having been apprenticed, he joined wicked companions. A fourth convict, born in a village in Warwickshire, lost both parents, joined a band of musicians and, after being gaoled for six months for theft, was finally transported for seven years. A Welsh prisoner remarked that he was brought into contact with people who drank too much. Another blamed unemployment for his present unfortunate position.[6]

So the explanations continue. One person, observing to a convict that he had found his way to Van Diemen's Land through the door of a public-house, was answered by a fervent 'You say right'; and the same writer was told by another prisoner that, though he had respectable parents, intemperance had led him to join a gang of thieves in Tothill Fields. Another prisoner also blamed his fate on drink: when in Van Diemen's Land he still thirsted for it, and sold his shirt for liquor and even parted with the skin off his back for it, being several times flogged for drunkenness.[7]

The views of a few convicts on why they were transported cannot end the question. Not enough spoke for one thing, and, for another, the attributing of motive is extremely difficult. Yet here is emphasis on bad company, temptation and drink. Were not distress, unemployment and poverty the root cause of men getting into trouble with the law? Not according to one prisoner, who said that many prisoners came from Birmingham because of drinking, and bad habits caused when wages were paid in a public-house, or the wages of several persons paid together, so that they had to visit a public-house for change;[8] and not according to many witnesses before committees of enquiry. There was a surprising unanimity about this. Poverty was a very much smaller cause of crime than usually supposed, declared a court recorder with thirty years' experience in Birmingham. Scarcely one prisoner in eight, said the governor of Newgate gaol, committed offences through pressure of want, and the chief magistrate of Bow Street declared that depraved character caused more crime than want of employment.[9] If, for argument's sake, the word of these three is accepted (and their evidence covers the twenty-five years which saw most convicts transported), is there any agreed reason for crime?

There does indeed appear a certain amount of agreement, though it is tempting to laugh at nineteenth-century ideas that offences were caused by 'moral destitution', and to point out the Calvinist implications of this judgment, especially when the persons advancing it speak of idleness, and lack of training.[10] Yet there is something to be said for this view, and for understanding what early nineteenth-century commentators meant by it. The offenders were, in fact, 'morally destitute', and evidently seldom thieves because of immediate want. But it is the causes of the destitution that are interesting, because the term, although a useful one, really only implies that persons committed crimes either through original sin, or because they were not trained properly. This is hard to disagree with, assuming that the number of mentally unbalanced people among the convicts was small (it was very rare that men appeared insane).

If by 'lack of training' it is meant that young persons were turned out on the streets of cities when very young by careless and thoughtless parents, or were turned out by criminals to steal, or were being spoilt by indulgent parents, then it could be expected that such people would become 'morally destitute'. That such juveniles were tempted and fell, the secretary of a society concerned with delinquency found to be the case. Members of his organization visited eight hundred boys lodged in prison and found the causes of their embarking on a life of thieving to be improper conduct of parents, the want of education, the want of suitable employment, violation of the Sabbath, and gambling in the public streets.[11]

Respecting the juvenile offenders who formed such a proportion of those transported for 'other larcenies', this point of 'improper conduct of parents' seems the crucial one. If the persons are ignored who, through some unexplained reason, suddenly committed an offence though brought up well, there can be no doubt that parental control and example must have been most important in keeping children out of the courts.

Let it be assumed that parental control was lacking or non-existent. Of course, the child concerned could grow up, however roughly, without committing crimes. This could be due to innate revulsion against commission of breaches of the law, or because of few bad examples, or because there was lack of temptation in the form of goods worth stealing. There were plenty of goods worth stealing, and plenty of bad examples, in the towns or cities of Britain during the transportation era.

The question is, why did parents neglect their children? As one answer, the Recorder of Birmingham gave evidence in 1852 in which he listed the following classes of children as prospective criminals: the children of criminals, illegitimate children, orphans, and the children of the very poor.[12] This list is an interesting one, for all these classes of juveniles might commit offences because of lack of parental control, one of the reasons for commission of illegal acts. What proportion of 'other larcenies' was committed by convicts because of indifferent or non-existent parental control, there is no way of knowing, but the evidence is overwhelming that there existed a professional class of thieves who taught children, not always their own but waifs and strays, how to pick pockets. *Oliver Twist* is only partly a work of fiction, and the illegitimate and orphaned child, as well as the Noah Claypoles, fell a ready prey to the Fagins of the metropolis.

We do not know to what extent the 'children of the very poor' were liable to be sent to Australia from the cities for thieving. This raises the whole question of poverty as a source of crime, and although it has been observed that witnesses decried the effect of poverty, the subject must be looked into more closely. Before this is done, the other three main causes of crime can be glanced at, namely, the want of education, violation of the Sabbath, and gambling in the streets. The two last-mentioned are rather manifestations of neglect by parents or guardians, and should properly be regarded not as fundamental causes of crime. As to want of education, there is a correlation between degree of education and criminal activity, and in the early nineteenth century it seems fair to say that compulsory education would have been effective in keeping children off the streets, though by 'education' people probably meant moral education, to be imparted at home.

Those who said poverty was the cause of transportation were both right and wrong because there is a difference between the immediate and fundamental causes of an offence. For instance, there are plenty of examples of picking pockets, and the theft of all sorts of objects, for which it is impossible that want was the immediate cause. No one steals a barrel which turns out to have oysters in it because he is hungry, and this is what the observers of the day remarked. However, the person could have stolen the barrel with the object of getting money by selling it, and this is almost certainly what did occur. Though theft was not for immediate gain in the sense of filling the belly, there is no doubt that it was seldom for sheer fun and the excitement of risk.

Once the youthful thief had started leading a double life by thieving part-time while he was an apprentice, or fell in with gangs of thieves and committed offences professionally, there were plenty of opportunities for him to continue. Among these was the want of an effective police force till Peel's police in London in 1829, the vicious system of rewards which led police officers to overlook minor depredations, the prevalence of receivers of stolen property, the number of 'flash houses' which studded London around the City, and the existence throughout the country of cheap lodging-houses, which harboured at least semi-criminal if not fully criminal people. As persons who had been in prison said, these lodging-houses were calculated only to encourage immorality and crime, especially among the young.

Some people chose to be poor and miserable. The youth who ran away from a good position because he sought adventure in London, did not do so because his parents were poverty-stricken, but there were not many youthful convicts who appear to have had good homes. The necessary conditions for commission of offences leading to transportation were many, but poverty was the principal one. It was not, however, so much individual poverty that bred an atmosphere of lawlessness, as its concentration. Together with crowded conditions and the other factors mentioned, such as inadequate and sometimes corrupt policing of the law, poverty must be regarded as a principal cause of crime. There is little doubt that only the few adventure-minded youths chose to live in the way they did in St Giles's lodging-houses. For the rest, they were victims of the times. As a police magistrate said at the end of the eighteenth century, the increase in crime 'may fairly be attributed to the demand for labour being much less than the supply, and from the greater number of depraved characters . . .

periodically discharged'.[13] It is highly significant that such an experienced magistrate as Patrick Colquhoun felt unable to explain crime in terms of one cause only.

Explanations of why convicts committed larceny apply with almost equal relevance to other forms of crime such as housebreaking and burglary. There is a difference, however, in that the burglar would probably act with more premeditation; he would be a more determined man than the pickpocket who acted on impulse and purloined a tempting watch. That such offences reflected a more serious hurt to the community than did petty larceny was recognized in the severity of the punishment.

Some convicts explained why they broke into houses, and there is no reason to suppose that initial parental carelessness or individual misfortune did not start the felon on the road to transportation. There could be a strong case made out that chance alone, i.e. the sort of person he first encountered, directed the potential Australian convict to burglary or housebreaking; crime was, at least in London, highly specialized. There was a certain inevitability about the law-breaker's progress once he started and tasted the sweets of easy money.

In the cases of 'other larcenies' and housebreaking and burglary, it is clear that human motive is not easily or conveniently analysed. Ideally, each individual case should be examined, a motive allotted and a conclusion drawn. But the records seldom hint at motive and we are forced back all too often to a subjective judgment. Nevertheless, it is clear that want was not the immediate cause of conviction and transportation, though it played a part in creating the necessary conditions for commission of crimes to become a possibility in some cases and a necessity in others. The parent inured to a semi-criminal existence himself, or who was unable to look after his children because he had to work very long hours to earn enough to live, probably neglected his children because of poverty and his miserable housing. Yet this charitable explanation does not fit all convicts. There is evidence that some were no more or less than 'wasters'.

It is not necessary to speculate much concerning why the two offences of 'other larcenies' and burglary/housebreaking were committed in the country. Some indications have been given earlier of the conditions of agricultural workers, and there is firmer ground for supposing that poverty was a direct cause of criminal acts. Especially in the case of Ireland does this appear so, though a heritage of lawlessness should not be overlooked. In England, too, some prisoners committed offences as an indirect result of agricultural distress in the period after the struggle with Napoleon had ended. For instance, one youthful prisoner said that he committed a theft because his father, an agricultural labourer with ten children, had no money,[14] and an observer thought that the increase in crime was due to distress among the farm workers, together with vicious habits created by poaching, which was in turn stimulated by the great increase in game. In some parishes unemployment was so widespread that in the late 1820s single men were not employed at all by farmers,[15] and by 1836 it was said that crime had increased in the country because there was more unemployment, and because men given relief were 'all thrown together into gravel pits and stone pits' to work, and thus were able to murmur and plot mischief.[16]

Not all country convicts were victims of the hard times. Approximately one-third of all the prisoners had been born outside the county in which they were tried and, though there is little information from the convicts themselves as to why they were on the move, descriptive evidence shows that at least some of them were not travelling because they were compelled to do so in order to earn a living: one convict admitted that 'I was what might be called a travelling thief'.[17] And a similar person made a detailed statement of his life which pertains very much to men who were transported.

This man began his statement by remarking that if he spoke in the cant of his brotherhood, the listener would be no more able to understand him than if he spoke a foreign language. He then, without hesitation, named all the fairs and 'statties' (fairs held by statute where servants were hired) which he followed up and down the country. He had started in Manchester with two other young men who had each received a transportation sentence for theft, and who 'had been at it for eight or nine years' (i.e. had been thieving). He had then proceeded to Leek fair with a young man from Kidderminster, who was subsequently transported for stealing a piece of cloth. Two other accomplices were later transported for stealing wet linen, and another yet again for picking pockets at Leicester cheese fair. This thief then went on to the York 'statties', where there was on hand that most important person in the world of law-breakers, a 'fence', or receiver of stolen property. This man went about the country with his wife ('since transported') and a horse and cart, and had been seen in three different guises in one day at Boston.

Most travelling thieves worked in 'mobs', disclosed this man, and assumed the countryman's dress—green smock-coats for Wiltshire, Somerset and Gloucestershire; blue and drab for Nottinghamshire and the Midland counties; and whites and drabs in Staffordshire and Lincolnshire. 'Jerry-shops' were started by thieves for the accommodation of their friends, he asserted. Such proprietors were sometimes transported, including one at Chester 'who had gone sixteen or seventeen years, and used to boast that the ship was never made, nor the wood grown to make one that would carry him over the water "lagged" (ironed)'.[18]

There is no way, however, of knowing how many of the convicts were travelling thieves, though they existed. For instance, in Northumberland at the end of the 1830s, of 2,168 prisoners tried by jury or magistrates, 261 were stated to be strangers to the town, or trampers travelling up and down the country. Of the total number committed to trial, 25 per cent were strangers, and 10 per cent of the persons summarily convicted were also unknown locally.[19]

Other sorts of offences apart from the main ones need not be commented on at length. Earlier conclusions were directed towards Irish agrarian offences, and it was shown that a climate of lawlessness and rural distress made the Irish convict from the country rather a different sort of person from his town brother. Nevertheless, doubtless the Irish countryside had its quota of men for whom crime would have been attractive, famine or no famine, evictions or no evictions. But evidence suggests that the Irish countryman sent to Australia was not hardened to crime in the same way as the city thief.

Of offences against the person, little also need be said: men who committed these explained their actions in a great deal of detail. In the case of the Irish, once again land troubles and local family feuds were prominent as a cause of assaults, and it is difficult to have much sympathy with convicts who beat people almost to death, no matter what the provocation, and despite the fact that there was no evidence of malice aforethought.

There were so few political offenders that they are scarcely worth troubling about among the mass of convicts, but their motives were clear in most cases.

Running through the history of transportation as reflected in the literature concerning it, is the question of how many convicts tried to get transported. Accounts of this are contradictory. The convicts themselves scarcely ever said they had been induced to commit offences in order to get transported. Typical of the few who did is the statement by a man transported for stealing a parcel out of a cart, and who was noted as having formerly been transported. This he denied: 'I said that to get transported.' Statements by convicts are available for Van Diemen's Land only, and there is, of course, no reason for a convict to admit that he wished to be transported. What evidence is there, by those who should have known, that men sought to be sent to Australia in chains?

In 1812 evidence was recorded from a hulk official that it was necessary for the safety of the hulks to remove those who had been guilty of the most atrocious crimes. Because the same individual said in 1819 that only approximately one-third of those on the hulks would actually be transported to Australia,[20] it appears that the convict determined on transportation would first have to commit an offence for which he would not be hanged, and then behave in such a way on the hulks that his superiors would be glad to be rid of him. All in all, courting transportation must have been a very risky business, and the man concerned would have to misbehave very cleverly even to get to some of the hulks, for it is noteworthy that in 1822 the hulks were receptacles for the worst characters.[21]

Hulk officials, questioned in 1835, said that convicts appeared to have a general wish for transportation,[22] and a boy aged ten announced that he would like to go to Australia, although he had heard that the prisoners worked in chains, and 'that those who had good characters were sold to Masters'.[23] Another person, a chaplain at Millbank penitentiary, said he found some men anxious to be off because they conceived they would enjoy good employment, and have good masters.[24] The governor of Newgate gaol declared that men did not dread transportation, and that nineteen out of twenty were glad to go,[25] and a prisoner sentenced to seven years' transportation said that, in his experience, his fellows did not fear transportation, except for two men who had been out previously.[26] Some country offenders, as well as those from the towns, were not deterred by transportation, observed one Bedfordshire magistrate: letters from men in New South Wales as prisoners made the people at home very careless about transportation, and the witness had seen one letter from a Bedford man, now in Australia, who was the owner of a large estate.[27]

Contrary views were held, however, by the Keeper of Newgate. He said that persons sentenced to transportation dreaded it, and used every means in their power to stay in the country and behaved well for that purpose.[28] An Australian resident thought otherwise yet again; he was in no doubt that men committed offences to get sent out, fancying it was an easy life.[29] Governor Arthur contradicted him: he did not think any convict got himself deliberately transported, for 'if it had operated to any extent, I must have heard of it'.[30]

So the difference in views goes on, and there is no way of proving the matter one way or the other. Obviously all these people could speak only from their own experience, which might have been extensive or limited. It would be more rewarding to regard the subject as one concerning the two groups of convicts distinguished in earlier chapters, namely, the English and Irish. There are grounds for supposing that the Irish would fear transportation more than the English, being not so accustomed to crime, and probably more attached to their families, for the Irish were older than the English and included more married men. The Lord-Lieutenant of Ireland summed up these differences when he commented that transportation was viewed with the greatest terror by the Irish, and the severance of home ties, except where starvation was the alternative to transportation, had been regarded with more fear than any term of imprisonment.[31]

A neat division between the two nationalities over-simplifies the case. Who can doubt that the Dublin thief thought differently of transportation than the married man with a family in Co. Sligo, transported to Australia for a fight concerning a piece of land, or that the man of Kent transported for machine-breaking did not look upon his fate rather differently than a fifteen-year-old pickpocket from London, who had been previously in trouble more times than he could remember? There is little evidence that men tried to be transported, and what a prisoner said to his fellow-prisoners after he was in gaol is not a very safe guide to his actions and thoughts prior to apprehension. The town thief was probably not deterred by transportation, but when he was caught and transported, he made the best of his fate. Wakefield records hearing men in Newgate sentenced to transportation looking forward to going out to Botany Bay,[32] but this was when they were not in a position to do anything else.

The man who committed an offence as a result of need or in desperation, and who had not been imprisoned previously would be the man to dread transportation when awaiting his trial, not the man whose life consisted of constant risk of such a fate. As was pronounced in 1837, the London thieves did not worry about transportation, but the agricultural workers entertained a vague and ignorant horror of it.[33]

The evidence of offences committed in Van Diemen's Land, which received the worst of the convicts, does not demonstrate that convicts were vicious criminals incapable of reformation, or unable to cease their criminal activity. There is no evidence that Australia received an element of the British population which was incapable of work or intelligent exertion. A shipload of prisoners who gave every indication in their home land of being desperate men, or persistent criminals at least, were subjected to a profound change in terms of their environment. Being uprooted from old haunts and companions, good or bad, shipped around the world, and set down as a shepherd on a sheep station, must have been a salutary shock to all convicts. There is evidence that this shock treatment was not unsuccessful, and that despite bad masters and the stresses and strains of life in a penal colony, the twenty-five-year-old urban convict transported for theft, though addicted to the bottle more than his free fellow-settlers, nevertheless was presented with a golden opportunity to make a fresh start. It could be done and it was done. Backsliders and vicious criminals there were, but the abundance of hard work, the relative abundance of food, and the lack of temptations 'up country' all tended to favour redemption. That he probably remained a bachelor and eked out his last days in a home, or lived in a humpy doing odd jobs, or remained a jealous and crotchety old retainer to a landed family, was not altogether the convict's fault, but a factor explained by the demographic history of Australia. Given the severity of transportation, and a bad master, it must still be asked of the convict, what would have become of him in Britain had he stayed after being imprisoned instead of transported? Would he have spent his life in and out of gaol, or would he have emigrated? Or would he have died in the work-house?

The convicts were neither simply 'village Hampdens' nor

merely 'ne'er-do-wells from the city slums'. But if the Hampdens are placed on one side of a scale and ne'er-do-wells on the other, the scale must tip toward the ne'er-do-wells.

APPENDICES

APPENDIX 1

Sampling and statistics

A statistical sample is not a specific that can conclusively prove or disprove anything, but it can enable probabilities to be adduced. Distrust of statistical analysis of observable data is a feeling expressed by the saying that 'statistics can prove anything'. This feeling has no basis in logic. Such analysis employed as an instrument to extract the data available in a sample of the convict intake to the Australian colonies, providing the sample chosen is a random one, is necessarily objective because nothing but chance has chosen the units to be discussed and analysed. In an attempt to discover the truth of the origins of the convicts, then, intuitive reasoning cannot be defended when objective methods are at hand. Historians have tended either to come into possession of an hypothesis, and then find cases to 'prove' its validity, or else inspected the material, picked out what suited their purpose, and then concluded that the pieces examined were representative of the whole. The latter technique may result in partly true conclusions, and the first may stimulate rewarding speculations. This is not enough in the case of the men and women transported to Australia, and it is not enough if only because there exists adequate material and a valid methodology to come to a more satisfactory conclusion.

Nearly all our knowledge derived by induction and analogy is fundamentally the result of an assessment of probabilities,[1] and when confronted with data on more than 150,000 convicts it is difficult to know what method other than statistical analysis can be used to answer sensibly the question, who were the convicts?

A sample of the sort suggested must be taken from all the men and women transported, and not from a list which excludes some. Such omissions will very likely result in conclusions being biassed, the degree of bias becoming graver according to the numbers omitted from the original 'population'. Such exclusion would not be of much importance if it could be proved very small, but there is always a reason for certain units not appearing in the records from which sampling is conducted, and that reason may be a significant one. It is conceivable, for instance, that the researcher might assume that shipping lists or indentures transmitted to the colonies included the names of all prisoners leaving Britain, whereas it may be that the Irish convicts were not represented at all in those registers. Again, it may be possible to be sure that all felons sent out from England and Ireland are accounted for, but to be unaware that some came directly to Australia from such places as India and Mauritius, in which case there has been omitted from consideration a special group of prisoners. The higher the degree of omission, the more likely is it that the investigator will come to a conclusion that is only partly true, though it is possible that he will by chance secure a representative sample from an incomplete population. If the number of people left off his sampling list is large, this is unlikely.

Australia is possibly the only nation in the world for which there exists a comprehensive record of a large proportion of the first settlers, both free and bond, because New South Wales and Van Diemen's Land were administered as virtual police states in the first years of their settlement, and thus it is not surprising that dossiers of one sort or another formed a large proportion of records, and that convict administration occupied much of the attention of the early governors.[2]

It has been observed that sampling, to be effective, demands population lists which are complete. The principal relevant documents are in the Public Record Office, London, among the Home Office papers.[3] These records, which are the transportation registers, list the name of the convict, place and date of conviction, and period for which transported, and are apparently complete except in the case of the felons on the First Fleet, which left England in 1787. Fortunately there is in the public records a list of prisoners on that fleet,[4] and although it has been claimed that this is not complete the numbers reckoned to be missing are no more than twenty.[5]

The completeness of these registers was checked in several ways, but mainly by noting the despatches of the various governors of the colonies, for the chief executives recorded the arrival of convict vessels, and the numbers on board. These records, allowing for deaths on the way out,[6] agree with the Home Office lists very closely in general, and exactly in the great majority of cases. Secondly, examination of the Blue Books disclosed a high degree of agreement, and thirdly, a publication listing all the convict vessels from Britain, with the details of numbers, also agrees very closely with Home Office documents.[7]

It is unfortunate for the purposes of this enquiry into the origins of the convicts that the transportation registers do not include those vessels departing from Ireland, and it is doubly unfortunate that during the uprising of 1922 the insurgents destroyed a quantity of records, among them the convict records for the period prior to 1837. However, names of convicts and some other particulars were despatched to the colonies, usually, but not always, with the ship in question, and nearly all reached Australia, though sometimes late. There are lists of one sort and another for all the ships leaving Ireland except one to New South Wales, the *Friendship* (99).[8] A partly complete list of men on this ship was compiled from later musters for the purpose of sampling.

Thus there are two sets of records which account for nearly all convicts transported: H.O. 11, and the indentures and associated papers. On the basis of these it was possible to secure a population which included, or made allowance for, all convicts despatched to Australia from Britain. For all convicts there were available name, place and date of trial, and period for which transported. From other sources in Australia it was possible to add to this framework, in many cases,[9] other details such as offence, age, religion, marital status, native place, occupation, former offences, and in some cases qualitative comments by gaol, hulk or ship officials.

Over and above the ships from England and Ireland, there were a number of vessels which brought prisoners to Australia from British overseas possessions. Some of these men came in small numbers on merchant vessels, and do not appear on the records so far mentioned.[10] Documents transmitted with them, and other sources of information, are intricate in the case of New South Wales, but in Van Diemen's Land a consolidated register of all arrivals was kept. Sampling was conducted also from these records.

Criterion for admission to the sampling list was a prisoner's presence on board a ship when it left the port of origin. These ports included all outside the present-day boundaries of the Commonwealth of Australia. Men transported within Australia, e.g. from South Australia to Van Diemen's Land, were omitted, because if they had arrived free they were outside the frame of reference of the sample, and if they had arrived bond then they had already been on an original transport that had been sampled. Thus men pardoned at the last minute, or taken off the convict vessels for health reasons or for any other reason, were omitted. Convicts who died on the way to Australia, or were on board vessels that were captured, or sunk, or otherwise prevented from reaching their destination, were still included in the sample: having left the port of origin they were assumed to be part of the convict numbers destined for the Antipodes. That they should not get there was not the intention of the home government.

In order to simplify sampling, a systematic sample of every twentieth convict was undertaken. This form of sampling is different from a random sample, in that the latter amounts to putting the numbers one to 150,000 (or whatever the total population is) into a container, and then drawing out one-twentieth of them, as in a lottery, it having been decided that 5 per cent of the total was the maximum possible to handle and analyse. However, because such random sampling supposes that the convicts are all numbered consecutively, and because the prisoners were not so identified in a running series, it was decided to take every twentieth convict from a total list based on H.O. 11 and the indentures and associated documents.

It might be supposed that selecting every twentieth unit from a total of approximately 150,000 could not help but be tantamount to a random sample, but this will not be so if there is a regularity throughout the data. In the present case, H.O. 11 and the other sources of convicts' names are so organized that each ship had a section to itself, convicts being enumerated not in alphabetical order but in order of county of conviction.[11] Thus men convicted in Bedfordshire are followed by those from Berkshire, and so on through to Scottish prisoners, who were listed at the end, and to any court-martial cases, which completed the register of names. If it could be shown that there was a regular number from each county, and that each ship carried the same number of prisoners, then systematic sampling could conceivably be unsatisfactory in that it might select in a biassed way, though such bias in the case here discussed is unlikely because of the large numbers involved. In fact, the numbers on each ship varied, and the numbers convicted in the counties were also different. Therefore, by selecting a random starting number between one and twenty, sampling could be carried forward with the assurance that it was equivalent to a random sample.

The data were recorded on a punched card designed for the purpose. When it seemed that sources of relevant information were all known, sampling began with the First Fleet and proceeded through to the last vessel to leave for Van Diemen's Land, the *St Vincent* (52). From various sources, the variables in the survey were completed as far as possible, and then coded on to the punched cards, which were counted, and totals drawn up for the categories distinguished. Since the sampling technique is essentially a quantitative one at this level, such a method of recording data is satisfactory. Qualitative comments concerning convicts in the sample were added to the card in writing.

One of the difficulties in writing this account of the origins of the convicts arises from use of the sampling technique. This methodology, unusual in an historical framework, has its own specialized terminology, and thus the reader accustomed to historical narration and analysis could find himself not only baffled but misled. Especially is the word 'significant' important, and throughout this enquiry its use in a statistical sense has been replaced by the word 'relative'. To understand the importance of 'relative' the reader should note the following paragraphs of explanation.

To explain fully the use of tests of statistical significance would take too much space, but briefly, when the observed and expected frequencies of variables are compared, a 'null hypothesis' is postulated. This hypothesis assumes that any divergence between observed and expected frequencies may be attributed to chance. When the chi-squared test of significance demonstrates that the probability of a difference from the anticipated frequency could occur by chance only once in twenty times, that difference is termed *significant* at the five per cent level, i.e. it is considered that there may be an association between the variables other than that due to chance. When the test shows that chance could account for the difference between expected and observed frequencies once in one hundred times, or more, that difference is termed *highly significant* at the one per cent level. The word 'significant' thus has a highly precise meaning in statistical work.

Consider the following example. Say there were 3,000 English convicts in the sample, and 1,000 Irish, making a total of 4,000 men altogether. The men who stole animals are being investigated, and it is desired to know whether the Irish were more likely to be convicted and transported for this than expected. There were say 400 such men all-told transported for stealing animals, and 200 were English and 200 Irish, making a total of 400 animal thieves. This figure of 200 is the *observed frequency* of Irish, but the *expected frequency* in this case is clearly 100 Irish and 300 English, if the men transported for stealing animals are distributed proportionately, as would be expected if there were no relationship between nationality and animal thieves among the convicts. Having ascertained the observed frequency, we have to ask: what is the probability of such a difference from the expected frequency arising by chance? To discover this, the null hypothesis is postulated, i.e. there is no (null) difference between the two sets of figures that cannot be explained away by chance alone; that is to say, there is nothing intrinsic about 'Irishness' among the prisoners that made them more likely to steal animals than the English, though it certainly appears from the figures of the sample that the number of Irish is much higher than expected, thus demonstrating the probability of an association between the variables of nationality and animal theft. The chi-squared test shows that the probability of such a difference between observed and expected frequencies could arise by chance only once in some thousands of times. It is possible to be on fairly firm ground, then, to conclude that some other factor or factors apart from chance are involved in the association between men tried in Ireland and those who stole animals. Such a result would be expressed by stating that the Irish who stole animals were more than expected to a highly significant level, or, in this work, by saying that *relatively* many Irish stole animals.

Thus observed frequencies, as they approached nearer to the 'perfect' relationship of 100 Irish and 300 English, would be attributable less and less to chance (and such a 'perfect' relationship, too, would be highly improbable). Where is the line between chance and other relationships drawn? Throughout, the chance of one in twenty or over has been adopted as a signpost that causal relationships appear likely, but there is, of course, nothing magical about this point.

An association that is significant in the statistical sense may not be significant in the ordinary meaning of the word, however: for instance, there could appear a relationship between a man's height and the number of his previous offences. If there could be found other evidence that made such an apparently nonsensical association worth considering, we should not discard it, but common sense and knowledge of the subject must come first in assessments. The statistical technique outlined should be viewed as illuminating the problem, and pointing out lines of investigation.

Reference is made throughout to *no response*. The term means that the convict or convicts in question did not have certain data recorded. It is clear that, providing 'no response' is not high, it will not greatly affect a test of significance, particularly if the value of chi-squared is very high, and the result highly significant. If, however, 'no response' is high, it will vitiate tests of significance, for it must be allowed that all the non-respondents fall into one category and are not distributed proportionately. It is generally more reasonable than not (particularly in a survey of this nature) to assume 'no response' distributed proportionately, and this assumption has usually been followed because there appeared no reason to suppose anything else.[12]

APPENDIX 2

The number of convicts transported

Many estimates have been made of the number of convicts transported to Australia. For instance, Henry Melville in 1851 computed the figures as '47,092 males and 7,491 females' transported in the years to 1843,[1] and Alexander Marjoribanks remarked that 'about 100,000' prisoners had been transported from 1788 to 1840.[2] Another writer calculated the total number of males sent to New South Wales as 51,082 and of females, 8,706,[3] and Mundy claimed that 'not less than 60,000 had been introduced and diffused throughout these colonies'.[4] A more recent estimate is approximately 157,000.[5]

The 1812 committee on transportation printed in its report a total of convicts landed in New South Wales from 1795 to 1810,[6] and the 1837 committee also listed totals.[7] More recently Bateson[8] has given an evidently exhaustive list of numbers of felons sent to Australia, and these three sources, together with a return of 1851,[9] and the sample totals, are set side by side in the following tables. The 1812 figures appear very much astray from 1814 onwards when compared with Bateson's figures and those of the sample, which agree closely. The 1837 figures are probably incorrect because of omission of the Irish, not noted on the Home Office transportation registers. Adding them in results in the following comparison:

| | Bateson | | | | Sample | |
	Males	Females	Total	Males	Females	Total
1810-19	11,650	1,934	13,584	10,900	1,920	12,820
1820-9	19,608	2,348	21,956	19,280	2,500	21,780
1830-9	26,714	4,947	31,661	27,460	5,000	32,460

| | 1837 Committee | | |
	Males	Females	Total
1810-19	11,612	1,896	13,508
1820-9	19,200	2,814	22,014
1830-9	24,163	4,474	28,637

If we allow for the omission of the last three years of transportation to New South Wales in the 1837 totals, we can see that the three sources agree fairly closely, when once the Irish are added in. That they were not recorded on Home Office lists probably explains some earlier underestimations of numbers of prisoners transported. Internal discrepancies are to be explained by conflicting totals on some ships, the division of convicts between New South Wales and Van Diemen's Land prior to 1825, and by inclusion in the sample of some military and colonial convicts who did not arrive on regular convict vessels, and were therefore not counted by the Home Office.

Two official returns are used to compare the number of convicts sent to Van Diemen's Land with the total derived from the sample. One is printed in the report of the 1837 committee, and the other is a return of 1851. These totals, together with the computed totals from Bateson, are in Table 2(b) and the New South Wales figures in Table 2(a).

It will be observed that the official returns are apparently incorrect in the case of Van Diemen's Land, though there do not appear the serious differences which exist in the New South Wales figures. Bateson's totals and the sample agree closely. The discrepancy in the period 1815-19 and 1820-4 is to be explained by the division of convicts between the two colonies: men who were sent on directly to the southern colony from Sydney after arriving from Britain were sampled as Van Diemen's Land convicts; though, strictly speaking, they were not sent directly from Britain to that colony, they spent their period of transportation there.

The main conclusion from these tables is that, according to the exhaustive work done by Bateson on the number of convicts transported, the sample totals are not astray unless it is held that the official returns are correct. It should be emphasized that computed figures relate to prisoners transported directly to New South Wales (to 1842) and Van Diemen's Land (to 1852) from overseas. They do not refer to convicts transported within Australia or to Western Australia, Norfolk Island, Port Phillip or Moreton Bay.

TABLE 2(a)

CONVICTS TRANSPORTED TO NEW SOUTH WALES ACCORDING TO
YEARS OF DEPARTURE

(i)

	1812 Committee				1837 Committee		
	Males	*Females*	*Total*		*Males*	*Females*	*Total*
1787-9					1,178	345	1,523
1790-4					2,471	399	2,870
1795-9	1,629	388	2,017		915	251	1,166
1800-4	1,412	407	1,819		1,743	450	2,193
1805-9	1,100	724	1,824		864	502	1,366
1810-14	539	140	679ᵃ		2,300	737	3,037
1815-19					6,252	579	6,831
1820-4					5,023	549	5,572
1825-9					6,857	925	7,782
1830-4					9,994	1,357	11,351
1835-9					5,909	697	6,606ᵇ
					43,506	6,791	50,297

(ii)

	Bateson				Sample		
	Males	*Females*	*Total*		*Males*	*Females*	*Total*
1787-9	593	417	1,010		700	320	1,020
1790-4	3,891	526	4,417		4,020	600	4,620
1795-9	1,244	418	1,662		1,300	400	1,700
1800-4	1,844	452	2,296		2,100	640	2,740
1805-9	1,123	611	1,734		1,120	640	1,760
1810-14	3,131	891	4,022		2,800	920	3,720
1815-19	8,519	1,043	9,562		8,100	1,000	9,100
1820-4	8,196	684	8,880		8,400	680	9,080
1825-9	11,412	1,664	13,076		10,880	1,820	12,700
1830-4	14,888	2,351	17,239		14,600	2,380	16,980
1835-9	11,826	2,596	14,422		12,860	2,620	15,480
1840-2	1,221	463	1,684		1,100	440	1,540
	67,888	12,116	80,004		67,980	12,460	80,440

ᵃ *En route.*
ᵇ 1835-7 only.

TABLE 2(b)

CONVICTS TRANSPORTED TO VAN DIEMEN'S LAND ACCORDING TO YEARS OF DEPARTURE

(i)

	1837 Committee			1851 Return		
	Males	*Females*	*Total*	*Males*	*Females*	*Total*
1803						
1805-9						
1810-14						
1815-19	1,460		1,460[a]			
1820-4	4,478	256	4,734	1,596	167	1,763[b]
1825-9	4,244	734	4,978	4,066	736	4,802
1830-4	9,184	1,269	10,453	8,832	1,185	10,017
1835-9	5,419	715	6,134[c]	8,955	1,315	10,270
1840-4				16,067	2,999	19,066
1845-9				6,884	2,607	9,491
1850-2				2,087	807	2,894[d]

(ii)

	Bateson			Sample		
	Males	*Females*	*Total*	*Males*	*Females*	*Total*
1803	307		307	260		260
1805-9						
1810-14	200		200	200		200
1815-19	1,110		1,110	2,140		2,140
1820-4	4,048	419	4,467	4,480	480	4,960
1825-9	4,334	921	5,255	4,220	820	5,040
1830-4	9,191	1,267	10,458	9,200	1,220	10,420
1835-9	8,677	1,334	10,011	8,200	1,320	9,520
1840-4	14,116	2,957	17,073	14,780	2,980	17,760
1845-9	4,783	3,423	8,206	4,900	3,420	8,320
1850-2	6,133	2,246	8,379	6,260	2,260	8,520
	52,899	12,567	65,466	54,640	12,500	67,140

[a] 1817-19 only.
[b] 1823-4 only.
[c] 1835-7 only.
[d] To June 1850 only. Arrived July-December 1850: 1,413 males, 198 females = 1,611.

APPENDIX 3

The convict records

From the indents* and associated papers transmitted with the convicts to Australia, together with statements made by the prisoners themselves, the consolidated registers held by the Tasmanian State Archives and the Archives Authority of New South Wales were formed.

A document of the first importance transmitted with the prisoners was the indent, which made over the labour and services of the convicts to the ship's master and then to the governor. This was not despatched with the First Fleet: 'The masters of the transports having left with the agents the bonds and whatever papers they had received that related to the convicts, I have no account of the time which the convicts are sentenced, or the dates of their convictions'.[1]

Two years later Phillip again asked 'that the necessary instructions may be sent out respecting those convicts who say their terms of transportation are expired'; and he repeated that request later in the same year.[2] The transport *Kitty* (92),† however, had on board a list of convicts which included their occupations, and *Indispensable* (95) also had transmitted with it a list of convicts on board, specifying their names, ages, crimes and sentences.[3]

Upon Governor Hunter complaining of the careless way in which lists of convicts were sent from Ireland, Portland gave instructions that an account of all the convicts who had been or should be sent from that kingdom should be regularly made out, together with the terms of their transportation and the assignment of their services.[4] These required lists were forwarded in H.M.S. *Buffalo,* which arrived at Sydney in 1799.[5] But next year Hunter complained again concerning the records sent out, and announced that 'we continue ignorant of those [crimes] of every other convict sent to this country, because the particular crimes are never in-

* The term 'indent' seems to have had different meanings at different times. Strictly speaking, it referred to the document transferring a property in the prisoners to the governor of the relevant colony, but usually appears to apply to a list of prisoners together with their descriptions.
† See Appendix 1, note 8.

serted in the list sent with them. We, therefore, can not so well judge of the character as we ought.'[6] Two years later the Lord-Lieutenant of Ireland caused to be sent 'accurate lists . . . of all convicts sent previous to the sailing of *Friendship*'.[7] Occupations of the convicts per *Calcutta* (03) were sent, however, together with names. These convicts had been especially selected with a view to their usefulness in the new settlement at Port Phillip, and subsequently Van Diemen's Land.

To this point, then, it appears that name, date of trial and period of transportation, and perhaps age and county of trial, was the only consistent information transmitted after the confusion of the first years, except in the case of the Irish where, after a very bad start, the documents appear more complete and include offences for which prisoners were transported.[8]

The best account of information sent out with the convicts is that of J. T. Bigge at the end of Macquarie's administration. He said that the muster of convicts at the end of their voyage was 'of a very detailed nature', resulting in the colonial authorities at Sydney or Hobart Town knowing the name, time and place of conviction, sentence, native place, age, and trade. The answers volunteered by the convicts were 'compared and corrected if necessary by the description in the Indent and in the lists transmitted from the hulks'. These hulk lists were probably identical with the registers preserved among the Admiralty papers. Bigge noted that such musters had been taken by Secretary Campbell since 1810.[9]

Therefore, some time prior to, or during, 1810 hulk lists were transmitted, and a detailed account of the prisoners' particulars noted. It has not been possible to discover when such information was first noted, but internal evidence suggests that it was only with the coming of Macquarie that much more than name, place and date of trial, and period of transportation of convicts, was noted in registers. It is possible that the four pieces of information came out as the indent, and that supplementary data were gathered from the hulk list, and from questioning the convicts. Offences for which convicts were transported were listed on New South Wales records for the first time in 1826, though such data may have been collected earlier and subsequently destroyed. It is difficult to know now how much material has been destroyed; certainly some has.

Bigge was not satisfied with the information sent out for he recommended that further particulars, especially number of former convictions,[10] be added to the hulk lists, but the main point to be noticed is that Bigge gave no indication that important particulars were being incorrectly recorded, though he cast doubts on whether the convicts told the truth about their marital status, and therefore recommended that such particulars also be recorded at home.[11] Presumably the information in these lists was determined from the gaol report and questions the prisoners answered on the hulks.

The position was clarified in 1825, for by an Act of the preceding year (5 George IV, c. 84) it was laid down that the sheriff or gaoler should deliver to the contractor, concerning felons 'a Certificate specifying concisely that Description of his or her Crime, his or her Age, whether married or unmarried, his or her Trade or Profession, and an account of his or her Behaviour in Prison before and after Trial, and the Gaoler's Observations on his or her Temper or Disposition, and such Information concerning his or her Connexions and former course of Life as may have come to the Gaoler's Knowledge'.[12]

This Act was a milestone in the administration of convict affairs in Australia, and especially in New South Wales (Van Diemen's Land records were consistently better organized and kept, it appears); and it was no doubt due to Bigge's recommendations, the erection of Van Diemen's Land into a separate government in 1825, and a new administration, that Brisbane was able to say in that year: 'Alphabetical references are compiling from the quarterly returns of fines and punishments, transmitted to the Secretary's office, which, when accomplished, will be an index to the moral history of the Colony. Thus . . . means will be afforded of pursuing the history, conduct and condition of a convict in his various situations in the Colony from his arrival to his emancipation or death'.[13]

A similar series of registers was compiled in Van Diemen's Land, for a memorial by a convict named Edward Cook discloses that this man compiled the first registers in May 1827. This was done, he said, under the superintendence of Josiah Spode, the superintendent of convicts, and Cook wrote up the careers of 12,305 felons in what he described as 'a new set of Black Books'. These were the conduct registers, for the handwriting of the memorialist and the first entries in the registers is the same.[14]

Thus the position by 1827 was as follows: from data drawn

from the indents and associated documents, and from information gained from the convicts by interrogation, their names and particulars were entered in the 'Black Books', or conduct registers, and some of these particulars were consolidated in other registers. It is not known for how long such comprehensive registers of conduct were kept in New South Wales.

That the procedure of recording information was thorough may be gathered from Arthur's evidence before the committee on transportation in 1837. At the Derwent, he stated, the surgeon-superintendent of the transport presented to the authorities on the spot hulk lists and his own comments on the prisoners. These were placed in the hands of the muster-master, who, armed with this information, usually gathered further particulars: 'The man perceives at once that the officer who is examining him knows something of his history, and, not being quite conscious of how much of it is known, he reveals, I should think, generally a very fair statement of his past life, apprehensive of being detected in stating what is untrue'.[15]

Other records concerning convicts exist in bewildering variety (see bibliography for a further discussion of them), but a most important set is in H.O. 26 and 27 which note offences, and sometimes other information, of London men from 1791 onwards, and for provincial offenders from 1805. Prior to these dates, and in isolated cases later, it was possible to discover offences only through a press report of the trial, or through the Assize or Quarter Sessions records.

APPENDIX 4

Basic tables and comments

The following tables should be read in conjunction with chapter 1. Most of them are self-explanatory, but in some cases comments have been added. The sample was one of 5 per cent, and therefore an *indication* of the true totals may be obtained by multiplying by twenty. Figures for percentages have been rounded.

Occupations of female prisoners have been omitted because virtually all were domestic servants.

TABLE 4(a)

MALE SAMPLE: YEARS OF DEPARTURE

	Total	Percentage
1787-9	35	1
1790-9	266	4
1800-9	174	3
1810-19	662	11
1820-9	1,400	23
1830-9	2,242	36
1840-9	1,039	17
1850-2	313	5
	6,131	100

TABLE 4(b)

MALE SAMPLE: FORMER OFFENCES

	Total	Percentage
0	1,360	22
1	1,355	22
2	434	7
3	176	3
4+	153	3
No response	2,653	43
	6,131	100

The level of 'no response' here is so high that it makes any conclusion concerning number of former offences a cautious one. The question of what is known of the non-respondents is too complex to go into here, but there is no reason to suppose that they were any different in respect of former offences to other convicts. However, if all were never previously punished, the total previously in the hands of the police is 33 per cent. If all were formerly punished, then the figure over all is 78 per cent. That is to say, the number of men formerly punished by public justice must vary between 33 per cent and 78 per cent. The true figure is probably close to 60 per cent.

TABLE 4(c)

MALE SAMPLE: PERIOD OF TRANSPORTATION

	Total	Percentage
7 years	3,141	51
10 years	441	7
14 years	711	11
15 years	147	3
Other	25	–
Life	1,632	27
No response	34	1
	6,131	100

TABLE 4(d)

MALE SAMPLE: COUNTIES OF TRIAL

	Total	Percentage			Total	Percentage
London	1,062	17		*Westmeath	37	
Lancs.	414	7		*Roscommon	36	
*Dublin	286	5		*Kilkenny	36	
Yorks.	241	4		Northumb.	33	
Warwicks.	185	3		Beds.	31	
Surrey	176			Bucks.	31	
Glos.	167			*Kerry	31	
Kent	151			*Cavan	29	0·5
*Cork	151			*Clare	29	
Overseas	140			Dorset	28	
Somerset	132			*Mayo	28	
Staffs.	129			*Queen's	27	
Essex	117	2		Durham	26	
Cheshire	108			*Down	25	
Norfolk	107			†Perth	25	
*Tipperary	104			*Longford	23	
Hants.	92			Cornwall	22	
†Midlothian	90			*Armagh	22	
†Lanarks.	89			*Kildare	20	
Wilts.	87			*Tyrone	20	
*Limerick	84			†Aberdeen	17	
Sussex	81			*Wexford	16	
Worcs.	80			*Wicklow	15	
Devon.	78			Hunts.	15	
Wales	77			*Carlow	15	
Lincs.	71			*Louth	15	
Suffolk	71			*Sligo	15	
Leics.	66			†Ayrshire	15	
Notts.	66			†Dumfries	13	
*Antrim	60	1		†Other Scottish	13	
Derbys.	58			*Londonderry	12	
Herts.	53			*Monaghan	12	
*Galway	53			*Fermanagh	11	
Berks.	49			Cumberland	10	
Northants.	47			*Donegal	10	
Salop	46			*Leitrim	9	
*King's	45			†Inverness	7	
Cambs.	42			†Stirling	6	
*Meath	41			Westmorland	6	
Oxford	39			No response	30	
*Waterford	38					
Hereford	37				6,131	100

Summary:	tried in England	4,331	71 per cent
	tried in Ireland	1,355	22 per cent
	tried in Scotland	275	5 per cent
	tried overseas	140	2 per cent
	no response	30	–
		6,131	100

All percentages are cumulative, e.g. totals range upwards from Cavan (0·5%) to Antrim (1%). The detailed figures are not given in this table nor in some of those which follow.

*Denotes an Irish county. †Denotes a Scottish county.

TABLE 4(e)

MALE SAMPLE: OFFENCES

	Total	Percentage
Offences against property		
Larceny (other than specified)	2,117	
Burglary; housebreaking	907	
Theft of animal or fowl (not poaching)	813	
Robbery (so designated)	402	
Theft of wearing apparel	379	
Receiving stolen goods	97	
Robbery with violence	68	
Wilful destruction	49	
Stealing by a trick	41	
Forgery	35	
Embezzlement	34	
Poaching	23	4,965	81
Offences of a public nature		
Coining; uttering	121	
Ribbonism; Whiteboyism; combination	37	
Riot	31	
Treason; sedition	17	
Perjury	14	
Sacrilege	11	
Bigamy	10	
Smuggling	4	245	4
Offences against the person		
Murder; manslaughter	81	
Assault (other than specified)	80	
Rape	25	
Kidnapping; abduction	9	
Other sexual offences	3	198	3
Military offences		
Insubordination; breach of the Articles of War	155	155	2·5
Other offences		
Theft, habit and repute	94	
Vagrancy; appearing armed	44	
Threatening letter; compelling to quit	12	150	2·5
No response		
	418	418	7·0
		6,131	100·0

Table 4(e)[1] leaves no doubt that a large proportion of the convict men were transported for the various forms of theft, and especially that designated 'other larcenies', i.e. forms of stealing such as picking pockets, stealing in a dwelling-house, and 'larceny' with no other explanation of the circumstances. Four per cent of the prisoners were transported for such 'larceny', and there is nothing to suggest that these offences were not typical of the ones we know more about. For instance, Thomas Tailby was transported in 1790 for 'grand larceny', and a newspaper noted that he had been found guilty of stealing several articles from a house; and William Keightley in 1816 was transported for 'larceny', which, according to a report in the press, was the theft of a piece of worsted cord. Again, Samuel Onions came out in 1821 from Norfolk on a charge of 'larceny' which, according to a newspaper, concerned him and three others, who were convicted of stealing £4 worth of silver, a double nankeen purse containing one £10 and nineteen £1 notes, and about £5 worth of silver.

Most of the offences need no explanation, but a few in the above table call for comment. For example, 'Ribbonism' and 'Whiteboyism' were names given to those offences committed by members of the Ribbon-men and Whiteboys, proscribed Irish organizations pledged to prevent eviction of tenants. The transmission of threatening letters, or the posting of threatening notices, were other Irish offences caused by the struggle to gain or hold a piece of land in the face of a great deal of subletting and eviction. These offences are discussed in chapter 3, but here is an example of one threatening letter: 'Ther is one fomily in this town that has not taken wornig by my last notise, and this is to let them now that if they works any more in that land of Armstrongs, or sets potatoes any more, or buys hay, or has any dalings in any one way with him or his, let them look up at ther last starting post — Tomy Downshire.' The last starting post was a sketch on the notice of the gallows with a body hanging.[2]

'Compelling to quit' was another Irish offence caused sometimes by feuds dating back for years, but generally by the pressure of population on arable land.

'Appearing armed' was an Irish offence linked with 'compelling to quit' and 'assaulting habitations' (wilful destruction). The sequence of events was the transmission of a threatening letter or notice, and, if this did not succeed in intimidating the party concerned, the appearance of armed persons who compelled the offending tenant to quit by threats, and, if necessary, knocked his house down.

TABLE 4(f)

MALE SAMPLE: OCCUPATIONS

	Total	*Percentage*
Agricultural worker	1,239	20
Labourer	1,154	19
Transport and communications	594	10
Metal manufacture and allied trades	323	5
Textile worker	295	5
Personal service	240	4
Worker in wood, cane or cork	213	3
Tanner, shoemaker	207	3
Defence personnel	194	3
Worker in building or contracting	156	3
Maker of textile goods, not boots	129	2
Maker of food, drink or tobacco	105	2
Commercial or financial	98	2
Brickmaker	93	2
Butcher	81	1
Mining, quarrying	78	1
Painter or decorator	61	1
Clerk	58	1
Worker in paper; printer	53	1
Professional and technical	24 ⎫	
Miller; shipwright	19 ⎪	
Warehouseman; packer	12 ⎬	1
Fisherman	9 ⎪	
Entertainer	6 ⎭	
Other	85	1
No response	605	10
	6,131	100

The classification which is adopted in Table 4(f) is based on one used in the 1951 census of the United Kingdom.[3] Though this is sophisticated, its use was necessary because convicts' records were often precise, and because the census categories used in the nineteenth century were too generalized.

The two most prominent categories—those of labourers and farm labourers—need little comment because entries on the records were unambiguous. Nevertheless, it is worthwhile noting the experience of one surgeon-superintendent on the question of occupations. Towards the end of his first voyage in charge of prisoners, he asked a man to make out a list of trades and the various particulars of the convicts: 'He came to me in a doubtful mood, scratching his head, and observing, "When I ask what their *trades* are, all the answer I can get from three-fourths of them is 'a thief, a thief'; shall I put them down as *labourers, sir?*" '4

The 'other' trades include such occupations as factory boy, flax dresser, harness cleaner, and drover. If a record noted two occupations, such as weaver and labourer, the first mentioned was used in allocation of the category. Though a great many youths were transported, only one did not have some specific calling noted. He was Thomas Clarke, who was transported from Dublin in 1820 for the theft of bank notes. He was fourteen years old, and recorded as 'boy at school' when he was sent to New South Wales.

TABLE 4(g)

MALE SAMPLE: AGE GROUPS

	Total	Percentage
10-14	76	1
15-19	1,117	18
20-24	1,934	32
25-29	1,085	18
30-34	554	9
35-39	328	5
40-44	211	3
45-49	119	2
50-54	77	1
55-59	38	
60-64	22	2
65-69	3	
70-74	4	
No response	563	9
	6,131	100

Table 4(g) shows that, far from being 'old lags', the convicts were numerically dominated by men in their early twenties, and that half were under twenty-five years of age, even supposing that all the men whose ages were not recorded were over that age. Most of these non-respondents were transported in the period prior to 1810, after which convict records become more complete, and there is no reason to suppose that the men transported in the early years were atypical in respect of age. If it is assumed that the 9 per cent of non-respondents were typical of the whole sample, then the mean age of the prisoners was 25·9 years.

TABLE 4(h)

MALE SAMPLE: MARITAL STATUS

	Total	Percentage
Married	1,072	17
Widower*	109	2
Single	3,056	50
No response	1,894	31
	6,131	100

* In the tables which follow this Appendix, 'married' includes widowers or widows.

Although, in Table 4(h), 'no response' amounted to not less than 31 per cent, there can be little doubt, in view of the data on age, that considerably more than half the total number of convicts were unmarried. Some of the men transported to Van Diemen's Land (where their statements upon arrival are still extant) denied what was on the records sent out with them. For instance, prisoners made such statements as 'I lived with a young woman who came to see me at the gaol, I never was married'. In other cases, it is likely that clerical errors exist. Some convicts divulged convincing details of the names of wife and children to the examining officials, together with corroborative data, but the official list noted the subject of the report as single. Such cases were placed in the category of 'no response'. It is impossible to know how many false statements were made, but there is no evidence for supposing that any but a few prisoners tricked the officials in both Britain and Australia. As Governor Arthur of Van Diemen's Land stated, prisoners were too apprehensive to tell lies.[5]

TABLE 4(i)

MALE SAMPLE: RELIGION

	Total	Percentage
Protestant	2,487	41
Roman Catholic	1,183	19
Other	18	–
No response	2,443	40
	6,131	100

It is impossible to read much into the data on religion, but it would be true to say that the great majority of men tried in

Ireland were Roman Catholic, and that a large proportion of those tried in England were Protestant. If non-respondents are typical, then 32 per cent of the male convicts were Roman Catholic, 27 per cent Irish-born, and 22 per cent Irish-tried. These findings are consistent with Irish-born having been tried in England and Scotland and overseas.

TABLE 4(j)

MALE SAMPLE: NATIVE PLACE

	Total	Percentage
England	3,462	56
Ireland	1,389	23
Scotland	247	4
Overseas	63	1
No response	970	16
	6,131	100

The difficulty in Table 4(j) is the proportion of the total number of convicts whose place of birth is unknown, but even if the non-respondents are discounted the percentage of Irish-born is still higher than the percentage of Irish-tried.

TABLE 4(k)

FEMALE SAMPLE: YEARS OF DEPARTURE

	Total	Percentage
1787-9	16	1
1790-9	50	4
1800-9	64	5
1810-19	96	8
1820-9	190	15
1830-9	377	30
1840-9	342	28
1850-2	113	9
	1,248	100

TABLE 4(l)

FEMALE SAMPLE: FORMER OFFENCES

	Total	Percentage
0	281	23
1	271	22
2	117	9
3	67	5
4+	70	6
No response	442	35
	1,248	100

TABLE 4(m)

FEMALE SAMPLE: PERIOD OF TRANSPORTATION

	Total	Percentage
7 years	925	74
10 years	102	8
14 years	106	8
15 years	19	2
Other	–	–
Life	94	8
No response	2	–
	1,248	100

TABLE 4(n)

FEMALE SAMPLE: COUNTIES OF TRIAL

	Total	Percentage		Total	Percentage
London	257	20	*Kildare	8	
Lancs.	99	8	*Fermanagh	8	
*Dublin	88	7	Lincs.	7	
*Cork	54	4	*Kilkenny	7	
†Lanarks.	44		Wilts.	6	0·5
Yorks.	30	3	Sussex	6	
†Midlothian	29		*Waterford	6	
Warwicks.	25	2	Cornwall	6	
Glos.	25		*Carlow	6	
*Limerick	25		Essex	5	
Surrey	24		Leics.	5	
Cheshire	21		Suffolk	5	
Devon	21		Derbys.	5	
*Galway	20		Hereford	5	
Somerset	19		*Westmeath	5	
*Antrim	17		*Queen's	5	
*Tipperary	16		*Longford	5	
*Down	16		*Londonderry	5	
*Tyrone	16		Cumberland	5	
†Perth	15		*Donegal	5	
Kent	14		Cambs.	4	
Worcs.	14		Durham	4	
Staffs.	13		*Louth	4	
Wales	13		†Stirling	4	
*Armagh	13		Herts.	3	
Norfolk	11	1	*Leitrim	3	
Notts.	11		Berks.	2	
*Mayo	11		Northants.	2	
Hants.	10		Dorset	2	
North'land	10		*Sligo	2	
*Kerry	10		†Ayr	2	
*Clare	10		†Other Scottish	2	
*Wexford	10		†Inverness	2	
*Wicklow	10		*King's	1	
*Monaghan	10		Beds.	1	
*Meath	9		Hunts.	1	
*Cavan	9		†Dumfries	1	
†Aberdeen	9		Overseas	—	
*Other Irish	9		Bucks.	—	
Salop	8		Westmorland	—	
Oxford	8		No response	2	
*Roscommon	8			1,248	100

Summary:	tried in England	707	57	per cent
	tried in Ireland	431	34	per cent
	tried in Scotland	108	9	per cent
	no response	2	—	
		1,248	100	

*Denotes an Irish county.   †Denotes a Scottish county.
'Other Irish' consists of those women who were drowned when the *Neva* was shipwrecked in 1835. The particular counties of trial are unknown.

TABLE 4(o)

FEMALE SAMPLE: OFFENCES

	Total	Percentage
Offences against property		
Larceny (other than specified)	587	
Theft of wearing apparel	199	
Robbery (so designated)	67	
Receiving stolen goods	52	
Theft of an animal (not poaching)	46	
Burglary; housebreaking	40	
Wilful destruction	27	
Robbery with violence	14	
Forgery	5	
Stealing by a trick	3	
Embezzlement	2	1,042	83
Offences of a public nature		
Coining; uttering	23	
Perjury	2	
Other	–	25	2
Offences against the person		
Murder; manslaughter	10	
Assault (other than specified)	4	
Aiding and abetting rape	1	15	1
Other offences		
Theft, habit and repute	39	
Vagrancy	17	56	5
No response	110	110	9
		1,248	100

TABLE 4(p)

FEMALE SAMPLE: AGE GROUPS

	Total	Percentage
10-14	5	–
15-19	184	15
20-24	355	28
25-29	227	18
30-34	125	10
35-39	76	6
40-44	54	4
45-49	35	3
50-54	21	2
55-59	4	–
60-64	6	1
No response	156	13
	1,248	100

TABLE 4(q)

FEMALE SAMPLE: MARITAL STATUS

	Total	*Percentage*
Married	223	18
Widowed	98	8
Single	624	50
No response	303	24
	1,248	100

TABLE 4(r)

FEMALE SAMPLE: RELIGION

	Total	*Percentage*
Protestant	369	29
Roman Catholic	347	28
No response	532	43
	1,248	100

TABLE 4(s)

FEMALE SAMPLE: NATIVE PLACE

	Total	*Percentage*
England	395	32
Ireland	428	34
Scotland	85	7
Overseas	6	–
No response	334	27
	1,248	100

APPENDIX 5

Tables classifying the number of male convicts tried in various countries

TABLE 5(a)

YEARS OF DEPARTURE

	England	Ireland	Scotland	Overseas	N.R.*	Total
1787-9	33	–	–	–	2	35
1790-9	213	45	2	–	6	266
1800-9	116	52	3	2	1	174
1810-19	478	153	16	15	–	662
1820-9	964	366	55	9	6	1,400
1830-9	1,646	413	110	58	15	2,242
1840-9	697	235	56	51	–	1,039
1850-2	184	91	33	5	–	313
	4,331	1,355	275	140	30	6,131

* 'N.R.' stands for 'no response', or 'unknown'. See Appendix 1.

TABLE 5(b)

FORMER OFFENCES

	England	Ireland	Scotland	Overseas	N.R.	Total
None	783	518	44	15	–	1,360
1+	1,665	253	156	43	1	2,118
N.R.	1,883	584	75	82	29	2,653
	4,331	1,355	275	140	30	6,131

TABLE 5(c)

PERIOD OF TRANSPORTATION

	England	Ireland	Scotland	Overseas	N.R.	Total
7 years	2,044	907	140	48	2	3,141
10 years	345	66	23	7	–	441
14 years	555	33	80	42	1	711
15 years	133	14	–	–	–	147
Other	19	1	1	4	–	25
Life	1,235	327	30	37	3	1,632
N.R.	–	7	1	2	24	34
	4,331	1,355	275	140	30	6,131

TABLE 5(d)

OCCUPATIONS

	England	Ireland	Scotland	Overseas	N.R.	Total
Agricultural	808	397	31	3	–	1,239
Labourer	741	356	56	1	–	1,154
Transport	449	117	24	4	–	594
Metal	269	30	24	–	–	323
Textile worker	225	39	30	1	–	295
Personal	170	57	11	2	–	240
Wood, cane and cork	171	31	11	–	–	213
Tanner, shoemaker	151	42	14	–	–	207
Defence	47	34	4	106	3	194
Building	139	14	2	1	–	156
Textile goods	94	27	8	–	–	129
Food, drink	86	13	6	–	–	105
Commercial	76	15	7	–	–	98
Brickmaker	89	2	2	–	–	93
Butcher	71	7	3	–	–	81
Mining	63	7	8	–	–	78
Painter	42	14	5	–	–	61
Clerk	43	12	3	–	–	58
Printer	47	3	3	–	–	53
Professional	15	6	2	1	–	24
Miller, shipwright	14	4	1	–	–	19
Warehouseman	12	–	–	–	–	12
Fisherman	8	1	–	–	–	9
Entertainer	5	1	–	–	–	6
Other	72	8	5	–	–	85
N.R.	424	118	15	21	27	605
	4,331	1,355	275	140	30	6,131

TABLE 5(e)

AGE GROUPS

	England	Ireland	Scotland	Overseas	N.R.	Total
10-14	53	20	3	–	–	76
15-19	813	226	76	2	–	1,117
20-24	1,427	406	87	14	–	1,934
25-29	747	262	45	30	1	1,085
30-34	369	162	9	12	2	554
35-39	208	94	17	9	–	328
40-44	135	66	6	4	–	211
45-49	86	25	6	2	–	119
50-54	45	27	4	1	–	77
55-59	29	6	3	–	–	38
60-64	11	9	2	–	–	22
65-69	3	–	–	–	–	3
70-74	1	3	–	–	–	4
N.R.	404	49	17	66	27	563
	4,331	1,355	275	140	30	6,131

TABLE 5(f)

MARITAL STATUS

	England	Ireland	Scotland	Overseas	N.R.	Total
Married	815	298	55	11	2	1,181
Single	2,196	613	173	74	–	3,056
N.R.	1,320	444	47	55	28	1,894
	4,331	1,355	275	140	30	6,131

TABLE 5(g)

RELIGION

	England	Ireland	Scotland	Overseas	N.R.	Total
Protestant	2,188	124	145	30	–	2,487
Roman Catholic	229	892	29	30	3	1,183
Other	16	–	–	2	–	18
N.R.	1,898	339	101	78	27	2,443
	4,331	1,355	275	140	30	6,131

TABLE 5(h)

NATIVE PLACE

(a) Tried in England

Born in county of trial	2,242
Born in England (except above)	1,158
Born in Ireland	151
Born in Scotland	27
Born overseas	43
N.R.	710
	4,331

(b) Tried in Ireland

Born in county of trial	843
Born in Ireland (except above)	339
Born in England	26
Born in Scotland	7
Born overseas	2
N.R.	138
	1,355

(c) Tried in Scotland

Born in county of trial	130
Born in Scotland (except above)	79
Born in England	7
Born in Ireland	27
Born overseas	3
N.R.	29
	275

(d) Tried overseas

Born overseas	15
Born in England	29
Born in Ireland	27
Born in Scotland	4
N.R.	65
	140

(e) N.R.

N.R.	28
Born in England	–
Born in Ireland	2
Born in Scotland	–
Born overseas	–
	30

(f) Totals

Born in county of trial	3,230
Born in country of trial (except above)	1,576
Born outside country of trial	353
N.R.	972
	6,131

APPENDIX 6

Tables classifying the number of male convicts transported for certain offences

TABLE 6(a)

YEARS OF DEPARTURE

Offences against property

	Larceny (other)	Burglary; housebreaking	Animal theft	Robbery	Theft of apparel	Other*
1787-9	6	5	4	1	2	4
1790-9	56	16	13	3	12	8
1800-9	24	24	13	4	5	10
1810-19	259	96	84	42	6	32
1820-9	533	219	213	123	65	54
1830-9	806	338	294	166	186	153
1840-9	348	153	139	45	90	63
1850-2	85	56	53	18	13	23
	2,117	907	813	402	379	347

	Offences of a public nature			Offences against the person	
	Coining	Other	Murder	Assault	Other
1787-9	–	–	–	–	–
1790-9	–	5	–	–	–
1800-9	3	1	2	–	2
1810-19	34	15	3	2	4
1820-9	40	43	13	5	9
1830-9	26	33	41	42	15
1840-9	13	20	21	25	4
1850-2	5	7	1	6	3
	121	124	81	80	37

	Military offences	Other offences	N.R.	Total
1787-9	–	1	12	35
1790-9	–	–	153	266
1800-9	4	1	81	174
1810-19	13	10	62	662
1820-9	12	18	53	1,400
1830-9	62	36	44	2,242
1840-9	55	51	12	1,039
1850-2	9	33	1	313
	155	150	418	6,131

* Numerically minor offences have been combined in this and the following tables.

TABLE 6(b)

FORMER OFFENCES

Offences against property

	Larceny (other)	Burglary; housebreaking	Animal theft	Robbery	Theft of apparel	Other
None	355	190	297	163	66	108
1+	920	334	191	106	233	90
N.R.	842	383	325	133	80	149
	2,117	907	813	402	379	347

	Offences of a public nature		*Offences against the person*		
	Coining	Other	Murder	Assault	Other
None	28	30	40	38	16
1+	22	12	16	13	5
N.R.	71	82	25	29	16
	121	124	81	80	37

	Military offences	Other offences	N.R.	Total
None	10	16	3	1,360
1+	71	96	9	2,118
N.R.	74	38	406	2,653
	155	150	418	6,131

TABLE 6(c)

PERIOD OF TRANSPORTATION

Offences against property

	Larceny (other)	Burglary; housebreaking	Animal theft	Robbery	Theft of apparel	Other
7 years	1,481	195	326	128	302	158
10 years	137	107	87	29	19	18
14 years	205	118	58	50	34	83
15 years	18	40	28	22	1	17
Other	7	7	2	–	3	2
Life	268	439	312	173	20	69
	2,117*	907*	813	402	379	347

	Offences of a public nature		*Offences against the person*		
	Coining	Other	Murder	Assault	Other
7 years	25	59	21	45	5
10 years	6	5	1	4	1
14 years	56	8	4	4	2
15 years	3	–	2	8	2
Other	–	–	–	–	–
Life	31	51	53	19	27
	121	124*	81	80	37

	Military offences	Other offences	N.R.	Total
7 years	67	103	226	3,141
10 years	2	22	3	441
14 years	54	5	30	711
15 years	–	4	2	147
Other	4	–	–	25
Life	28	16	126	1,632
N.R.	–	–	31	34
	155	150	418	6,131

* Denotes one non-respondent.

TABLE 6(d)

COUNTRY OF TRIAL

Offences against property

	Larceny (other)	Burglary; housebreaking	Animal theft	Robbery	Theft of apparel	Other
England	1,752	734	514	264	294	263
Ireland	296	90	287	115	74	67
Scotland	62	79	11	16	11	15
Overseas	7	4	1	7	—	2
N.R.	—	—	—	—	—	—
	2,117	907	813	402	379	347

	Offences of a public nature		Offences against the person		
	Coining	Other	Murder	Assault	Other
England	83	34	24	26	16
Ireland	23	80	49	46	18
Scotland	15	5	5	7	2
Overseas	—	5	3	1	1
N.R.	—	—	—	—	—
	121	124	81	80	37

	Military offences	Other offences	N.R.	Total
England	34	78	215	4,331
Ireland	23	41	146	1,355
Scotland	4	29	14	275
Overseas	91	2	16	140
N.R.	3	—	27	30
	155	150	418	6,131

TABLE 6(e)

OCCUPATIONS

Offences against property

	Larceny (other)	Burglary; house-breaking	Animal theft	Robbery	Theft of apparel	Other
Agricultural	274	193	378	70	51	83
Labourer	435	192	156	70	83	50
Transport	287	90	49	59	41	24
Metal	139	57	29	24	30	9
Textile worker	121	48	21	28	23	13
Personal	98	53	15	22	15	18
Wood, cane and cork	99	26	25	14	13	16
Tanner, shoemaker	92	24	10	12	24	12
Defence	7	3	–	–	7	4
Building	75	28	9	13	7	2
Textile goods	52	22	6	11	16	11
Food, drink	41	23	8	7	7	8
Other	264	99	77	54	43	70
N.R.	133	49	30	18	19	27
	2,117	907	813	402	379	347

	Offences of a public nature		Offences against the person		
	Coining	Other	Murder	Assault	Other
Agricultural	19	55	36	35	14
Labourer	21	23	18	15	12
Transport	8	5	1	1	–
Metal	7	6	3	7	1
Textile worker	17	7	3	6	2
Personal	5	2	1	–	–
Wood, cane and cork	4	2	–	3	1
Tanner, shoemaker	10	2	–	3	–
Defence	1	1	4	2	1
Building	7	2	–	1	2
Textile goods	–	1	1	2	1
Food, drink	2	1	2	1	–
Other	16	10	7	4	3
N.R.	4	7	5	–	–
	121	124	81	80	37

	Military offences	Other offences	N.R.	Total
Agricultural	–	24	7	1,239
Labourer	–	40	39	1,154
Transport	1	14	14	594
Metal	–	7	4	323
Textile worker	–	3	3	295
Personal	–	5	6	240
Wood, cane and cork	–	7	3	213
Tanner, shoemaker	–	12	6	207
Defence	154	–	10	194
Building	–	6	4	156
Textile goods	–	5	1	129
Food, drink	–	4	1	105
Other	–	14	16	677
N.R.	–	9	304	605
	155	150	418	6,131

TABLE 6(f)

AGE GROUPS

Offences against property

	Larceny (other)	Burglary; housebreaking	Animal theft	Robbery	Theft of apparel	Other
10-14	49	8	–	2	12	–
15-19	553	194	67	65	122	29
20-24	685	346	248	167	129	105
25-29	321	192	151	84	50	68
30-34	172	58	112	36	24	43
35-39	96	34	66	15	12	31
40-44	60	19	61	8	4	20
45-49	34	10	29	2	4	15
50-54	15	2	20	5	2	4
55-59	10	5	11	–	1	3
60-64	9	–	5	–	1	2
65-69	1	–	2	–	–	–
70-74	1	–	1	–	–	–
N.R.	111	39	40	18	18	27
	2,117	907	813	402	379	347

	Offences of a public nature		Offences against the person		
	Coining	Other	Murder	Assault	Other
10-14	–	–	–	--	–
15-19	6	5	5	4	2
20-24	27	32	24	20	13
25-29	24	39	21	25	10
30-34	14	18	12	10	4
35-39	13	14	5	6	3
40-44	7	5	3	4	3
45-49	8	3	5	3	–
50-54	13	3	2	3	–
55-59	4	–	1	1	–
60-64	–	–	1	1	1
65-69	–	–	–	–	–
70-74	1		–	–	–
N.R.	4	5	2	3	1
	121	124	81	80	37

	Military offences	Other offences	N.R.	Total
10-14	–	1	4	76
15-19	1	38	26	1,117
20-24	24	54	60	1,934
25-29	33	25	42	1,085
30-34	15	13	23	554
35-39	10	4	19	328
40-44	1	4	12	211
45-49	1	2	3	119
50-54	–	1	7	77
55-59	–	–	2	38
60-64	–	2	–	22
65-69	–	–	–	3
70-74	–	–	1	4
N.R.	70	6	219	563
	155	150	418	6,131

TABLE 6(g)

MARITAL STATUS

Offences against property

	Larceny (other)	Burglary; housebreaking	Animal theft	Robbery	Theft of apparel	Other
Married	345	125	284	65	51	134
Single	1,145	542	342	247	285	135
N.R.	627	240	187	90	43	78
	2,117	907	813	402	379	347

	Offences of a public nature		Offences against the person		
	Coining	Other	Murder	Assault	Other
Married	29	36	34	33	6
Single	30	34	39	43	23
N.R.	62	54	8	4	8
	121	124	81	80	37

	Military offences	Other offences	N.R.	Total
Married	12	25	2	1,181
Single	86	97	8	3,056
N.R.	57	28	408	1,894
	155	150	418	6,131

APPENDIX 7

*Tables classifying the number of female convicts
tried in various countries*

TABLE 7(a)

YEARS OF DEPARTURE

	England	Ireland	Scotland	N.R.	Total
1787-9	14	–	–	2	16
1790-9	36	13	1	–	50
1800-9	53	10	1	–	64
1810-19	64	29	3	–	96
1820-9	114	67	9	–	190
1830-9	220	121	36	–	377
1840-9	164	139	39	–	342
1850-2	42	52	19	–	113
	707	431	108	2	1,248

TABLE 7(b)

FORMER OFFENCES

	England	Ireland	Scotland	N.R.	Total
None	121	154	6	–	281
1+	282	165	78	–	525
N.R.	304	112	24	2	442
	707	431	108	2	1,248

TABLE 7(c)

PERIOD OF TRANSPORTATION

	England	Ireland	Scotland	N.R.	Total
7 years	466	378	81	–	925
10 years	74	22	6	–	102
14 years	80	9	17	–	106
15 years	12	7	–	–	19
Life	75	15	4	–	94
N.R.	–	–	–	2	2
	707	431	108	2	1,248

TABLE 7(d)

AGE GROUPS

	England	Ireland	Scotland	N.R.	Total
10-14	2	2	1	–	5
15-19	118	49	17	–	184
20-24	178	148	29	–	355
25-29	119	89	19	–	227
30-34	69	44	12	–	125
35-39	44	20	12	–	76
40-44	28	22	4	–	54
45-49	23	11	1	–	35
50-54	9	11	1	–	21
55-59	4	–	–	–	4
60-64	–	5	1	–	6
N.R.	113	30	11	2	156
	707	431	108	2	1,248

TABLE 7(e)

MARITAL STATUS

	England	Ireland	Scotland	N.R.	Total
Married	176	115	30	–	321
Single	328	232	64	–	624
N.R.	203	84	14	2	303
	707	431	108	2	1,248

TABLE 7(f)

RELIGION

	England	Ireland	Scotland	N.R.	Total
Protestant	266	49	54	–	369
Roman Catholic	62	272	13	–	347
N.R.	379	110	41	2	532
Total	707	431	108	2	1,248

TABLE 7(g)

NATIVE PLACE

(a) Tried in England

Born in county of trial	233
Born in England (except above)	159
Born in Ireland	66
Born in Scotland	9
Born overseas	6
N.R.	234
	707

(b) Tried in Ireland

Born in county of trial	218
Born in Ireland (except above)	135
Born in England	2
Born in Scotland	1
Born overseas	–
N.R.	75
	431

(c) Tried in Scotland

Born in county of trial	44
Born in Scotland (except above)	31
Born in England	1
Born in Ireland	9
Born overseas	–
N.R.	23
	108

(d) Tried overseas

Nil

(e) N.R.

N.R.	2
Born in England	–
Born in Ireland	–
Born in Scotland	–
Born overseas	–
	2

(f) Totals

Born in county of trial	495
Born in country of trial (except above)	325
Born outside country of trial	94
N.R.	334
	1,248

APPENDIX 8

Tables classifying the number of female convicts transported for certain offences

TABLE 8(a)

YEARS OF DEPARTURE

	Offences against property			
	Larceny (other)	Theft of apparel	Robbery	Receiving
1787-9	8	3	–	–
1790-9	15	4	–	1
1800-9	19	3	–	1
1810-19	57	4	2	4
1820-9	93	28	20	3
1830-9	203	59	32	20
1840-9	156	87	10	16
1850-2	36	11	3	7
	587	199	67	52

	Animal theft	Burglary; housebreaking	Wilful destruction	Other
1787-9	–	–	–	–
1790-9	–	1	–	1
1800-9	–	7	–	1
1810-19	2	2	–	2
1820-9	6	7	1	3
1830-9	11	8	1	3
1840-9	13	10	12	8
1850-2	14	5	13	6
	46	40	27	24

	Offences of a public nature		Offences against the person	
	Coining; uttering	Perjury	Murder	Other
1787-9	–	–	–	–
1790-9	–	–	–	1
1800-9	4	–	–	1
1810-19	5	–	2	1
1820-9	10	–	1	–
1830-9	2	1	6	2
1840-9	2	1	1	1
1850-2	–	–		
	23	2	10	5

	Other offences			
	Theft, habit	Vagrancy	N.R.	Total
1787-9	–	–	5	16
1790-9	–	–	28	50
1800-9	–	–	28	64
1810-19	–	3	15	96
1820-9	–	2	14	190
1830-9	13	6	17	377
1840-9	12	4	3	342
1850-2	14	2	–	113
	39	17	110	1,248

TABLE 8(b)

FORMER OFFENCES

	Offences against property			
	Larceny (other)	Theft of apparel	Robbery	Receiving
None	125	42	31	18
1+	272	116	19	21
N.R.	190	41	17	13
	587	199	67	52

	Animal theft	Burglary; housebreaking	Wilful destruction	Other
None	19	9	12	5
1+	21	11	8	7
N.R.	6	20	7	12
	46	40	27	24

	Offences of a public nature		Offences against the person	
	Coining; uttering	Perjury	Murder	Other
None	2	–	8	2
1+	4	1	2	–
N.R.	17	1	–	3
	23	2	10	5

	Other offences			
	Theft, habit	Vagrancy	N.R.	Total
None	–	8	–	281
1+	38	4	1	525
N.R.	1	5	109	442
	39	17	110	1,248

TABLE 8(c)

PERIOD OF TRANSPORTATION

Offences against property

	Larceny (other)	Theft of apparel	Robbery	Receiving
7 years	462	172	40	30
10 years	47	13	4	4
14 years	37	11	8	17
15 years	2	–	1	1
Life	39	3	14	–
	587	199	67	52

	Animal theft	Burglary; housebreaking	Wilful destruction	Other
7 years	29	19	11	12
10 years	10	7	5	4
14 years	–	4	–	5
15 years	2	1	9	2
Life	5	9	2	1
	46	40	27	24

	Offences of a public nature		Offences against the person	
	Coining	Perjury	Murder	Other
7 years	8	2	1	2
10 years	1	–	1	–
14 years	13	–	2	–
15 years	–	–	–	1
Life	1	–	6	2
	23	2	10	5

Other offences

	Theft, habit	Vagrancy	N.R.	Total
7 years	31	17	89	925
10 years	5	–	1	102
14 years	2	–	7	106
15 years	–	–	–	19
Life	1	–	11	94
N.R.	–	–	2	2
	39	17	110	1,248

TABLE 8(d)

Offences against property

	Larceny (other)	Theft of apparel	Robbery	Receiving
England	398	99	34	34
Ireland	159	86	24	18
Scotland	30	14	9	–
N.R.	–	–	–	–
	587	199	67	52

	Animal theft	Burglary; housebreaking	Wilful destruction	Other
England	6	21	7	14
Ireland	39	6	19	4
Scotland	1	13	1	6
N.R.	–	–	–	–
	46	40	27	24

	Offences of a public nature		Offences against the person	
	Coining; uttering	Perjury	Murder	Other
England	13	2	4	3
Ireland	7	–	5	2
Scotland	3	–	1	–
N.R.	–	–	–	–
Total	23	2	10	5

Other offences

	Theft, habit	Vagrancy	N.R.	Total
England	13	3	56	707
Ireland	–	14	48	431
Scotland	26	–	4	108
N.R.	–	–	2	2
	39	17	110	1,248

TABLE 8(e)

AGE GROUPS

Offences against property

	Larceny (other)	Theft of apparel	Robbery	Receiving
10-14	2	2	–	–
15-19	95	39	12	3
20-24	166	71	28	7
25-29	115	31	12	10
30-34	68	17	6	4
35-39	44	9	5	7
40-44	15	12	2	9
45-49	14	5	–	6
50-54	9	5	–	3
55-59	2	–	–	–
60-64	3	1	–	–
N.R.	54	7	2	3
	587	199	67	52

	Animal theft	Burglary	Wilful destruction	Other
10-14	–	–	–	–
15-19	2	7	5	6
20-24	11	13	13	3
25-29	11	4	7	6
30-34	7	6	1	5
35-39	1	1	–	–
40-44	5	1	–	1
45-49	2	1	–	–
50-54	2	1	–	–
55-59	1	–	–	–
60-64	1	–	–	–
N.R.	3	6	1	3
	46	40	27	24

	Offences of a public nature		Offences against the person	
	Coining	Perjury	Murder	Other
10-14	–	–	–	–
15-19	5	1	–	–
20-24	7	1	3	3
25-29	1	–	5	1
30-34	2	–	1	–
35-39	3	–	1	–
40-44	–	–	–	–
45-49	1	–	–	–
50-54	–	–	–	–
55-59	–	–	–	1
60-64	–	–	–	–
N.R.	4	–	–	–
	23	2	10	5

| | *Other offences* | | | |
	Theft, habit	Vagrancy	N.R.	Total
10-14	1	–	–	5
15-19	4	2	3	184
20-24	14	5	10	355
25-29	9	5	10	227
30-34	4	–	4	125
35-39	2	1	2	76
40-44	2	2	5	54
45-49	1	1	4	35
50-54	–	–	1	21
55-59	–	–	–	4
60-64	1	–	–	6
N.R.	1	1	71	156
	39	17	110	1,248

TABLE 8(f)

MARITAL STATUS

| | *Offences against property* | | | |
	Larceny (other)	Theft of apparel	Robbery	Receiving
Married	158	54	16	28
Single	297	128	46	18
N.R.	132	17	5	6
	587	199	67	52

	Animal theft	Burglary; housebreaking	Wilful destruction	Other
Married	18	7	7	5
Single	24	25	20	13
N.R.	4	8	–	6
	46	40	27	24

| | *Offences of a public nature* | | *Offences against the person* | |
	Coining	Perjury	Murder	Other
Married	5	–	3	4
Single	4	2	7	–
N.R.	14	–	–	1
	23	2	10	5

| | *Other offences* | | | |
	Theft, habit	Vagrancy	N.R.	Total
Married	12	2	2	321
Single	27	11	2	624
N.R.	–	4	106	303
	39	17	110	1,248

APPENDIX 9

*Tables classifying the number of male convicts sent to
New South Wales and Van Diemen's Land*

TABLE 9(a)

YEARS OF DEPARTURE

	N.S.W.	V.D.L.	Total
1787-9	35	–	35
1790-9	266	–	266
1800-9	161	13	174
1810-19	545	117	662
1820-9	965	435	1,400
1830-9	1,374	868	2,242
1840-9	53	986	1,039
1850-2	–	313	313
	3,399	2,732	6,131

TABLE 9(b)

FORMER OFFENCES

	N.S.W.	V.D.L.	Total
None	1,190	170	1,360
1+	587	1,531	2,118
N.R.	1,622	1,031	2,653
	3,399	2,732	6,131

TABLE 9(c)

PERIOD OF TRANSPORTATION

	N.S.W.	V.D.L.	Total
7 years	1,771	1,370	3,141
10 years	53	388	441
14 years	395	316	711
15 years	23	124	147
Other	6	19	25
Life	1,117	515	1,632
N.R.	34	–	34
	3,399	2,732	6,131

TABLE 9(d)

COUNTRY OF TRIAL

	N.S.W.	*V.D.L.*	*Total*
England	2,181	2,150	4,331
Ireland	1,024	331	1,355
Scotland	100	175	275
Overseas	64	76	140
N.R.	30	–	30
	3,399	2,732	6,131

TABLE 9(e)

OFFENCES

	N.S.W.	*V.D.L.*	*Total*
Offences against property			
Larceny (other)	1,052	1,065	2,117
Burglary; housebreaking	460	447	907
Animal theft	488	325	813
Robbery	297	105	402
Theft of wearing apparel	161	218	379
Receiving	58	39	97
Robbery with violence	32	36	68
Wilful destruction	19	30	49
Stealing by a trick	21	20	41
Forgery	15	20	35
Embezzlement	19	15	34
Poaching	12	11	23
Offences of a public nature			
Coining; uttering	78	43	121
Ribbonism, etc.	36	1	37
Riot	14	17	31
Treason	14	3	17
Perjury	5	9	14
Sacrilege	4	7	11
Bigamy	5	5	10
Smuggling	2	2	4
Offences against the person			
Murder; manslaughter	48	33	81
Assault (other)	42	38	80
Rape	17	8	25
Kidnapping; abduction	9	–	9
Other sexual offences	1	2	3
Military offences	70	85	155
Other offences			
Theft, habit and repute	2	92	94
Vagrancy, etc.	33	11	44
Threatening letter, etc.	6	6	12
N.R.	379	39	418
	3,399	2,732	6,131

TABLE 9(f)

RELIGION

	N.S.W.	V.D.L.	Total
Protestant	1,407	1,080	2,487
Roman Catholic	779	404	1,183
Other	9	9	18
N.R.	1,204	1,239	2,443
	3,399	2,732	6,131

APPENDIX 10

Tables classifying the number of female convicts sent to New South Wales and Van Diemen's Land

TABLE 10(a)

YEARS OF DEPARTURE

	N.S.W.	V.D.L.	Total
1787-9	16	–	16
1790-9	50	–	50
1800-9	64	–	64
1810-19	96	–	96
1820-9	125	65	190
1830-9	251	126	377
1840-9	21	321	342
1850-2	–	113	113
	623	625	1,248

TABLE 10(b)

FORMER OFFENCES

	N.S.W.	V.D.L.	Total
None	217	64	281
1+	116	409	525
N.R.	290	152	442
	623	625	1,248

TABLE 10(c)

PERIOD OF TRANSPORTATION

	N.S.W.	V.D.L.	Total
7 years	489	436	925
10 years	5	97	102
14 years	65	41	106
15 years	4	15	19
Life	58	36	94
N.R.	2	–	2
	623	625	1,248

TABLE 10(d)

COUNTRY OF TRIAL

	N.S.W.	*V.D.L.*	*Total*
England	344	363	707
Ireland	252	179	431
Scotland	25	83	108
N.R.	2	–	2
	623	625	1,248

TABLE 10(e)

OFFENCES

	N.S.W.	*V.D.L.*	*Total*
Larceny (other)	299	288	587
Theft of wearing apparel	76	123	199
Robbery	44	23	67
Receiving	24	28	52
Theft of an animal	17	29	46
Theft, habit and repute	–	39	39
All other offences	63	85	148
N.R.	100	10	110
	623	625	1,248

TABLE 10(f)

RELIGION

	N.S.W.	*V.D.L.*	*Total*
Protestant	160	209	369
Roman Catholic	175	172	347
N.R.	288	244	532
	623	625	1,248

APPENDIX 11

Particulars of convicts mentioned in the text

Ships marked with an asterisk (*) were sent to Van Diemen's Land, and all others to New South Wales. Particulars of the Van Diemen's Land prisoners were obtained from the Home Office papers, the conduct registers, and, in some cases, from supplementary documents in the Tasmanian State Archives (see bibliography). Particulars of New South Wales convicts were obtained from the Home Office papers and the convict indents held by the Archives Authority of New South Wales. The other main source of information about convicts is the census of New South Wales in 1828, the musters which preceded it (see bibliography) and newspaper references to trials. Particulars of the offences for which convicts were transported from England may be found in the Home Office papers (H.O. 26 and H.O. 27).

Men transported on the Second and Third Fleets were not distinguished in the Home Office lists by name of ship, though this can often be established from later documents. I have spelt 'Surrey' in the modern manner, though it is usually spelt 'Surry' on the convict registers. Particulars of Irish convicts give only county of trial. For further information on source material, see bibliography.

Abbreviations are as follows:

A.A.N.S.W.—Archives Authority of New South Wales
Adm.—Admiralty Papers
C.C.C.—Central Criminal Court
C.J.—Court of Justiciary (Scotland)
C.M.—Court Martial
C.O.—Colonial Office
E.R.—East Riding
G.D.—Gaol Delivery
G.Q.S.—General Quarter Sessions
G.S.—General Sessions
H.O.—Home Office
H.T.Q.S.—Hobart Town Quarter Sessions
H.T.S.C.—Hobart Town Supreme Court
L.G.D.—London Gaol Delivery
L.Q.S.—Launceston Quarter Sessions

L.S.C.—Launceston Supreme Court
M.G.D.—Middlesex Gaol Delivery
M.S.P.—Middlesex Session of Peace
Nat. Lib. Aust.—National Library of Australia, Canberra
O.B.S.P.—Old Bailey Sessions Papers (names of convicts are
    listed alphabetically in each session)
O.S.C.—Oatlands Supreme Court
O.T.G.D.—Oyer, Terminer and Gaol Delivery
P.R.O.—Public Record Office
Q.S.—Quarter Sessions
S.P.—Session of Peace
W.R.—West Riding

Adams, John, per *Lady Harewood* (30), Bristol Q.S., 19 April
    1830.
Aldhouse, Stephen, per *John Renwick* (42)*, C.C.C., 22 August
    1842; *The Times,* 1 September 1842.
Alexander, Henry, per *Rodney* (51)*, Birmingham Q.S., 17 April
    1847.
Allen, Sarah, per *Emma Eugenia* (43)*, Sussex Assizes, 20 March
    1843.
Allman, William, per *Earl Cornwallis* (00), M.G.D., 15 January
    1800; *O.B.S.P.*
Andrew, John, per *Medina* (25)*, M.G.D., 15 July 1824.
Ankin, Thomas, per *Emperor Alexander* (33)*, Cambs. (Isle of
    Ely) Q.S., 17 October 1832.
Archer, Isaac, per *Alexander* (87), 'came free'.
Armitage, Thomas, per *Lord Lyndoch* (33), Yorks. (W.R.) Q.S.,
    18 October 1832; Adm. 6/421, no. 2538.
Armstrong, Thomas, per *North Briton* (42)*, Mayo, 20 June 1842.
Arnold, Mary, per *Lady Juliana* (89), M.G.D., 12 December 1787;
    O.B.S.P.
Ashford, Benjamin, per *Pestonjee Bomanjee* (46)*, Somerset
    Assizes, 31 March 1846; *Sherborne, Dorchester and Taunton
    Journal,* 9 April 1846.
Askins, James, per *Coromandel* (38)*, Lancs. Assizes, 9 August
    1837.
Asquith, Constantine, per *Oriental Queen* (52)*, C.C.C., 2 July
    1849; *The Times,* 5 July 1849.
Attiwell, John, per *Recovery* (37)*, Brecon Assizes, 22 March
    1837.

Audery, Joseph, per *Pitt* (91), L.G.D., 16 February 1791; *O.B.S.P.*

Austin, James, or John, per *Minerva* (99), Dublin, March 1798.

Avery, Albert James, per *Baring* (19), L.G.D., 9 September 1818; *O.B.S.P.*

Avery, John, per *Moffatt* (34)*, Kent Q.S., 6 April 1832; *Kent Herald,* 12 April 1832.

Bailey, Paul, per *Active* (91), L.G.D., 7 July 1790; *O.B.S.P.*

Baker, Ann, per *Britannia* (98), M.G.D., 22 June 1796; *O.B.S.P.*

Banks, Solomon, per *Batavia* (17), L.G.D., 21 May 1817; *O.B.S.P.*

Barker, George, per *Susan* (34), Yorks. (W.R.) Q.S., 23 October 1833; Adm. 6/421, no. 484.

Barr, Mary, per *Aurora* (51)*, Nether Knutsford Q.S., 12 August 1850.

Barrington, George, per *Active* (91), M.G.D., 15 September 1790.

Becket, Ellen, per *Kinnear* (48)*, Cork, 14 March 1848.

Bellett, Jacob, per *Scarborough* (87), M.G.D., 12 January 1785; *O.B.S.P.*

Bence, Robert, per *Second Fleet* (90), Glos. Assizes, 16 July 1788; P.R.O., Assizes 25.

Biggs, George, per *Henry* (23), L.G.D., 17 April 1822; H.O. 10/16.

Blacker, Titus, per *Lord Lyndoch* (36)*, Yorks. Assizes, 18 July 1835.

Bleathman, Richard, per *Circassian* (32)*, Dorset Assizes, 10 March 1832; *Dorchester Chronicle,* 22 March 1832.

Booth, John, per *Hindostan* (40)*, Flint Q.S., 9 April 1840.

Bowing, James, per *Lord Sidmouth* (18), M.G.D., 17 June 1818; *O B.S.P.*

Bratt, Samuel, per *Asia* (35)*, M.G.D., 27 July 1835.

Bray, William, per *Henry Tanner* (34), Hereford Q.S., 30 December 1833; Adm. 6/421, no. 672.

Breckenridge, Thomas, per *Eden* (36)*, Edinburgh C.J., 18 March 1836; *Scotsman,* 19 March 1836.

Brennan, Mary Ann, per *Elizabeth and Henry* (48)*, C.C.C., 20 September 1847.

Buckley, James, per *Prince Regent* (41)*, Armagh, 13 March 1841.

Burdo, Sarah, per *Lady Penrhyn* (87), M.G.D., 25 October 1786; *O.B.S.P.*

Burns, Catherine, per *Morley* (20)*, Southampton Assizes, 28 February 1820; H.T.Q.S., 11 July 1835.

Burns, James (1), per *Orator* (43)*, Longford, 1 March 1843.

Bushell, Paul, per *Surprize* (90), Warwicks. (Coventry) Assizes, 3 April 1789; *H.R.A.,* I. vi. 574, vii. 113, x. 741, xviii. 473; A.A.N.S.W.

Butler, Mary, per *Neptune* (90), M.G.D., 9 September 1789; *O.B.S.P.*

Button, William, per *Asiatic* (43)*, Suffolk (Ipswich) G.Q.S., 10 June 1842; *Ipswich Journal,* 18 June 1842.

Callicott, John, per *Countess of Harcourt* (21)*, M.G.D., 6 December 1820.

Cameron, James, per *Glatton* (02), M.G.D., 17 September 1800; *O.B.S.P.*

Campion, William, per *Ratcliffe* (45)*, Kilkenny, 17 January 1844.

Capps, Robert Thomas, per *Bussorah Merchant* (28), L.G.D., 13 September 1827; *The Times,* 21 September 1827.

Carr, Andrew, or Brady, or Byrnes, Patrick, per *Susan* (42)*, Meath, 28 December 1841.

Carthy, Sylvester, per *Westmorland* (38), Carlow, 20 March 1838.

Cartland, James, per *Active* (91), L.G.D., 24 February 1790; *O.B.S.P.*

Cass, Thomas, per *John* (33)*, Warwicks. Assizes, 30 March 1833.

Cash, Martin, per *Marquis of Huntley* (27), Wexford, 13 March 1827.

Cassidy, Edward, per *Hercules* (30), Fermanagh, 23 March 1830.

Chalkley, Thomas, per *Marmion* (27)*, Kent Assizes, 25 July 1827.

Chambers, Mary, per *Isabella* (18), M.G.D., 17 September 1817; *O.B.S.P.*

Chandler, Thomas, per *Morley* (18), M.G.D., 3 December 1817; *O.B.S.P.*

Chapman, William, per *Morley* (16), M.G.D., 29 May 1816; H.O. 27.

Chetwode, Thomas, per *Lady Harewood* (30), Salop Assizes, 7 August 1830; *Salopian Journal and Courier of Wales,* 11 August 1830.

Clapton, Ann, per *Lady Juliana* (89), L.G.D., 10 December 1788; *O.B.S.P.*

Clare, Samuel, per *Gilmore* (38)*, Northants. Q.S., 19 October 1837.

Clarke, Thomas, per *Almorah* (20), Dublin, 6 July 1820.

Cleveland, Elizabeth, per *Rajah* (41)*, C.C.C., 17 August 1840; *The Times,* 21 August 1840.

Clogherty, Mary, per *Kinnear* (48)*, Galway, 12 April 1848.

Coin, John, per *General Hewart* (13), Kent Assizes, 15 March 1813; H.O. 26.

Coles, William, per *Gilmore* (38)*, Somerset Assizes, 31 March 1838; H.T.S.C., 22 July 1845; *Hobart Town Courier,* 26 July 1845.

Conean, Michael, per *Blenheim* (51)*, Galway, 16 July 1849.

Cooper, Jonathan, per *Tottenham* (18), M.G.D., 2 July 1817; H.O. 27.

Coulson, Thomas, per *Lady Kennaway* ex *Norfolk* (34)*, Northumb. Assizes, 26 February 1834.

Crehan, Patrick, per *Prince Regent* (24), Tipperary, 23 May(?) 1823; *P.P.,* 1824, vol. 22, p. 236.

Crighton, Joseph, per *Triton* (42)*, Lancs. Assizes, 24 March 1842.

Crighton, Mary, per *Sir Robert Seppings* (52)*, Glasgow C.J., 30 September 1851.

Crittle, John, per *Surrey* (42)*, C.C.C., 19 November 1841; *The Times,* 3 December 1841.

Davis, Charles, per *Hillsborough* (98), Middx. (Westminster) G.D., 12 July 1797; *O.B.S.P.*

Davis, John, per *General Hewart* (18), M.G.D., 1 April 1818; *O.B.S.P.*

Davis, William (2), per *Mandarin* (40)*, C.C.C., 4 February 1839.

Davison, Agnes, per *Lady Shore* (97), M.G.D., 22 June 1796; *O.B.S.P.*

Dean, Robert, per *Albemarle* (91), M.G.D., 24 February 1790; *O.B.S.P.*

Dennis, James, per *Coromandel* (38), C.C.C., 14 May 1838.

Dickens, William, per *Morley* (18), M.G.D., 18 February 1818; *O.B.S.P.*

Dixon, Jane, per *Competitor* (28), M.G.D., 10 April 1828.

Donahue, John, per *Ann and Amelia* (24), Dublin City, April 1824.

Donohue, Martin, per *Portland* (33), Galway Summer Assizes, 1832.

Donohue, Patrick, per *Ratcliffe* (45)*, Kilkenny, 15 March 1845.

Donney, David Henry, per *Marion* (45)*, C.C.C., 3 March 1845; *The Times,* 6 March 1845.

Downes, Charles, per *Elphinstone* (35)*, C.C.C., 6 April 1835; *The Times,* 15 April 1835.

Driscoll, William, per *Norfolk* (35)*, M.S.P., 17 June 1833; H.T.S.C., 7 April 1847 and 22 January 1856; *Hobart Town Advertiser,* 23 January 1856.

Dwyer, James, per *Richard Webb* (41)*, Tipperary, 29 July 1841.

Dwyer, John, per *Surrey* (16), Tipperary, January 1816.

Dyster, Thomas, per *Asia (IV)* (27)*, Essex Special Session of G.D., 9 December 1826; *Colchester Gazette,* 23 December 1826.

Edmondson, Benjamin, per *Royal Admiral* (92), L.G.D., 14 September 1791; *O.B.S.P.*

Edwards, Ann, per *Providence* (25)*, M.G.D., 15 September 1825; *The Times,* 22 September 1825.

Emblin, Jeremiah, per *Calcutta* (03)*, L.G.D., 14 August 1802.

Evans, Stephen, per *Morley* (16), Warwicks. Assizes, 12 August 1816; H.O. 26.

Everitt, James, alias Everard, per *Coromandel* (03), L.G.D., 28 October 1801; *O.B.S.P.*

Eyre, James, per *Layton* (39)*, Yorks. Assizes, 9 March 1839.

Fagan, Elizabeth, or Gibbs, per *Mexborough* (41)*, Down, 4 January 1841; L.S.C., 8 July 1851; *Launceston Examiner,* 9 July 1851.

Fallon, Patrick, per *Mary Anne* (35), Lancs. Assizes, 8 March 1834; *Lancaster Gazette,* 15 March 1834.

Farrell, Maria, or Henry, per *Maria* (49)*, Dublin, October 1848.

Fincham, Mary, per *Friendship* (17), M.G.D., 15 January 1817; *O.B.S.P.*

Finn, Dennis, junior, per *St Vincent* (36), Wexford, 7 June 1836.

Fitzgerald, Margaret, per *Hector* (35)*, Surrey Q.S., 27 March 1835.

Fitzgerald, Mary Jane, per *St Vincent* (49)*, C.C.C., 23 October 1848; *The Times,* 31 October 1848.

Fletcher, George, per *Tortoise* (41)*, Yorks. (W.R.) Q.S., 22 March 1841.

Flynn, John, per *Marion* (43), Edinburgh C.J., 26 July 1843.

Forbes, Catherine, per *Glatton* (03), L.G.D., 20 May 1801; *O.B.S.P.*

Fowler, William, per *Sir Godfrey Webster* (23)*, Hereford Assizes, 24 March 1823.

Gale, William, per *Henry Porcher* (36)*, Suffolk Q.S., 12 April 1836.

Galloway, Thomas, per *Marquis of Hastings* (25), Surrey Q.S., 11 January 1825.

Gardner, Ann, per *Lloyds* (45)*, Oxford Assizes, 5 March 1845.

Gibson, George, per *Anson* (43)*, C.C.C., 28 November 1842.

Gibson, William Hay, per *Equestrian* (52)*, Durham Assizes, 27 February, 1849; *Durham Advertiser,* 2 March 1849.

Glasgow, Eliza, per *Edward* (34)*, M.G.D., 20 February 1834.

Gordon, Thomas, or Cordon, per *Equestrian* (52)*, C.C.C., 26 November 1849; *The Times,* 1 December 1849.

Goulder, Elias, per *Emperor Alexander* (33)*, Surrey S.P., 15 October 1832; H.T.S.C., 22 October 1844.

Green, George, per *Indefatigable* (12)*, Notts. Assizes, 13 March 1812; *Nottingham Journal,* 21 March 1812.

Green, Patrick, per *Asia* (24), Limerick, 12 August 1823; *P.P.,* 1824, vol. 22, p. 246.

Green, Richard, per *William Jardine* (50)*, Derby Q.S., 27 June 1848.

Griffith, Anne, or Griffin, per *Elizabeth* (18), Meath, August 1817.

Grundell, John William, per *Red Rover* (30)*, M.G.D., 16 September, 1830.

Guion, William, per *William Miles* (28)*, L.G.D., 6 December 1827.

Haig, George, per *Woodford* (28)*, L.G.D., 13 September 1827; *The Times,* 20 September 1827.

Haines, William, per *Alibi* (51)*, Bombay, 25 March 1850.

Halfpenny, John, per *Lord Lyndoch* (33), Staffs. Q.S., 5 January 1831.

Hallett, John Major, per *Pestonjee Bomanjee* (52)*, C.C.C., 20 August 1849; *The Times,* 27 August 1849.

Harley, David, per *Asia (IV)* (27)*, Aberdeen C.J., 15 April 1822.

Harris, James, per *Runnymede* (39)*, Bristol (City) Q.S., 5 April 1839.

Harris, John (2), per *General Stewart* (18), L.G.D., 1 April 1818; *O.B.S.P.*

Hart, Thomas Henry, per *Ocean* (15), M.G.D., 14 September 1814; H.O. 26; C.O. 201/138; *The Times,* 22 September 1814; A.A.N.S.W.

Haydon, John, per *Cressy* (43)*, London (Canada) C.M., 11 September 1841.

Hayes, Mary, per *Glatton* (02), M.G.D., 20 May 1801; *O.B.S.P.*

Haynes, Ann, or Foss, per *William Pitt* (05), M.G.D., 11 April 1804; *O.B.S.P.;* C.O. 201/138.

Herwick, Ann, per *America* (30)*, M.G.D., 16 September 1830; H.T.Q.S., 27 August 1836.

Heucher, Thomas, per *Lord Lyndoch* (40)*, C.C.C., 3 February 1840.

Hickie, James, per *Barossa* (41)*, Edinburgh C.J., 23 April 1841; *Scotsman,* 28 April and 19 May 1841.

Higgins, Martin, per *Commodore Hayes* (23)*, Lancs. Q.S., 4 November 1822; H.T.S.C., 1 March 1827; *Hobart Town Gazette,* 23 June and 7 July 1827.

Hindle, John, alias Thorpe, per *Lord Auckland* (44)*, C.C.C., 6 May 1844.

Hinks, Henry, per *Arab* (34)*, M.G.D., 17 October 1831; *The Times,* 22 October 1833.

Hipsley, Hannah Augusta, per *Tasmanian* (44)*, C.C.C., 13 September 1843.

Hobbs, John, per *Earl St Vincent* (52)*, C.C.C., 10 May 1847.

Holbrook, Jane, per *Navarino* (40)*, Surrey Q.S., 6 July 1840.

Holder, William, or Holden, per *Glory* (18), M.G.D., 2 July 1817; *O.B.S.P.*

Holt, John, per *Asiatic* (43)*, Lancs. (Preston) G.S., 19 October 1842.

Hope, Henry, per *Tortoise* (41)*, Staffs. Assizes, 10 March 1841.

Horton, Benjamin, per *Dromedary* (19)*, Lincs. (Parts of Lindsey) Q.S., 27 April 1819.

Howlett, Richard, per *Elphinstone* (36)*, St Christopher, 24 August 1835.

Hughes, Patrick, per *Emily* (44)*, Mayo, 17 October 1843.

Humphries, James, per *John Barry* (34)*, Somerset Assizes, 28 March 1833.

Hutchinson, John, per *Maria Soames* (44)*, C.C.C., 5 February 1844.

Jobbins, John, per *Fanny* (15), Glos. Assizes, 5 April 1815; H.O. 26; *Gloucester Journal,* 17 April 1815; A.A.N.S.W.

Johnson, Joseph, per *Egyptian* (39)*, C.C.C., 26 November 1838.

Johnston, Isabella, per *Lord Auckland* (46)*, Fermanagh, 2 March 1848.

Johnston, William, per *Richard Webb* (41)*, Antrim, 26 June 1841.

Joiner, Elizabeth, per *Speke* (08), M.G.D., 8 April 1807; *O.B.S.P.*

Jones, John, per *Eliza* (19), M.G.D., 21 April 1819; H.O. 10/16; Nat. Lib. Aust. MS. 67.

Jones, Richard, per *Gilmore* (38)*, Monmouth Assizes, 28 March 1838.

Jones, Robert, per *Albemarle* (91), M.G.D., 16 February 1791; *O.B.S.P.*

Joseph, Moses, per *Albion* (26), Warwicks. Assizes, 25 March 1825.

Keightley, William, per *Sir William Bensley* (16), Leics. Q.S., 23 April 1816; H.O. 26; *Leicester Journal,* 26 April 1816.

Kelly, James (2), per *Kinnear* (42)*, Londonderry, 17 March 1842.

Killick, Ann, per *Sydney Cove* (07), Southampton Assizes, 4 March 1806; H.O. 26.

Kilmartin, Dennis, per *Samuel Boddingtons* (45)*, Limerick, 26 July 1845.

Kenny, Charles, per *Countess of Harcourt* (27), Dublin, 22 September 1826.

King, Henry, per *Lady Feversham* (30), M.G.D., 10 September 1829; *The Times,* 19 September 1829.

King, James, per *General Stewart* (18), Somerset Assizes, 28 March 1818; *Taunton Courier,* 2 April 1818; *Sydney Herald,* 8 August 1838.

Kinsila, William, per *Blenheim* (39), Kildare, 27 March 1839.

Knott, Ann, alias Carringdon, or Mary Purdy, per *America* (30)*, Surrey Q.S., 25 October 1830; H.T.Q.S., 2 July 1849; *Hobart Town Advertiser,* 3 July 1849.

Lacey, Joseph, per *Asia (V)* (27)*, Yorks. Assizes, 24 March 1827.

Lawlor, Bridget, or McGarry, per *Earl Grey* (49)*, Kilkenny, 31 March 1849.

Lawrence, Nathaniel, per *Ganges* (96), Somerset Assizes, 11 August 1792; A.A.N.S.W.

Le Noble, Maria, per *Elizabeth and Henry* (46)*, St Helier, Jersey, 21 April 1846.

Lews, Robert, per *Lord William Bentinck* (32)*, M.G.D., 5 January 1832.

Littler, Thomas, per *Stakesby* (33)*, M.S.P., 11 February 1833.

Lord, Simeon, per *Atlantic* (91), Lancs. Q.S., 22 April 1790; *Australian Encyclopaedia.*

Lyon, Levy, per *Ann* (09), M.G.D., 13 July 1808; *O.B.S.P.*

Lyons, John, per *Atlas* (02), Tipperary, April 1800.

Madden, Bridget, per *Gilbert Henderson* (39)*, Lancs. Q.S., 16 October 1839.

Mahony, Abigail, per *Lady Rowena* (26), Cork, 9 August 1825.

Mandeville, Elizabeth, per *Eolus* (08), M.G.D., 6 April 1808; *O.B.S.P.*

Marginson, James, per *Norfolk* (35)*, Yorks. (E.R.) Q.S., 30 June 1834.

Marlin, Ellen, per *Atwick* (37)*, Chester Assizes, 5 August 1837.

Marshall, Luke, per *John Renwick* (42)*, Yorks. (Wakefield) Q.S., 5 January 1842.

Martin, Elizabeth, per *Harmony* (28)*, M.G.D., 29 May 1828.

Martin, Margaret, per *Sir Robert Seppings* (52)*, Liverpool Assizes, 22 March 1851; *Manchester Guardian,* 5 April 1851.

Mason, John, per *Isabella* (18), M.G.D., 17 September 1817; *O.B.S.P.*

Mayo, Elizabeth, per *Neptune* (90), Hereford Assizes, 20 March 1788.

McAllister, Robert, per *Prince Regent* (41)*, Antrim, 6 March 1841.

McCallum, James, per *Pestonjee Bomanjee* (45)*, Perth C.J., 25 April 1845.

McCormack, Catherine, per *Asia* (29), Dublin, 10 January 1829.

McDonald, Patrick, per *Richard Webb* (41)*, Cavan, 23 July 1841.

McGaverin, Thomas, per *William Jardine* (44)*, Stirling C.J., 25 April 1844.

McGuire, Elizabeth, per *Margaret* (43)*, Glasgow C.J., 19 September 1842.

McInally, James, per *Blenheim* (37)*, Glasgow C.J., 4 January 1837.

McKay, Robert Abercromby, per *Lady Kennaway* (34)*, Aberdeen C.J., 30 April 1834.

McLeod, Margaret, alias Fleming, per *Westmorland* (36)*, Edinburgh C.J., 14 December 1835.

McMahon, Mary, per *Margaret* (37), Clare, 5 July 1836.

McShane, John, per *John Brewer* (41)*, C.C.C., 14 June 1841; *The Times,* 19 June 1841.

Meredith, Jane, per *Mary Anne* (15), Devon Assizes, 20 March 1815; H.O. 26; *uxor* Thomas Parmeter per *Fanny* (15).

Millican, Sarah, per *Elizabeth and Henry* (46), Ipswich Q.S., 29 July 1846.

Million, Edward, per *Active* (91), Middx. (Westminster) G.D., 3 January 1790; *O.B.S.P.*

Moore, Thomas, per *Equestrian* (44)*, C.C.C., 23 October 1843.

Moroney, John, per *Guildford* (15), Tipperary, October 1815.

Mugan, Honor, per *Tasmania* (45)*, Mayo, 27 June 1845.

Mullett, Mary, per *Indispensable* (95), Southampton (Portsmouth) Assizes, 29 July 1794; *uxor* James Austin per *Minerva* (99).

Murray, Edward, per *Forth* (34), Roscommon, 10 July 1834.

Newton, William, per *Pyramus* (38)*, Kent Q.S., 19 October 1838; *Kent Herald,* 25 October 1838.

Nodes, Maria, per *Indispensable* (09), M.G.D., 11 January 1809; *O.B.S.P.*

Norris, John, per *Royal Admiral* (00), Dorset G.D., 15 March 1798.

Oare, Randall, per *Indian* (10), Salop Assizes, 23 March 1809; H.O. 26; *H.R.A.,* III. ii. 576; Ingleton, *True Patriots All,* p. 69.

O'Grady, Michael, per *Layton* (41)*, Lower Canada C.M., 10 September 1840.

O'Hara, Samuel, per *Minerva* (17)*, Carrickfergus, 7 July 1817; H.T.S.C., 25 January 1821.

O'Neill, John, per *Earl St Vincent* (52)*, Preston, 21 February 1850; H.T.S.C., 3 September 1856; *Tasmanian Daily News,* 4 September 1856.

O'Neill, Mary, per *Isabella* (40)*, Cavan, 13 July 1839.

O'Neill, Terence, per *Eden* (36)*, Nova Scotia (Halifax) C.M., 7 December 1835.

Onions, Samuel, per *Minerva* (21), Norfolk (Norwich) Q.S., 15 May 1821; *Norwich and Norfolk Chronicle,* 19 May 1821; H.O. 26.

O'Shaughnessy, Edward, per *Asia* (24), City of Dublin, 12 July 1824; Mudie, *Felonry of N.S.W.,* ch. VII; A.A.N.S.W.

Page, Mary, per *Experiment* (04), Worcs. Assizes, 5 March 1803; *uxor* John Lyons per *Atlas* (02).

Parment, or Parmeter, or Parmeton, Thomas, per *Fanny* (15), M.G.D., 21 June 1815.

Parish, William, per *Alexander* (87), M.G.D., 20 October 1784; *O.B.S.P.*

Parr, William, per *Fortune* (12), Kent Assizes, 6 August 1812; H.O. 26; A.A.N.S.W.

Pearce, William, per *Commodore Hayes* (23)*, M.G.D., 15 January 1823; *The Times,* 16 January 1823.

Peeler, Charles, per *Admiral Gambier* (08), M.G.D., 15 September 1806; *The Times,* 26 September 1806.

Perry, Phillis, per *Lady of the Lake* (29)*, Worcs. Q.S., 2 April 1829.

Pevett, Thomas, per *Perseus* (02), M.G.D., 14 January 1801; *O.B.S.P.*

Phillips, George, per *Frances Charlotte* (37)*, C.C.C., 13 June 1836.

Player, William, per *Phoenix* (24)*, M.G.D., 10 September 1823.

Plunkett, Charles, per *Anson* (43)*, Staffs. Q.S., 5 April 1843.

Pocock, William, per *Nile* (50)*, C.C.C., 15 December 1845; *The Times,* 17 December 1845.

Potter, William, per *Elphinstone* (37)*, Devon Assizes, 16 March 1837.

Preston, Mary, per *Canada* (10), M.G.D., 20 September 1809; *O.B.S.P.*

Purcell, Edward, per *Hyderabad* (49)*, King's, 28 February 1848.

Purcell, James, per *Lady Harewood* (29)*, M.G.D., 12 July 1827.

Pye, John, per *Britannia* (91), Warwicks. Assizes, 23 March 1790; *H.R.A.,* I. ii. 456, x. 564, xxiv. 724-5; A.A.N.S.W.

Randall, Mary, per *Bellona* (92), M.G.D., 23 May 1792; *O.B.S.P.;* *uxor* Paul Randall per *Admiral Barrington* (91), Surrey Q.S., 13 April 1790.

Redman, Charles, per *John* (27), Glos. Assizes, 9 April 1827; Adm. 6/420, no. 2345.

Reid, James, alias Terry, John, per *Phoenix* (24)*, Edinburgh C.J., 4 November 1823.

Reilly, Mary, per *Waverley* (47)*, Fermanagh, 24 October 1846.

Reilly, Thomas, per *Cadet* (44)*, Leitrim, 10 January 1844.

Richardson, Richard, per *Active* (91), L.G.D., 8 December 1790; *O.B.S.P.*

Roberts, David, per *Fortune* (06), Glos. (City) Assizes, 27 July 1803.

Robinson, James, per *Castle Forbes* (19)*, City of Dublin, 17 August 1819.

Robley, Christopher, per *Indian* (10), Cumberland Assizes, 31 July 1807; C.O. 201/138.

Robson, Thomas, per *Fortune* (06), M.G.D., 15 February 1804; *O.B.S.P.*

Roffey, George, per *Coromandel* (38)*, C.C.C., 1 January 1838.

Rogers, Thomas, per *Second Fleet* (90), M.G.D., 25 June 1788; *O.B.S.P.*

Rolands, or Rawlins, Ralph, per *Adrian* (30), M.G.D., 14 January 1830; Nat. Lib. Aust. MS. 67.

Rorke, Thomas, per *Hyderabad* (49)*, Longford, 7 July 1847.

Routh, Henry, per *Tenasserim* (44)*, Bombay(?), 20 August 1843.

Rowley, Elizabeth, per *Persia* (27)*, Chester Q.S., 17 October 1826.

Ruffler, John, per *Scarborough* (87), M.G.D., 23 February 1785; *O.B.S.P.*

Ryan, Anthony, per *Waverley* (41)*, Limerick, 3 March 1841.

Sampson, Isaac, per *Grenada* (19), M.G.D., 9 September 1818; H.O. 10/16; *O.B.S.P.*

Samuels, Abraham, per *Susan* (37)*, C.C.C., 8 May 1837.

Sandlant, William, per *Augusta Jessie* (38)*, Leics. Q.S., 2 July 1838; *Leicester Chronicle,* 6 July 1838.

Saurien, Carl Leopold, per *Southworth* (33), Kent (Sandwich) S.P. and G.D., 29 August 1833; *Kentish Chronicle*, 5 September 1833.

Scholes, James, per *Eliza* (28), Yorks. Assizes, 22 March 1828; Adm. 6/420, no. 2966.

Semple, Elizabeth, per *Elizabeth and Henry* (46)*, Glasgow C.J., 28 April 1846.

Shead, Richard, per *Lord William Bentinck* (32), Cambs. Assizes, 19 July 1831; *Cambridge Chronicle and Journal,* 22 July 1831.

Silverthorn, John, per *Alexander* (87), Wilts. (New Sarum), 6 March 1784; Cobley, *Sydney Cove 1788,* p. 79.

Simfield, Charles, per *Jane* (47)*, King William's Town, 9 February 1847.

Simmons, Joshua, per *Earl St Vincent* (52)*, C.C.C., 20 August 1849; *The Times,* 24 and 25 August 1849.

Sinner, Ann, alias Ruffey, alias Hedges, per *Asia* (47)*, C.C.C., 26 October 1846.

Slough, Frederick John, per *Elphinstone* (42)*, C.C.C., 28 April 1841.

Slow, Sarah, per *Westmorland* (36)*, C.C.C., 13 June 1836; *The Times,* 17 June 1836.

Smith, Charlotte, per *Nile* (01), L.G.D., 17 September 1800; *O.B.S.P.*

Smith, Patrick, per *Chapman* (17), Dublin City, 17 February 1816.

Smith, Thomas, per *Pestonjee Bomanjee* (45)*, Cheshire (Knutsford) Q.S., 1 January 1845.

Somers, John, per *Bengal Merchant* (28)*, Glos. Assizes, 30 August 1827; H.T.S.C., 19 November 1831; *Hobart Town Courier,* 3 and 24 December 1831.

Sowden, John, per *John Barry* (34)*, Yorks. Assizes, 13 July 1833; *Yorkshire Chronicle,* 18 July 1833.

Sparks, Thomas (Benjamin?),† per *Neptune* (90), Somerset Q.S., 3 October 1786.

Speed, Thomas, per *Somerset* (41)*, Somerset Assizes, 3 April 1841; *Taunton Courier,* 14 April 1841.

Spencer, Esther, per *Indispensable* (95), M.G.D., 17 September 1794; *O.B.S.P.*

Spencer, Robert, per *Isabella* (33)*, L.G.D., 14 February 1833.

Stallard, Alfred, per *Bardaster* (35)*, Somerset Q.S., 23 March 1835.

Stevens, Margaret, alias McCarty, per *Jane* (35)*, M.G.D., 18 October 1832; L.S.C., 28 March 1871; *Launceston Examiner,* 1 April 1871.

Stevenson, William, per *Westmorland* (41)*, Kent Q.S., 15 March 1841; *Kent Herald,* 18 March 1841.

Strike, Frederick, per *Waterloo* (34)*, M.S.P., 4 September 1834.

Tailby, Thomas, per *Royal Admiral* (92), Leics. Assizes, 28 July 1790; *Leicester Journal,* 6 August 1790.

Tassiker, Peter, per *Eden* (42)*, Lancs. (Salford) G.S., 6 December 1841.

† I have not found Thomas Sparks in the convict lists. There was, however, a Benjamin Sparkes transported in the Second Fleet, with particulars as shown. This man may be, however, Thomas Parkes or Perks; he was tried in London on 10 December 1788, and came to the colony on the *Salamander* in 1791.

Taylor, Elizabeth, per *Experiment* (04), M.G.D., 20 April 1803; *O.B.S.P.*

Taylor, Robert, per *Waterloo* (33), M.G.D., 3 January 1833; *The Times,* 10 January 1833; *Sydney Herald,* 13 November 1839.

Terry, Samuel, per *Earl Cornwallis* (00), Lancs. Q.S., 22 January 1800; *Australian Encyclopaedia.*

Teysum, John, per *Moffatt* (42)*, Monmouth (Usk) G.Q.S., 3 January 1842.

Thomas, George, per *Lord William Bentinck* (38)*, Middx. Q.S., 16 May 1837.

Thomas, John, (2) per *Isabella* (42)*, Glos. Assizes, 31 March 1841; *Gloucester Chronicle,* 3 April 1841.

Thompson, Charles, per *Marquis of Huntley* (26), M.G.D., 27 October 1825; *The Times,* 28 October 1825; Adm. 6/420, no. 1594.

Tierney, Michael, per *Emily* (44)*, Galway, 17 June 1844.

Tinan, Thomas, per *John Renwick* (42)*, Lancs. Special Assizes, 10 October 1842.

Traill, Sarah Ann, per *New Grove* (34)*, M.G.D., 16 May 1834.

Tucker, John, per *Second Fleet* (90), M.G.D., 20 October 1789; *O.B.S.P.*

Turner, Robert, per *Aboukir* (51)*, Deal Q.S., 30 March 1849.

Turner, Samuel, per *Earl St Vincent* (26)*, Sussex Special Session of G.D., 20 December 1824; H.T.Q.S., 10 October 1831; *Colonial Times,* 19 October 1831.

Underwood, James, per *Charlotte* (87), Wilts. (New Sarum), 11 March 1786; *Australian Encyclopaedia.*

Vaux, James Hardy, per *Minorca* (01), L.G.D., 17 September 1800; *Australian Encyclopaedia.*

Wain, Jordan, per *Royal Admiral* (92), L.G.D., 7 December 1791; *O.B.S.P.*

Walsh, John, per *Sir Godfrey Webster* (25), Limerick, 7 March 1825.

Watkins, Alfred, per *Rodney* (50)*, Clerkenwell G.S., 9 May 1848.

Watkins, William, per *Mangles* (24), Berks. Assizes, 1 March 1824, Nat. Lib. Aust. MS. 67.

Watts, Charlotte, per *Frances Charlotte* (32)*, Oxford Q.S., 2 July 1832.

Webb, George, per *Earl Grey* (42)*, Devon Assizes, 21 July 1842; *Devonport Telegraph and Plymouth Chronicle,* 30 July 1842.

Webb, John, per *Canada* (01), M.G.D., 2 December 1795; *O.B.S.P.*

Webb, Joseph, per *Waterloo* (33), Surrey S.P. and G.D., 19 December 1832; Adm. 6/421, no. 2642.

Webb, William, per *Bengal Merchant* (28)*, Somerset Assizes, 5 April 1827.

Welch, George, per *Hindostan* (40)*, C.C.C., 25 November 1839; *The Times,* 3 December 1839.

Weyman, William, per *Somerset* (41)*, Glos. Assizes, 4 August 1841.

Whitburn, Susan, per *St Vincent* (49)*, Southampton Assizes, 10 July 1849.

White, Jophet, per *Surrey* (16), Dublin City, December 1815.

Whitehead, George, per *Bussorah Merchant* (28), Derby (Borough) Q.S., 1 March 1828; Adm. 6/420, no. 2893.

Williams, Susannah, per *Nile* (01), M.G.D., 14 January 1801; *O.B.S.P.; uxor* Thomas Sparks per *Neptune* (90).

Willoughby, Joseph, per *Minorca/Canada* (01)†; L.G.D., 26 February 1797; *O.B.S.P.*

Wilson, Charles Edward, per *Isabella* (42)*, C.C.C., 25 October 1841; *The Times,* 28 October 1841.

Winstan, Thomas, per *Neptune* (90), M.G.D., 12 December 1787; *O.B.S.P.*

Winstanley, Reuben, per *Sir Robert Peel* (44)*, Lancs. (Salford) G.S., 26 February 1844.

Wood, Frederick, per *Barossa* (41)*, Maidstone Q.S., 15 March 1841; *Maidstone Gazette,* 23 March 1841.

Wood, Joseph, per *Royal Charlotte* (24), Radnor Great Session, 24 August 1824; H.O. 26.

Wright, Joseph, per *Guildford* (20)*, Essex Assizes, 4 March 1820.

Wright, Joseph, per *Scarborough* (87), M.G.D., 26 May 1784; *O.B.S.P.*

Yeates, Charles, per *Lady Harewood* (29)*, M.G.D., 4 December 1828; *The Times,* 11 December 1828.

† I have not discovered on which of these two ships Willoughby was embarked.

Abbreviations

References are all cited by short titles and full particulars of them are in the bibliography. To reduce the number of footnotes concerning convicts, I have listed all those mentioned by name, together with details of sources, in Appendix 11.

Abbreviations and meanings of certain words are as follows:

A.A.N.S.W.	Archives Authority of New South Wales.
Australia	New South Wales and Van Diemen's Land. (The name of Van Diemen's Land was changed officially to that of Tasmania in 1856.)
Britain	England and Wales, Scotland, Ireland and the isles in the British seas.
England	England and Wales.
Governor Arthur	Properly Lieutenant-Governor of Van Diemen's Land 1824-36.
Overseas	Any territories outside Britain and the present Commonwealth of Australia.
C.O.	Colonial Office.
C.S.O.	Colonial Secretary's Office.
G.O.	Governor's Office.
H.O.	Home Office.
H.R.A.	*Historical Records of Australia.* The Series number is cited first, then the volume number, page number and date.
O.B.S.P.	*Old Bailey Sessions Papers.*
P.P.	*Parliamentary Papers* (British). The year of printing of the Paper is first cited, then the volume number and the page number of the volume (not the page number of the individual Paper).
T.S.A.	Tasmanian State Archives.

Notes

1 INTRODUCTION

[1] Hammond, *The Village Labourer,* p. 239.
[2] Arthur to Murray, 10 February 1829, T.S.A., G.O. 10, no. 3566.
[3] Mansfield, *The 1841 Census of N.S.W.;* Clark, *History of Australia,* vol. 1, pp. 236-7.
[4] Wood, 'Convicts', Royal Australian Historical Society, *Journal and Proceedings,* vol. 8, part 4 (1922); Shaw, *Sydney Morning Herald,* 29 June 1953, and 'The British Criminal and Transportation', Tasmanian Historical Research Association, *Papers and Proceedings,* vol. 2, no. 2 (1953); Clark, 'The Origins of the Convicts Transported to Eastern Australia 1787-1852', *Historical Studies,* vol. 7, nos. 26-7 (1956).
[5] Bateson, *The Convict Ships,* pp. 111, 152, 166, 236, 265.
[6] Smith, *Colonists in Bondage,* ch. 5 *passim.*
[7] Such a short discussion does less than justice to the subject. For further and more detailed accounts, see Holdsworth, *History of the English Law,* vol. 11, pp. 570-5; Radzinowicz, *History of the English Criminal Law,* vol. 1, pp. 105-10; O'Brien, *Foundation of Australia,* pp. 47-64.
[8] Radzinowicz, *History of the English Criminal Law,* vol. 1, pp. 526-601.

2 THE PLACES OF TRIAL

[1] Cunningham, *Two Years in N.S.W.,* vol. 2, pp. 52-3.
[2] Marjoribanks, *Travels in N.S.W.,* pp. 140, 154.
[3] The N.S.W. records do not note offences consistently until 1826, but there is no reason to suppose that convicts transported prior to that date had no former convictions.
[4] *H.R.A.,* I. iii. 330, 14 November 1801.
[5] *P.P.,* 1822, vol. 20, p. 551.
[6] George, *London Life in the XVIIIth Century,* ch. 2 and p. 105.
[7] Mayhew, *London Labour,* 'extra' vol., pp. 294-301.
[8] Ibid., pp. 311-16.
[9] *P.P.,* 1817, vol. 7, pp. 349-57.
[10] Ibid., p. 363.
[11] Ibid., pp. 377-81.
[12] Mayhew, *London Labour,* 'extra' vol., p. 313.
[13] *P.P.,* 1819, vol. 7, pp. 162-4.
[14] Backhouse, *Narrative,* p. 20.
[15] *P.P.,* 1852, vol. 8, p. 250.
[16] *P.P.,* 1819, vol. 7, pp. 162-4.
[17] Dickens, *Oliver Twist,* ch. 26.
[18] Radzinowicz, *History of English Criminal Law,* vol. 2, pp. 297-306.
[19] Vaux, *Memoirs,* p. 250.
[20] *P.P.,* 1828, vol. 6, pp. 54-5.
[21] Ibid., p. 63.
[22] Mayhew, *London Labour,* vol. 1, pp. 108-24.

23 Ibid., p. 466. The anonymous *Sinks of London Laid Open* notes that, in London thieves' kitchens, conversation centred upon such books.

24 Ibid.

25 *P.P.*, 1819, vol. 7, p. 158.

26 Ibid., p. 162.

27 *P.P.*, 1817, vol. 7, p. 429.

28 Ibid.

29 Marjoribanks, *Travels in N.S.W.*, p. 149.

30 Barrington, *Voyage to Botany Bay*, p. 20.

31 Cunningham, *Two Years in N.S.W.*, vol. 2, p. 253.

32 Holdsworth, *History of the English Law*, vol. 11, p. 568, citing Goldsmith, *The Vicar of Wakefield*. For the relevance of this judgment in the nineteenth century, see Webb, *The English Prisons Under Local Government*.

33 *P.P.*, 1819, vol. 7, p. 159.

34 Ibid., p. 168.

35 Ibid., p. 171.

36 *P.P.*, 1852, vol. 7, p. 246.

37 *P.P.*, 1828, vol. 6, pp. 48-51.

38 *P.P.*, 1817, vol. 7, p. 430.

39 *P.P.*, 1852, vol. 7, p. 427.

40 Backhouse, *Narrative*, p. 276.

41 This was also noted by Lieut.-Governor Sorell in Van Diemen's Land in 1821. See *H.R.A.*, III. iv. 26, 8 August 1821.

42 Ashton, *Modern Street Ballads*, pp. 399-402.

43 *P.P.*, 1819, vol. 7, p. 218.

44 Ibid., pp. 385-6.

45 An example of this occurred in London. Thomas King, an errand or kitchen boy, aged sixteen, was transported for seven years with many others for picking pockets. Several of the prisoners then said, 'Thank you, your Lordship, we are much obliged to you.' (*The Times*, 17 September 1832.)

46 *P.P.*, 1828, vol. 6, pp. 444-9.

47 Clapham, *Economic History of Modern Britain*, vol. 1, p. 61.

48 Engels, *Condition of the Working Class*, p. 53.

49 *P.P.*, 1839, vol. 19, pp. 93-4.

50 Clapham, *Economic History of Modern Britain*, vol. 1, p. 40.

51 Engels, *Condition of the Working Class*, p. 40.

52 Maxwell, *Dublin Under the Georges*, p. 115.

53 Ibid., ch. 4 *passim*.

54 *P.P.*, 1852, vol. 7, p. 98.

55 Clapham, *Economic History of Modern Britain*, vol. 1, p. 38.

56 Engels, *Condition of the Working Class*, p. 46.

57 It is difficult to know in some cases whether a convict was from the 'countryside' or not, though the number of men noted as 'farm labourers' in the records suggests country and village dwellers, as do accounts of some trials. *P.P.*, 1833, vol. 37, p. 832, shows that in 1831 57 per cent of families in Bedfordshire were employed chiefly in agriculture, 44 per cent in Dorset, 53 per cent in Cambridgeshire, and 49 per cent in Wiltshire.

58 Hasbach, *History of the English Agricultural Labourer*, p. 208.

59 *P.P.*, 1826-7, vol. 6, p. 8.
60 Ibid., pp. 58-65.
61 *P.P.*, 1824, vol. 6, pp. 438-9.
62 Ibid., pp. 404-5, 435.
63 *P.P.*, 1839, vol. 19, p. 146.
64 Ibid., p. 73.
65 Ibid., p. 147.
66 Ibid., p. 148.
67 Ibid., p. 19.
68 Ibid., p. 22.
69 Ibid., p. 73.
70 Ibid., p. 22.
71 Cunningham, *Two Years in N.S.W.*, vol. 2, pp. 237-9.
72 *P.P.*, 1845, vol. 19, p. 35.
73 *P.P.*, 1822, vol. 20, p. 551.
74 Woodham-Smith, *The Great Hunger*, pp. 30-1. For an authoritative account of the famine and the condition of Ireland on the eve of the famine, see *The Great Famine* (ed. Edwards and Williams).
75 O'Brien, *Economic History of Ireland from the Union to the Famine*, p. 32, citing Curwen's *Observations*.
76 Freeman, *Pre-Famine Ireland*, p. 16. See especially the maps on pp. 18-19
77 Woodham-Smith, *The Great Hunger*, p. 24.
78 Ibid., p. 40. Population figures for Ireland in the eighteenth century are approximate, and the increase of 100 per cent appears incredible, though so do some other aspects of Ireland's history.
79 Carty, *Ireland from Grattan's Parliament to the Great Famine*, pp. 158-60, citing William Carleton, *The Black Prophet*.

3 THE OFFENCES

1 Dickens, *Oliver Twist*, ch. 46. For tables relevant to this and the following chapters concerning offences, see Appendix 7.
2 *The Whole Proceedings of the King's Commission of the Peace, Oyer and Terminer, and Gaol Delivery for the City of London; and also the Gaol Delivery for the County of Middlesex held at Justice Hall in the Old Bailey.*
3 Breton, *Excursions*, p. 279.
4 *P.P.*, 1852, vol. 7, pp. 20-1.
5 Vaux, *Memoirs*, chs. 12-13.
6 Dickens, *Oliver Twist*, ch. 26.
7 Mayhew, *London Labour*, vol. 3, p. 396.
8 Ibid., p. 392.
9 *P.P.*, 1819, vol. 8, p. 22.
10 Radzinowicz, *History of the English Criminal Law*, vol. 1, pp. 94-5. There is no doubt that the criminal law was not nearly as severe as it appeared on paper. On this, see in particular O'Brien, *Foundation of Australia*, pt I, and Radzinowicz, op. cit., vol. 1, p. 83, 'Application of Capital Statutes by the Courts'.
11 *P.P.*, 1852, vol. 8, p. 86.

12 Goddard, *Memoirs of a Bow Street Runner*, pp. 138-42.
13 Cunningham, *Two Years in N.S.W.*, vol. 2, p. 248.
14 Vaux, *Memoirs*, p. 218.
15 *P.P.*, 1819, vol. 7, p. 323.
16 Ibid., p. 218.
17 Ibid., p. 284.
18 *P.P.*, 1828, vol. 6, p. 463.
19 Ibid., p. 484.
20 Ibid., p. 494.
21 Vaux, *Memoirs*, p. 195; see also *P.P.*, 1819, vol. 7, pp. 299-300.
22 *P.P.*, 1812, vol. 2, pp. 9-10.
23 *P.P.*, 1835, vol. 11, pp. 670-1.
24 Mayhew, *London Labour*, 'extra' vol., pp. 376-7.
25 *P.P.*, 1839, vol. 19, pp. 13-14.
26 Redgrave, 'Abstract of the Criminal Tables for England and Wales, 1837', *Journal of the Statistical Society of London*, vol. 1 (1839).
27 *P.P.*, 1835, vol. 11, p. 674.
28 Mayhew, *London Labour*, vol. 1, pp. 456-8, cf. *Oliver Twist*, ch. 8. Coldbath Fields House of Correction was known as the 'Bastille' (hence the 'steel') to the criminal classes.
29 *P.P.*, 1837, vol. 22, p. 188.
30 *P.P.*, 1819, vol. 7, pp. 164-7.
31 Ibid., p. 168.
32 Ibid., p. 171.
33 *P.P.*, 1852, vol. 7, pp. 20-1.
34 Maxwell, *Country and Town in Ireland*, pp. 263-4, citing the *Hibernian Magazine* of April 1791.
35 Burke (ed.), *Adventures of Martin Cash*, p. 10.
36 *P.P.*, 1839, vol. 19, p. 218.
37 Mayhew, *London Labour*, 'extra' vol., p. 349.
38 For further comment on this see *P.P.*, 1839, vol. 19, Paper 169.
39 *P.P.*, 1839, vol. 19, pp. 19-21.
40 *P.P.*, 1819, vol. 8, pp. 95-6.
41 *P.P.*, 1850, vol. 45, p. 103.
42 *P.P.*, 1839, vol. 19, pp. 118-20.
43 Ibid., p. 143.
44 *P.P.*, 1826-7, vol. 6, p. 25.
45 *P.P.*, 1828, vol. 6, pp. 443-5.
46 Mayhew, *London Labour*, 'extra' vol., p. 325.
47 Mayhew, *London Labour*, 'extra' vol., pp. 377-90.
48 Ibid., pp. 380-1; Mayhew thought that forgeries of Bank of England notes emanated from Birmingham, and were uttered casually by pretended horse-dealers and travellers. Thomas Shelton, clerk of the arraigns of Oyer and Terminer and Gaol Delivery at the Old Bailey for thirty-five years, said (*P.P.*, 1819, vol. 8, p. 27) that the same persons came up to trial over and over again for forgery and disposal of forged bank notes, and that sometimes a whole family appeared in the dock, one after the other, for forgery of money or for coining.
49 *P.P.*, 1824, vol. 22, pp. 236, 246.
50 For Whiteboy offences, see, for example, *P.P.*, 1846, vol. 25, Paper 181.
51 *P.P.*, 1831-2, vol. 16, pp. 11-13.

52 *P.P.*, 1845, vol. 21, pp. 911-12.
53 For an account of these incidents, see Hammond, *The Village Labourer*.
54 *P.P.*, 1850, vol. 45, p. 103.
55 *P.P.*, 1828, vol. 12, pp. 207-9.
56 *P.P.*, 1845, vol. 19, p. 42.
57 *P.P.*, 1845, vol. 20, pp. 631-7.
58 Ibid., pp. 974-5. See also Woodham-Smith, *The Great Hunger*, pp. 71-2.
59 Maxwell, *Country and Town in Ireland*, p. 22.
60 *P.P.*, 1837, vol. 18, p. 129.
61 See Hammond, *The Village Labourer*, ch. 11.
62 *P.P.*, 1846, vol. 35, p. 181.
63 The vindictive offence of maiming livestock is noted in *P.P.*, 1846, vol. 35, p. 324: a filly about one and a half years old was maliciously injured, so as to render it useless, by some person or persons unknown. The owner had been attacked about twelve months previously by an armed party, in consequence of decrees which he had obtained. At the time of the attack on his filly, he held such decrees against persons in the neighbourhood, and this was reckoned to be the cause of the outrage.
64 *P.P.*, 1826-7, vol. 6, p. 39.
65 *P.P.*, 1846, vol. 35, pp. 181, 322.
66 *P.P.*, 1845, vol. 19, pp. 402-6.
67 *P.P.*, 1845, vol. 21, pp. 911-13.

4 THE FEMALE CONVICTS

1 Breton, *Excursions*, pp. 210-11.
2 For tables relevant to this chapter, see Appendix 9.
3 Mayhew, *London Labour*, vol. 3, p. 424.
4 Bonwick, *Curious Facts*, p. 283.
5 Mayhew, *London Labour*, vol. 1, p. 535, and vol. 3, p. 413.
6 Cunningham, *Two Years in N.S.W.*, vol. 2, pp. 261-75.
7 Backhouse, *Narrative*, p. 492.
8 Therry, *Reminiscences*, pp. 217-19.
9 Bonwick, *Curious Facts*, p. 281.
10 Fitzpatrick, *Sir John Franklin in Tasmania*, pp. 80-1.
11 *P.P.*, 1837, vol. 19, p. 42.
12 Ibid., p. 68.
13 *P.P.*, 1822, vol. 20, p. 553.
14 If such comments were made concerning N.S.W. female convicts, they have not been discovered.
15 Mayhew, *London Labour*, vol. 3, pp. 412-14. It was estimated (Mayhew, op. cit., 'extra' vol., pp. 211-13) that there were 80,000 prostitutes in London alone, but extent of prostitution is notoriously difficult even to estimate.
16 George, *London Life in the XVIIIth Century*, p. 113, citing *Brief Description of London and Westminster*.
17 Nicol, *Life and Adventures*, pp. 116-28.
18 *P.P.*, 1817, vol. 7, pp. 360-2.
19 Bonwick, *Curious Facts*, p. 114.

5 THE MALE CONVICTS

1 *Launceston Examiner,* 1 May 1852.

2 Irish were sent on from Sydney to Van Diemen's Land per *Minerva* in 1818 and *Castle Forbes* in 1819. *Bencoolen* was despatched from Ireland to New South Wales in 1819, and a number of its convicts were sent down to Hobart Town almost immediately by Macquarie.

3 Legislative Council of N.S.W., *Votes and Proceedings,* Committee on Immigration, 1838, p. 177.

4 Lang, *Transportation and Colonization,* pp. iv-v.

5 Therry, *Reminiscences,* p. 146.

6 McQueen, *Australia as she is,* p. 17.

7 *P.P.,* 1837, vol. 19, pp. 283, 292.

8 *H.R.A.,* I. xiv. 653, 18 February 1829.

9 Ibid., xv. 273, 6 December 1829. I am indebted to Russel Ward's *The Australian Legend* for some of the above references.

10 Personal communication from Mr A. G. L. Shaw, Department of History, University of Sydney.

11 See bibliography.

12 For an account of this under Governor Arthur see Forsyth, *Governor Arthur's Convict System.* During and after Arthur's time, 'mechanics' (trained artisans) were not, strictly speaking, assigned, but only loaned to settlers for stated periods.

13 See Syme, *Nine Years in Van Diemen's Land;* West, *History of Tasmania;* Barry, *Alexander Maconochie;* Shaw, 'The Origins of the Probation System in Van Diemen's Land', *Historical Studies,* vol. 6, no. 21 (1953).

14 In 1841 seven-year men could be indulged with a ticket-of-leave after serving four years of their sentence, fourteen-year men after six years, and men sent out for life after eight years (T.S.A., C.S.O. 16/1/8, memo. by Matthew Forster, 30 June 1841).

15 *Hobart Town Gazette,* 23 June and 7 July 1827.

16 Backhouse, *Narrative,* p. 167.

17 T.S.A., C.S.O., 16/1/8, 30 June 1841.

18 *H.R.A.,* III. iv. 43, 13 December 1821.

19 Byrne, *Twelve Years' Wandering in the British Colonies,* vol. 2, pp. 58-9, noted that 'since the suppression of the Assignment System, flogging has been abolished, and the male convicts are punished either by solitary confinement, working on the roads, or transportation to the settlements'.

20 Backhouse, *Narrative,* p. liv, Appendix F (note).

21 Mayhew, *London Labour,* vol. 3, pp. 397-8.

22 A document in the National Library of Australia, Canberra, MS. 280, concerning runaways, suggests that the number of absconders gazetted was much less than 15 per cent of the men transported.

23 Mundy, *Our Antipodes,* pp. 537-8.

24 *P.P.,* 1837, vol. 19, p. 312.

25 T.S.A., 2/286, memo. from commandant at Port Arthur, 24 November 1866.

26 Bonwick, *Curious Facts,* p. 274.

27 Backhouse, *Narrative,* p. liii.

28 Ibid., Appendix F, p. 476.

29 Ibid., p. xliii, Appendix E.

30 Ibid., p. lxii, Appendix F.

31 Ibid., p. liii, Appendix F.
32 *H.R.A.*, III. v. 650, 23 March 1827.
33 Backhouse, *Narrative*, p. lix, Appendix F.
34 *P.P.*, 1837, vol. 19, p. 284.
35 Barrington, *Sequel*, p. 20.
36 Vaux, *Memoirs*, p. 194.
37 Byrne, *Twelve Years' Wandering in the British Colonies*, vol. 2, pp. 45-6. See also Earnshaw, *Thomas Muir*, Appendix 3.
38 *P.P.*, 1837, vol. 19, p. 27.
39 *H.R.A.*, I. iii. 22, Encl. 5, 10 March 1805.
40 Ibid., ii. 25, 20 June 1797.
41 *P.P.*, 1819, vol. 7, pp. 14, 26.
42 Bonwick, *Curious Facts*, p. 116.
43 Rusden, *History of Australia*, vol. 1, p. 143; Bateson, *The Convict Ships*, p. 113; Cunningham, *Two Years in N.S.W.*, vol. 1, pp. 203-4.
44 National Library of Australia, Canberra, MS. 67.
45 *H.R.A.*, I. xi. 765, 803-6, 11 August 1825.
46 *Sydney Herald*, 7 February 1840.
47 Melville, *Present State of Australia*, p. 159.
48 For the musters and their nature, see bibliography. The following case studies are sketches from the musters.
49 Cunningham, *Two Years in N.S.W.*, vol. 2, p. 180.
50 Ibid., p. 289.
51 Therry, *Reminiscences*, pp. 24-6. Such separation was, of course, carried to its logical extreme in the establishment of penal settlements for incorrigibles.
52 Breton, *Excursions*, pp. 277-8.
53 Byrne, *Twelve Years' Wandering in the British Colonies*, vol. 1, p. 215.
54 Backhouse, *Narrative*, pp. 341, 420-1.
55 Vaux, *Memoirs*, p. 280; Marjoribanks, *Travels in N.S.W.*, pp. 55-8, 73.
56 *P.P.*, 1837, vol. 19, p. 64. See also Breton, *Excursions*, p. 269.
57 Byrne, *Twelve Years' Wandering in the British Colonies*, vol. 1, pp. 245-51. See also Backhouse, *Narrative*, p. cxxviii, Appendix O, for an account of the ironed gangs, their severe punishment and miserable existence.

6 THE FEMALE CONVICTS

1 Cunningham, *Two Years in N.S.W.*, vol. 2, p. 275.
2 See Appendix 11.
3 Bonwick, *Curious Facts*, p. 280, citing 'the autobiography of Goodridge, a runaway sailor'.
4 See bibliography.
5 Bateson, *The Convict Ships*, pp. 134-9.

7 CONCLUSION

1 *P.P.*, 1837, vol. 19, p. 294: evidence of Sir George Arthur.
2 Lang, *Transportation and Colonization*, p. 77.
3 *P.P.*, 1819, vol. 7, p. 164.
4 *P.P.*, 1828, vol. 6, p. 39.

[5] *P.P.*, 1819, vol. 7, p. 171.

[6] *P.P.*, 1835, vol. 11, p. 581; Browning, *The Convict Ship*, pp. 69, 96, 106, 119-20, 124.

[7] Backhouse, *Narrative*, pp. 23, 161, 492-3.

[8] Ibid., p. 67.

[9] *P.P.*, 1852, vol. 7, p. 44; 1839, vol. 19, p. 73; 1828, vol. 6, p. 38.

[10] *P.P.*, 1852, vol. 7, p. 44.

[11] *P.P.*, 1817, vol. 7, p. 429.

[12] *P.P.*, 1852, vol. 7, p. 44.

[13] *P.P.*, 1819, vol. 8, p. 67.

[14] *P.P.*, 1835, vol. 11, pp. 336-7.

[15] *P.P.*, 1826-7, vol. 6, p. 31.

[16] *P.P.*, 1836, vol. 8, part I, p. 155.

[17] Browning, *The Convict Ship*, p. 55.

[18] *P.P.*, 1839, vol. 19, pp. 23-9.

[19] Redgrave, 'Abstract of the Criminal Tables for England and Wales, 1837', *Journal of the Statistical Society of London*, vol. 1 (1839), pp. 324-6.

[20] *P.P.*, 1812, vol. 2, p. 649; 1819, vol. 7, pp. 229-300.

[21] *H.R.A.*, I. x. 618, 4 February 1822 (encl.).

[22] *P.P.*, 1835, vol. 11, p. 673.

[23] Ibid., pp. 676-7.

[24] Ibid., First Report, p. 61.

[25] Ibid., p. 306.

[26] Ibid., Second Report, p. 508.

[27] *P.P.*, 1826-7, vol. 6, p. 41.

[28] *P.P.*, 1828, vol. 6, p. 53.

[29] *P.P.*, 1831-2, vol. 7, p. 592.

[30] *P.P.*, 1837, vol. 19, p. 294.

[31] *P.P.*, 1850, vol. 45, p. 103.

[32] Wakefield, *Facts Relating to the Punishment of Death*, pp. 190, 195.

[33] *P.P.*, 1837-8, vol. 22, p. 20.

APPENDIX 1

[1] Simon, *Philosophical Essay on Probabilities*, p. 1.

[2] For the nature of the documents transmitted see Appendix 3 and bibliography.

[3] H.O. 11: transportation registers.

[4] H.O. 10/6 and 10/7.

[5] Tench (ed. Fitzhardinge), *Sydney's First Four Years*, pp. 83-4, n. 4. I am also doubtful about the list of prisoners per *Lady Juliana* in 1789, and think that some who apparently came out in that vessel embarked on other ships.

[6] It must be stressed that the sample was of convicts leaving Britain and certain places abroad, and not only of those who arrived.

[7] Bateson, *The Convict Ships*, particularly pp. 326-41. See also O'Brien, *Foundation of Australia*, p. 287.

[8] Figures in brackets after the name of a ship refer to the year of departure. Australian records refer to ships by date of arrival.

[9] For the number, see Appendix 4.

10 Some soldiers and native inhabitants of British possessions were shipped from their place of trial to England and sent on with convicts tried at home, and thus appear in H.O. 11.
11 Irish lists vary, and some are alphabetical. They were not rearranged for sampling purposes.
12 For the theory of sampling, see Yates, *Sampling Methods;* Karmel, *Applied Statistics;* Moroney, *Facts from Figures.*

APPENDIX 2

1 Melville, *Present State of Australia,* p. 87.
2 Marjoribanks, *Travels in N.S.W.,* pp. 109-10.
3 Braim, *History of N.S.W.,* vol. 2, pp. 121-3.
4 Mundy, *Our Antipodes,* p. 44.
5 Article, 'Convicts and Transportation', *Australian Encyclopaedia,* vol. 3, p. 24. The writer calculates that 80,000 prisoners were sent to New South Wales and 67,500 to Van Diemen's Land.
6 *P.P.,* 1812, vol. 2, p. 689.
7 *P.P.,* 1837-8, vol. 22, p. 376.
8 Bateson, *The Convict Ships,* Appendices 1-6; O'Brien, *Foundation of Australia,* p. 279.
9 *P.P.,* 1851, vol. 46, pp. 3, 14.

APPENDIX 3

1 *H.R.A.,* I. i. 57, 9 July 1788.
2 Ibid., i. 171, 15 April 1790; i. 187, 10 July 1790.
3 Ibid., i. 335, 10 February, 1792; i. 545-6, 30 October 1795.
4 Ibid., ii. 9, 2 March 1797.
5 Ibid., ii. 707, note 20.
6 Ibid., ii. 190-1, 20 April 1800.
7 Ibid., iii. 569, 29 August 1802.
8 Ibid., iv. 10, note 9. See also A.A.N.S.W. 4/4558 (Irish documents), X30-34 (Irish indents).
9 *P.P.,* 1822, vol. 20, pp. 555-6. Adm. 6/420-2.
10 *P.P.,* 1822, vol. 20, p. 698.
11 Ibid., p. 647.
12 *Statutes at Large,* 4-5 George IV, 1823-4, p. 785.
13 *H.R.A.,* I. xi. 574, 14 May 1825.
14 T.S.A., C.S.O., 1/431/9687 (1829).
15 *P.P.,* 1837, vol. 19, pp. 281-2.

APPENDIX 4

1 The division of offences in this table is based on Turner, *Russell on Crime.*
2 *P.P.,* 1845, vol. 21, p. 864.
3 H.M. Stationery Office, *Classification of Occupations, 1950.*
4 Cunningham, *Two Years in N.S.W.,* vol. 2, p. 234.
5 *P.P.,* 1837, vol. 19, pp. 281-2.

Select Bibliography

INTRODUCTION

The convict records consolidated as 'Convict Indents', and held by the Archives Authority of New South Wales, vary from little more than lists of convicts' names in the early years to much fuller descriptions after 1825. From that point not only are offences for which prisoners were transported included, but also a physical description, together with number of former offences, native place, occupation, and the like. Another set of records, on parchment, includes details of Irish prisoners transported from 1823 to 1836. These records list offences and other information such as occupation. A third series consists of miscellaneous indents in boxes. These include details of some ships that arrived in the eighteenth century, and of others which brought prisoners from places other than Britain.

Convict records in the Tasmanian State Archives are organized differently from those in Sydney. The most important series is the conduct registers, in alphabetico-chronological order to 1840. Thereafter, a separate volume is devoted to each ship. Indent details after 1840 (1844 in the case of female prisoners) are similar to those in Sydney, though not as comprehensive to that date. However, the Van Diemen's Land records include throughout not only the offence for which prisoners were transported, but their statements upon arrival, as well as details of offences committed during their period as convicts in the colony. Separate volumes are devoted to male and female prisoners. There is also a number of associated documents, some details of which have been copied into the conduct registers.

The New South Wales musters and the census of 1828 vary a good deal in the nature of the data recorded. The 1806 muster,* for instance, gives names of prisoners in alphabetical order (but by first letter of surname only) and ship by which they arrived, together with varying other information such as current civil condition, by whom employed, and in what capacity. There is appended a list of landholders, organized according to the area of land held. The 1811

---

* The muster of 1806 is incorrectly classified in the Public Record Office as the muster of 1837. There are some other similar misclassifications.

muster lists prisoners in no recognizable order, and in most cases limits 'remarks' to 'in the Colony'. Subsequent musters vary in information recorded and in accuracy of alphabetical order. Though some musters may appear at first sight to be strictly alphabetical, it is never safe to assume this. In short, information given in the musters generally increased, but it would be misleading to generalize on such a varied batch of records. The 1825 muster lists married women by their maiden names, but the 1828 census does not. This census is particularly valuable because it notes extent of land held, age of subject, civil condition and current employment, number of livestock owned, place of domicile and so on. Even here, however, it is not unusual to find blanks in the record.

The Van Diemen's Land musters are not so comprehensive. Though they include some information on current employment and civil condition, there appears to be extant no such valuable records of prisoners' whereabouts and position in society as there are for New South Wales.

Manuscript sources held in the Public Record Office, London, were examined on microfilm at the National Library of Australia, Canberra. Manuscript material marked with an asterisk (*) and held in Britain was examined there. British newspapers were also examined in London. British *Parliamentary Papers* and New South Wales newspapers are held in the National Library of Australia, Canberra, and the Van Diemen's Land newspapers in the Tasmanian State Archives, Hobart. Printed sources listed in the Select Bibliography are those cited in footnotes, together with a few other works consulted but not cited. Books are first editions published in London unless otherwise stated. *Parliamentary Papers* are cited by short titles.

MANUSCRIPT SOURCES

PUBLIC RECORD OFFICE, LONDON

ADMIRALTY PAPERS

Adm. 6/418-21—convicts with particulars, 1819-34.

COLONIAL OFFICE PAPERS

C.O. 201/4—female convicts per *Lady Juliana.*
C.O. 201/21—list of convicts from settlers, 1801.
C.O. 201/118—ships and numbers of convicts, 1812-20.
C.O. 201/138—births, deaths and marriages in N.S.W., 1816-21.
C.O. 207/1—list of convicts with particulars, 1788-1825.
C.O. 207/2—list of convicts with particulars, 1823-5.

HOME OFFICE PAPERS

H.O. 10/1-2—N.S.W. muster, 1819.
H.O. 10/5—N.S.W. muster, 1811.
H.O. 10/6-7—convicts embarked, 1787.
H.O. 10/16—persons convicted in London, 1815-49.
H.O. 10/19-20—N.S.W. muster, 1825.
H.O. 10/21-8—N.S.W. census, 1828.
H.O. 10/32-5—N.S.W. and Norfolk Island prisoners, 1837.
H.O. 10/36—N.S.W. muster, 1821.
H.O. 10/37—N.S.W. muster and list of landholders, 1806.
H.O. 10/38—V.D.L. ledger returns, *c.* 1846.
H.O. 10/41—V.D.L. ledger returns, *c.* 1849.
H.O. 10/42—V.D.L. muster, 1811.
H.O. 10/43—V.D.L. convicts, 1817-21.
H.O. 10/44-5—V.D.L. muster, 1822-3.
H.O. 10/46—V.D.L. muster, 1825.
H.O. 10/49—V.D.L. muster, 1833.
H.O. 11/1-21—convicts transported, 1787-1868.
*H.O. 26—persons convicted in counties other than London, 1805-92.
*H.O. 27—persons convicted in London, 1791-1849.

* CLERK OF ASSIZE RECORDS, CLASS LIST *c.* 1784-1805

Assizes 5, Oxford Circuit—bundles 107, 108, 110, 111, 120, 121, 123.
Assizes 25, Western Circuit—bundle 1.

Assizes 35, South-East Circuit—bundles 227-31, 237-41.

Assizes 44, North-East Circuit—bundles 102-6, 109, 110, 114-6.

*JUSTICIARY COURT RECORDS, EDINBURGH

Particulars of Scottish prisoners transported, *c.* 1802-24.

†TASMANIAN STATE ARCHIVES, HOBART

2/58-60, 199/4-5, 2/467-73—assignment lists and associated papers, 1810-26, 1830-6, 1845-52.

199/2, 93/7096, 53/4328, 2/61-4, 2/66-105—indents of male convicts arriving in V.D.L. on *c.* 30 November 1827, 3, 5, 19 August, 1 November 1831, 1 August 1835, 5 February 1841-26 May 1853.

2/114-20, 53/4329, 2/114-9, 2/120—indents of female prisoners arriving in V.D.L. on 19 April 1842-21 April 1853.

2/106-8—indents of male prisoners arriving in V.D.L. from Norfolk Island, 6 June 1844-7 September 1852.

2/109-12—indents of convicts arriving in V.D.L. on minor ships, 30 October 1842-6 March 1853.

2/113—indent of miscellaneous convicts arriving in V.D.L.

2/122-30—comprehensive alphabetical registers of convicts arriving in V.D.L., 1804-53.

26/2763-5—alphabetical lists of male convicts, 1804-30 (A-F, P-Z), 1830-9 (G-M, O).

2/374-432—description lists of male convicts arriving in V.D.L., 1828-53.

2/444-5—description lists of male convicts arriving in V.D.L. from Norfolk Island, 1845-51.

2/446-50—description lists of convicts arriving on minor ships or convicted locally, *c.* 1842-53.

2/433-43—description lists of female convicts arriving in V.D.L., 1841-53.

2/131-56, 2/158-79—alphabetico-chronological conduct registers of male convicts arriving in V.D.L., 1807-41.

2/207-321—chronological conduct registers of male convicts arriving in V.D.L., 1840-53.

† Since the bibliography was prepared, Mr Peter Eldershaw, the State Archives Officer, has prepared a *Guide* to the records of the Convict Department, and converted the cited accession numbers into a fresh series.

2/195-203—conduct registers of convicts still on strength at the introduction of the probation system, 1818-40.

2/370-1—miscellaneous conduct records of convicts whose records were transferred from the probation series as a result of second conviction, and of certain other colonially convicted men, *c.* 1840-5.

2/180-4—supplementary conduct registers recording colonial offences in continuation (males and females).

2/359-69—chronological conduct registers of male convicts arriving in V.D.L. on minor ships or convicted locally, 1840-93.

2/185-94—alphabetico-chronological conduct registers of female convicts arriving in V.D.L., 1803-43.

2/322-58—chronological conduct registers of female convicts arriving in V.D.L., 1844-53.

ARCHIVES AUTHORITY OF NEW SOUTH WALES

4/3996-4058—convict indents of prisoners transported to N.S.W., 1787-1842.

4/4558-68—convict indents and associated papers of prisoners transported to N.S.W., *c.* 1790-1840.

X30-40—Irish indents and associated papers, 1823-36.

NATIONAL LIBRARY OF AUSTRALIA, CANBERRA

MS. 280—V.D.L. convicts gazetted as runaways, 1830-57.

MS. 67—Hunter River Magistrates' Bench Deposition Book, 1830-2.

Convict indents of prisoners transported to N.S.W., 1833-6, 1838-9.

PRINTED SOURCES

DICTIONARIES, ENCYCLOPAEDIAS, GUIDES, PRINTED DOCUMENTS

Chisholm, A. H. (ed.): *Australian Encyclopaedia*. 10 vols (Sydney, 1958).

General Index to the Accounts, Papers, Reports of Commissioners, Estimates &c &c Printed by order of the House of Commons or presented by Command 1801-1852 (1938).

Giuseppi, M. S.: *A Guide to the MSS. preserved in the Public Record Office* (1924).

Historical Records of Australia, Series I and III.

H.M. Stationery Office: *Classification of Occupations, 1950* (1956).

Oxford English Dictionary. 12 vols (1933).

Partridge, E.: *A Dictionary of Slang and Unconventional English . . .* (4th ed., 1951).

Statutes of the United Kingdom of Great Britain and Ireland 4-5 George IV, 1823-4.

BRITISH PARLIAMENTARY PAPERS

Transportation, 1812, vol. 2.

State of the Police of the Metropolis, 1817, vol. 7.

Criminal Laws, 1819, vol. 8.

State of the Colony of New South Wales, 1822, vol. 20.

Labourers' Wages, 1824, vol. 6.

Persons Committed in each County of Ireland, 1824, vol. 22.

Criminal Commitments and Convictions, 1826-7, vol. 6.

Criminal Commitments and Convictions, 1828, vol. 6.

Police of the Metropolis, 1828, vol. 6.

Courts in Ireland, 1828, vol. 12.

Secondary Punishments, 1831-2, vol. 16.

State of Ireland, 1831-2, vol. 16.

Census of 1831, 1833, vol. 37.

Gaols and Houses of Correction, 1835, vol. 11.

Agriculture, 1836, vol. 8.

Transportation, 1837, vol. 19.

Transportation, 1837-8, vol. 22.

Constabulary, 1839, vol. 19.

Occupation of Land in Ireland, 1845, vols 19-22.

Aggravated Assaults in Ireland, 1846, vol. 35.

Principal Outrages in Tipperary, Limerick, etc., 1846, vol. 35.
Convict Discipline and Transportation, 1850, vol. 45.
Criminal and Destitute Juveniles, 1852, vol. 7.

NEWSPAPERS

BRITAIN

Cambridge Chronicle and Journal
Chester Chronicle and Cheshire and North Wales Advertiser
Colchester Gazette
Derby Mercury
Devonport Telegraph and Plymouth Chronicle
Dorchester Chronicle
Dublin Morning Post
Durham Advertiser
Gloucestershire Chronicle
Gloucestershire Journal
Ipswich Journal
Jackson's Oxford Journal
Kent Herald
Kent Herald and Kentish Chronicle
Kentish Chronicle
Lancaster Gazette
Leicester Journal
Maidstone Gazette
Manchester Guardian
Newcastle Advertiser
Northampton Herald
Norwich and Norfolk Chronicle
Nottingham Journal
Salopian Journal and Courier of Wales
Scotsman
Sherborne, Dorchester and Taunton Journal
Taunton Courier
The Times
Truro Royal Cornwall Gazette
York Chronicle
York Chronicle and York Courant

NEW SOUTH WALES

Sydney Herald
Sydney Morning Herald

VAN DIEMEN'S LAND

Colonial Times
Cornwall Chronicle
Hobart Town Advertiser
Hobart Town Courier
Hobart Town Gazette
Hobart Town Mercury
Launceston Examiner
Tasmanian Daily News

ARTICLES IN PERIODICALS

Clark, M.: 'The Origins of the Convicts Transported to Eastern Australia 1787-1852', *Historical Studies, Australia and New Zealand*, vol. 7, nos. 26-7 (1956).

Redgrave, S.: 'Abstract of the Criminal Tables for England and Wales, 1837', *Journal of the Statistical Society of London*, vol. 1 (1839).

Shaw, A. G. L.: 'The Origins of the Probation System in Van Diemen's Land', *Historical Studies, Australia and New Zealand*, vol. 6, no. 21 (1953).

Shaw, A. G. L.: 'The British Criminal and Transportation', Tasmanian Historical Research Association, *Papers and Proceedings*, vol. 2, no. 2 (1953).

Wood, G. A.: 'Convicts', Royal Australian Historical Society, *Journal and Proceedings*, vol. 8, part 4 (1922).

OTHER HISTORICAL SOURCES

Anon.: *Sinks of London Laid Open: a Pocket Companion for the Uninitiated, to which is added a Modern Flash Dictionary containing all the Cant Words, slang terms and flash phrases now in vogue, with a list of the sixty orders of Prime Coves, Doings of the Modern Greeks, Snooking Kens depicted, the Common Lodging-House Gallants, Lessons to Lovers of Dice, the Gaming Tables* (1844).

Ashton, John: *Modern Street Ballads* (1888).

Backhouse, James: *A Narrative of a Visit to the Australian Colonies* (1843).

Barrington, George: *A Voyage to Botany Bay, with a description of the country, manners, customs, religion &c of the natives*. [n.d.]
————: *A Sequel to Barrington's Voyage to New South Wales, comprising an interesting narrative of the Transactions and Behaviour of the Convicts; the Progress of the Colony: an official register of the crimes, trials, sentences and executions that have taken place: A Topographical, Physical, and Moral Account of the Country, Manners, Customs &c of the Natives,—as likewise authentic anecdotes of the most Distinguished Characters, and Notorious Convicts that have been Transported to the Settlement at New South Wales* (1801).

Barry, J. V. W.: *Alexander Maconochie of Norfolk Island: a study of a pioneer in penal reform* (Melbourne, 1958).

Bateson, Charles: *The Convict Ships 1787-1868* (Glasgow, 1959).

Bonwick, James: *Curious Facts of Old Colonial Days* (1870).

Braim, T. H.: *A History of New South Wales from its settlement to the close of the year 1844*. 2 vols (1846).

Branch-Johnson, W.: *The English Prison Hulks* (1957).

Breton, W. H.: *Excursions in New South Wales, Western Australia and Van Dieman's [sic] Land during the years 1830, 1831, 1832 and 1833* (2nd revised ed., 1834).

Browning, C. A.: *The Convict Ship and England's Exiles* (2nd ed., 1847).

Burke, J. L. (ed.): *The Adventures of Martin Cash, comprising a faithful account of his exploits, while a bush ranger under arms in Tasmania, in company with Kavanagh and Jones, in the year 1843* (Hobart Town, 1870).

Byrne, J.: *Twelve Years' Wandering in the British Colonies from 1835-1847*. 2 vols (1848).

Carty, James: *Ireland: a documentary record. Vol. 2: Ireland from Grattan's Parliament to the Great Famine 1783-1850* (Dublin, 1949).

Clapham, Sir John: *An Economic History of Modern Britain*. 3 vols (Cambridge, 1949).

Clark, C. M. H.: *A History of Australia: I: From the Earliest Times to the Age of Macquarie* (Melbourne, 1962).

Clarke, Marcus: *For the Term of His Natural Life*. 2 vols (Sydney, 1929).

Cobley, John: *Sydney Cove 1788* (1962).
————: *Sydney Cove 1789-1790* (Sydney, 1963).

Cunningham, P. M.: *Two Years in New South Wales; comprising sketches of the actual state of society in that colony; of its peculiar advantages to emigrants; of its topography, natural history, etc.* 2 vols (3rd ed., 1828).

Dickens, Charles: *Oliver Twist* (Everyman ed., 1957).

Earnshaw, John: *Thomas Muir, Scottish Martyr: Some Account of his Exile to New South Wales, his Adventurous Escape in 1796 across the Pacific to California, and thence, by way of New Spain, to France* (Cremorne, N.S.W., 1959).

Edwards, R. D. and Williams, T. D. (eds): *The Great Famine: Studies in Irish History 1844-52* (New York, 1957).

Engels, Frederick (trans. and ed. W. O. Henderson and W. H. Chaloner): *The Condition of the Working Class in England* (1958).

Fitzpatrick, Kathleen: *Sir John Franklin in Tasmania 1837-1843* (Melbourne, 1949).

Forsyth, W. D.: *Governor Arthur's Convict System, Van Diemen's Land 1824-36: a study in colonization* (1935).

Freeman, T. W.: *Pre-Famine Ireland: a study in historical geography* (Manchester, 1957).

George, M. D.: *London Life in the XVIIIth Century* (1925).

Goddard, Henry: *Memoirs of a Bow Street Runner* (1956).

Gwynn, Denis R.: *Young Ireland and 1848* (Cork, 1949).

Hammond, J. L. and B.: *The Village Labourer 1760-1832: a study in the government of England before the Reform Bill* (new ed., 1913).

Hasbach, W. (trans. Ruth Kenyon): *A History of the English Agricultural Labourer* (1908).

Holdsworth, Sir William: *History of the English Law*. 14 vols (1932-52).

Ingleton, G. C.: *True Patriots All; or, News from Early Australia, as told in a collection of broadsides* (Sydney, 1952).

Ives, George: *A History of Penal Methods: criminals, witches, lunatics* (1914).

Kiernan, T. J.: *Transportation from Ireland to Sydney 1791-1816* (Canberra, 1954).

Lang, J. D.: *Transportation and Colonization, or the Causes of the comparative failure of the transportation system in the Australian Colonies; with suggestions for ensuring its future efficiency in subserviency to extensive colonization* (1837).

Mansfield, Ralph: *Analytical View of the Census of New South Wales for the year 1841; with tables showing the progress of the population during the previous twenty years* (Sydney, 1841).

Marjoribanks, Alexander: *Travels in New South Wales* (1847).

Maxwell, Constantia: *Country and Town in Ireland under the Georges* (2nd ed., Dundalk, 1949).

—————: *Dublin Under the Georges 1714-1830* (1946).

†Mayhew, Henry: *London Labour and the London Poor: Those that will not work, comprising prostitutes, thieves, swindlers, rogues: by several contributors.* 'extra' vol. (1862).

—————: *London Labour and the London Poor: the condition and earnings of those that will work, cannot work and will not work,* 3 vols (1864).

McQueen, T. Potter: *Australia as she is and as she may be* (1841).

Melville, Henry: *The Present State of Australia, including New South Wales, Western Australia, South Australia, Victoria and New Zealand, with practical hints on emigration: to which are added the land regulations and description of the aborigines and their habits* (1851).

Meredith, John: *The Wild Colonial Boy: the life and times of Jack Donahoe (1808?-1830)* (Sydney, 1960).

Mudie, James: *The Felonry of New South Wales, being a faithful picture of the real romance of life in Botany Bay, with anecdotes of Botany Bay society, and a plan of Sydney* (1837).

Mundy, G. C.: *Our Antipodes, or Residence and Rambles in the Australian Colonies, with a glimpse of the gold fields* (3rd ed., 1855).

Nicol, John: *The Life and Adventures of John Nicol, Mariner, His Service in King's Ships in War & Peace, His Travels and Explorations by Sea to remote & unknown Countries in Merchant Vessels, Whalers, and other Sundry Craft; together with copious Notes & Comments on Ships, the Officers and Shipmates with whom he served, the Customs & Traditions of the Sea and of the Inhabitants of Distant Lands both Savage and Civilized, their Religions, Culture, & Industries, etc. etc. etc. as Related by Himself* (New York, 1936; first published in Edinburgh, 1822).

† These four volumes were published in a uniform edition and have been cited as three volumes and an 'extra' volume for the sake of convenience. Some of Mayhew's interviews took place earlier than the 1860s.

O'Brien, Eris: *The Foundation of Australia (1786-1800): A Study in English Criminal Practice and Penal Colonization in the Eighteenth Century* (2nd ed., Sydney, 1950).

O'Brien, G.: *Economic History of Ireland from the Union to the Famine* (1921).

Old Bailey Sessions Papers (The Whole Proceedings of the King's Commission of the Peace, Oyer and Terminer, and Gaol Delivery for the City of London; and also Gaol Delivery for the County of Middlesex held at Justice Hall in the Old Bailey) (1782-1833).

Radzinowicz, Leon: *A History of the English Criminal Law and its Administration from 1750*. 3 vols (1948-56).

Redford, Arthur: *Labour Migration in Britain 1800-50* (Manchester, 1926).

Rusden, G. W.: *History of Australia,* 3 vols (1884).

Smith, A. E.: *Colonists in Bondage: White Servitude and Convict Labour in America 1607-1776* (Chapel Hill, Va., 1947).

Stephen, Sir James: *A History of the Criminal Law of England.* 3 vols (1883).

Syme, J.: *Nine Years in Van Diemen's Land, Comprising an account of its discovery, possession, settlement, progress, population, value of land, herds, flocks, &c; an essay on prison discipline; and the results of the working of the probation system; with anecdotes of bushrangers* (Perth, 1848).

Tench, Watkin (ed. L. F. Fitzhardinge): *Sydney's First Four Years, being a reprint of 'A Narrative of the Expedition to Botany Bay' and 'A Complete Account of the Settlement at Port Jackson'* (Sydney, 1961).

Therry, Sir Roger: *Reminiscences of Thirty Years' Residence in New South Wales and Victoria; with a supplementary chapter on Transportation and the ticket-of-leave System* (1863).

Townshend, William C.: *Modern State Trials; revised and illustrated with essays and notes.* 2 vols (1850).

Turner, J. W. Cecil: *Russell on Crime: A Treatise on Felonies and Misdemeanours* (10th ed., 1950).

Vaux, James Hardy: *Memoirs of James Hardy Vaux, a swindler and thief, now transported to New South Wales for the second time, and for life* (2nd ed., 1830).

Wakefield, E. G.: *Facts Relating to the Punishment of Death in the Metropolis* (1832).

Ward, R. B.: *The Australian Legend* (Melbourne, 1958).
Webb, S. and B.: *English Local Government, vol. 6—The English Prisons under Local Government* (1929).
West, John: *History of Tasmania.* 2 vols (Launceston, 1852).
Woodham-Smith, Cecil B.: *The Great Hunger: Ireland 1845-9* (1962).

STATISTICAL SOURCES

Karmel, P. H.: *Applied Statistics for Economists: a course in statistical methods* (Melbourne, 1957).
Moroney, M. J.: *Facts from Figures* (3rd ed., 1956).
Simon, Pierre, Marquis de Laplace (trans. F. W. Truscott and F. L. Emory): *A Philosophical Essay on Probabilities* (New York, 1951).
Tippett, L. H. C.: *Statistics* (1952, first published 1943).
Yates, F.: *Sampling Methods for Censuses and Surveys* (1949).

Index